New Urges in Postcolonial Literature

Widening Horizons

New Urges in Postcolonial Literature
Widening Horizons

Edited by
Sunita Sinha

ATLANTIC
PUBLISHERS & DISTRIBUTORS (P) LTD

Published by

ATLANTIC

PUBLISHERS & DISTRIBUTORS (P) LTD

7/22, Ansari Road, Darya Ganj,
New Delhi-110002
Phones : +91-11-23273880, 23275880, 23280451
Fax : +91-11-23285873
Web : www.atlanticbooks.com
E-mail : info@atlanticbooks.com

Branch Office
5, Nallathambi Street, Wallajah Road,
Chennai-600002
Phones : +91-44-64611085, 32413319
E-mail : chennai@atlanticbooks.com

ISBN 978-81-269-1203-2

Printed in India at Nice Printing Press, A-33/3A, Site-IV,
Industrial Area, Sahibabad, Ghaziabad, U.P.

Acknowledgements

Nothing compares to my grandfather, Dr. R.K. Sinha—the most truly humble teacher—whose very name casts a spell over all the lovers of English literature. Whether it was Eliot or Lawrence, whether it was Donne or Keats, whether it was Shakespeare or Shaw, it was with an equal felicity, ease and command that he dealt them all. I was privileged, no doubt, to have grown up amidst quotes from Milton, Eliot and Arnold, lines from Wordsworth and Shelley, that kept me familiar with the golden names of English literature since my earliest years. Whenever my imagination began to stagger or when I was at a complete loss, all he would say was—"compare and connect".

This book is in homage to a profound admiration for my grandfather.

Sunita Sinha

Preface

In the last decade postcolonialism has emerged as a major critical discourse and the most influential mode of socio-cultural analysis shaping the current climate of literary studies. The growing relevance of the postcolonial method in the context of globalization and empowerment has made it "the latest catch-all term to dazzle the academic mind", "a watchword for the fashionable study of cultural otherness" and "a distinctly viable commodity in the academic marketplace."

Like all other "post-isms", postcolonialism has caused a rigorous ongoing debate among its antagonists and protagonists over the precise parameters of the field and the definition of the term "postcolonial". However, no other literary term has evinced such diverse opinions as postcolonialism. On the one hand, it is acclaimed for the energy and ferment it has brought to the otherwise self-contained literary discipline, on the other, it is held responsible for ushering in new forms of economic and cultural oppression that have succeeded modern colonialism, sometimes called neo-colonialism, which is as dangerous as the former imperial colonialism.

It is true that the term postcolonialism has become so heterogeneous and diffuse that it has become "depressingly difficult." The difficulty is partly due to the multidisciplinary nature of postcolonial studies which incites interest from academics across the humanities and social sciences. What unifies the postcolonial landscape, however, is the object of its study. All postcolonial studies forward new theoretical domains of the colonizational relationship between East and West. With the question of identity as the central theme, creating spaces for the non-European in the Western academia, postcolonial studies seeks to deconstruct the eurocentricism of Western scholarship and cultural hegemonism and gives "emphasis and voice to what is silent or marginally present." Peter Barry identifies one of the major aims of postcolonial literature as "the rejection of the claims to universalism made on behalf of canonical Western literature" and more specifically to "show its limitations of outlook, especially its general inability to empathize across boundaries of cultural and ethnic difference."

Postcolonialism marked a growth of new literatures—literatures of the erstwhile colonies which had in common the shared experience of colonialism. In addition to absorbing the influence of imperial culture, such literatures also resisted this influence and colonial control by asserting their "differences from the assumptions of the imperial center." For them, it was a means of self-assertion and a bridge of dialogue across international audiences. In reaction to the rejection of anything "too local in interest" by the great tradition of established Western canon, postcolonial literature chose to "answer back." Re-examining the earlier literary tradition and reconstructing new mythologies, postcolonial literature has indeed afforded an enabling experience and generated an enormous corpus of specialized academic writing in the field of postcolonial studies. Thus, having expanded into relevant discussions of image culture and having represented studies of imperial and colonial history, anthropology, cultural studies, multiculturism, postcolonial literature "coolly claims half a millennium and most of the planet as its turf."

For Achille Mbembe, one of the brilliant theorists of postcolonial studies writing today, postcolonial thought is a dream, "the dream of a new kind of humanism". As he remarks:

> Postcolonial thinking stresses humanity in the making, the humanity that will emerge once the colonial figures of the inhuman and of racial difference have been swept away.

The book *New Urges in Postcolonial Literature: Widening Horizons* is a humble effort to encapsulate the enormous literary dynamism and debate that characterize the field of postcolonial studies. The twenty-one well-researched papers from India as well as abroad explore the vast array of themes and issues that constitute the postcolonial world. The papers included in the anthology encompass an in-depth analysis of the key trends and recent debates in the field of postcolonialism like feminism, hybridity, multiculturalism, diasporic and transnational migration, gender, otherness, decolonization, androgyny and ecofeminism. The miscellaneous research papers on African, Irish, Canadian, British, Australian and Indian English Literature aim at achieving a harmonious instance of academic homogeneity of themes and views related to postcolonialism.

Postcolonial literature is writing at the margins and has similarities to contemporary European thought like feminism. Feminist and postcolonialist theories share much common ground due to their examination of the voice and the position of subaltern in society. The impact of gender on postcolonial studies was belated but there is now a growing body of work that seeks to define postcolonial feminism and to revisit, if not to revive, ideas of a transnational or global solidarity. In her scholarly paper, "The Cultural Designation of Feminism: Theory and Praxis," Dr. Nandini Sahu offers an in-depth analysis of the multiple theories related to feminism—the single most powerful social movement of our times. Tracing the origin, development and meaning of feminism, Dr. Sahu goes on to examine the feminist theory and its related issues in detail.

In the highly perceptive article, "Spaces, Gender, and Healing in Alice Walker's *The Color Purple* (1982) and Mariama Bâ's *So Long a Letter* (1981)," Prof. Emmanuel N. Ngwang makes a comparative study between Alice Walker and Mariama Bâ's common concern for female marginalization and self-definition. Both the writers centre their work around the struggles of two female protagonists who in their attempt to find "a voice for themselves make a powerful statement about spaces, gender and healing."

In "Traditionalizing Christianity in Kenjo Jumbam's *The White Man of God*," Dr. Ernest L. Veyu examines the cultural-religious clash—the clash between the ingrained traditional worship system and Christianity. The paper brings out the difference between the humaneness of the indigenous traditions and harshness of Christianity and concludes with the picture of a compassionate and open-minded Christianity, "a form of Christianity, robbed of the strict Biblical and Catholic forms." The paper concludes with a peaceful co-existence of Tradition and Christianity in Nso which is achieved by traditionalizing Christianity or Christianizing tradition.

Dr. Devika's insightful paper, "Exquisite Depiction of Cultural Sensitivities in Doris Lessing," defines the writer's role as an interpreter of cultural sensitivities. The paper pivots tellingly on Doris Lessing's prime concern with the individual variations of culture in her works. Although Lessing's fiction is primarily rooted in the issues of feminism, one cannot ignore the undercurrents of twentieth century British culture in her works—it is apparent in the problems, the thinking process, the dressing sense and in the issues that her works point out. What makes Lessing an outstanding novelist is her universal appeal, the humanist approach which is appreciated by even those who are "alien to her native roots."

Kamala Das originated a vigorous and poignant feminine confessional poetry in which a common theme is the exploration of man-woman relationship. "The Poetry of Kamala Das: A Study in Radical Feminism" is a brilliant effort by Purnendu Chatterjee to establish Kamala Das as a radical feminist—a fervent feminist voice with rebellious dimensions, who in her quest for identity broke the fetters of conventions and traditions. In his exhaustive analysis, the author brings out the unabashed self-revelation, stringent protest against the patriarchal hegemony and the traditional concept of gender in the poems of Kamala Das.

Prof. Alessandro Monti's critical paper, "The Reactive Expatriate," traces the sense of loss arising out of the issues of failed migration and the expatriate experience in three rather different novels written by three significant writers of today—Hari Kunzru's *Transmission*, Nirpal Singh Dhalival's *Tourism* and Mohsin Hamid's *The Reluctant Fundamentalist*.

In "Demarcating a Marginalized Lineage: Reading *Robinson Crusoe* through *Roxana* and into *Foe*," Natalie Wall brings out the intertextual relationship of J.M. Coetzee's *Foe* with Defoe's *Robinson Crusoe* and *Roxana*. The paper points out that basically, an extension of Defoe's *Robinson Crusoe*, Coetzee's *Foe* recounts the story of Susan Barton's experiences on a desert island with Crusoe and Friday and her attempt to get Foe to write an account of these experiences. In Coetzee's story, we see a transformation of colonialism and its ideology into one of existing meaninglessness in *Foe*.

In her paper, "The Paradigm of Ambivalence in the Women Characters of Rohinton Mistry," Dr. Anita Myles observes in detail, the comprehensive portrayal of women characters in the writings of Rohinton Mistry, "successfully juggling between home life, motherhood, career and spiritual fulfilment." Dr. Myles presents Rohinton Mistry's women characters as symbols of growth as well as means of withdrawal and destruction. Not always victims, these women characters display remarkable grit, courage, understanding and forbearance in moments of crisis.

In her paper, "The Rewriting of Personal Narratives in the Exile's Quest for Home: Brian Friel's *Dancing at Lughnasa* and *The Loves of Cass McGuire*," Elisa Armellino explores the quest for home, the search for location and the need for a sense of belonging which characterize the experience of exile. Armellino's paper brilliantly captures the painful sense of displacement, portrayed effectively in the plays of Brian Friel, one of the eminent contemporary Irish writers.

Many Indian women novelists have explored female subjectivity in order to establish an identity that is not imposed by a patriarchal society. Anita Desai in her psychological novels presents the image of a suffering woman preoccupied with her inner world, her sulking frustration and the storm within. In their paper, "Inner Progression of a Repressed Soul in Anita Desai's *Fasting, Feasting*," Prof. Meenakshi Raman and Sushila Rathore offer a scholarly analysis of the inner recesses and the 'angst within' the women characters in Anita Desai's

Fasting, Feasting. The paper focuses on the sense of power attained by the powerless woman protagonist through self-sacrifice, tolerance and indomitable spirit.

Rosalyn M. Mutia's innovative paper, "Bridges in the Gap between British and American Women Poets: A Feminist Reading of Selected Poems of Sylvia Plath and Hilda Doolittle's *Helen in Egypt*," effectively traces the feminist issues which inform the poems of the 20th century British poet, Sylvia Plath and the poems of the American woman poet, Hilda Doolittle. In her comparative analysis, Rosalyn M. Mutia brings out the "heightened degree of unanimity with feminist concerns and themes" which bridges the gap between the British and the American women poets.

In "Immigrant Experience and Pain of Exile in Jhumpa Lahiri's *The Namesake*," Dr. Srutimala Duara discusses the immigrant experience, the question of identity and the sense of exile, alienation and assimilation in Jhumpa Lahiri's fiction. The author effectively captures the perpetual dilemma faced by immigrants as they struggle to maintain their identities, while trying to shake them off at the same time as presented in Lahiri's first novel, *The Namesake*.

Dr. Ranu Uniyal's innovative paper, "Re-writing the Myth: Romantic Love in Margaret Drabble's *The Waterfall*," concentrates on Margaret Drabble's attempt to rewrite or revise the myths and to alter the language that constructs and reconstructs the lives of women. The paper deals with the portrayal of the woman protagonist within the context of modern culture, ending in the self-awakening of the female protagonist and the feminization of its male protagonist. It also explores Romantic love which conveys a desire for wholeness and completion.

In an exhaustive study of feminism, "Third World Women and the Politics of Feminism," Prof. Anita Singh explores the meaning, the goals and the critique of Third World feminism. The paper focuses on the Third World women's struggle for new definition of power. In addition to analyzing their own situation, the Third World women are articulating powerful critiques of eurocentricism of Western feminism and urging the Third World feminine perspectives to a global feminism.

Prof. Shubha Tiwari in her competent analysis in "The Idea of Selling the Idea of India in Recent Indian English Fiction" draws our attention to the fact that a particular genre of Indian authors are milking a preset idea of India that unfortunately sells; portraying a negative and derogatory image of India. The highly innovative paper ends on a pertinent question as to whether we need the Western world to certify our literary merit.

In her innovative paper, "Nature as Metaphor: A Study of Anita Desai's *In Custody*," Dr. Reena Mitra presents Nature as the all-pervasive symbol to explore the moods, experiences and relationships in Anita Desai's *In Custody*. Though an interpreter of the "inner climate," Anita Desai makes an effective use of the "outer weather" to reinforce the experiences of the protagonists.

Dr. Pradeep Trikha's "Multiculturalism in the Recent Australian Short Fiction: An Indian Point-of-View," presents an academic analysis of the tradition of Australian short story which successively depicts those areas of Australian experience which have not been explored by the Australian novelists. With the breaking down of repressive censorship, legislation and the experience of eclecticism and rich literary culture, a new genre of writers arrived and short story in Australian short fiction got a new lease. Further, the short story writer and the reader enjoy a unique position of being a spectator rather than a participant. Thus, the paper effectively brings out the influence wielded by short fiction writer upon the masses.

Athanasius Ayuk-Ako in his innovative paper "Teaching Achebe and Conrad at the University of Burundi in Bujumbura" offers an interesting analysis of the various challenges faced in teaching Chinua Achebe's *Things Fall Apart* and Conrad's *Heart of Darkness*. The paper examines the problematic nature of the text and reflects the varying responses of the students of the Department of English, University of Burundi, who have been adversely affected by the conservative educational system.

In her brilliant comparative analysis, "White Man at the End of History: A Comparative Study of Nadine Gordimer's

The Conservationist and J.M. Coetzee's *Disgrace*," Dr. Arpa Ghosh observes critically the disintegration of oppressive white apartheid-ridden power and the growing powerlessness of the white colonizer as social entity, as projected in the novels of Gordimer and Coetzee.

In her scholarly paper, "Indigenous vs Non-Indigenous: A Cultural Interface in Multicultural Australia," Dr. Jaslene Dhaliwal surveys the unbridgeable evolutionary gulf between the indigenous and non-indigenous, between the civilized and uncivilized. The paper proposes to establish a society where people with different roots can co-exist, a society which looks across the frontiers of race, language, gender and age. Dr. Dhaliwal's article presents the Aborigines as still clinging tenaciously to their limping cultural identity seeking changes that sustain and not weaken their Aboriginal culture.

Prof. Basavaraj Naikar's article "The Dialectics of Enchained Sensibility in *The Foreigner*," explores the theme of alienation and rootlessness which engulfs the protagonist, a victim of the 'terror of indifference' and aloneness, which symbolizes the tragic predicament of the contemporary man.

Thus, placing its emphasis on literary as well as theoretical texts, the book explores a wide range of Anglophone postcolonial writing. It is a comprehensive collection spanning the literatures of Australia, Africa, Canada, India and America and offers an extensive focus on the emergence of many innovative non-European English language writers originating from former British colonies. The book attempts to situate postcolonial literary and theoretical material within the complex, diverse histories and cultures which constitute the "postcolonial world".

Representing the combined efforts of scholars, the book is multivocal and inclusive, which would not have come to fruition without the help of many people. Needless to say, *New Urges in Postcolonial Literature: Widening Horizons* would not have existed but for the efforts of the contributors who conscientiously and patiently wrote and sometimes rewrote their articles at my request. Hence, I wish to thank all the contributors from India as well as from Calgary (Canada), Mississippi (USA), Turin (Italy), and Yaoundé (Cameroon) for being an indispensable part of this venture and lending it a cosmopolitan outlook and a global approach.

I also wish to thank Atlantic Publishers and Distributors (P) Ltd. for the confidence evinced in me and for seeing the book through the press.

Sunita Sinha

Contents

The Cultural Designation of Feminism: Theory and Praxis

1

Nandini Sahu

Feminism is a vital area in contemporary intellectual literary discourse. This paper aims at an analysis of the impact of this theory that has given rise to issues like 'men in feminism', 'feminism without women', 'the origin and the types of feminism', keeping in view its fundamental significance and impact on literary studies during the second half of the twentieth century. Also, the paper discusses several major theories related to feminism as a whole, their origin and development across the years. Feminist theory can be compared with some major conceptual developments like Marxism and psychoanalysis. This theory helps one analyze and understand the major factors through which the two genders—male and female—have been constructed with specific languages and ideas in literature. Chronologically, 1960s and 1970s helped theorize a woman's discourse; in 1980s, feminism concentrated on changing the intellectual fields for women; and in 1990s it began and reached its culmination in playing a major role in directing women's feeling of themselves as the other sex.

The word "feminism" has so many meanings and directions in the current century that it is hardly possible to attribute it some precise definition. Janet Radcliff Richards observes: "women suffer from systematic social injustice because of their sex,"[1] and a voice against this social injustice is the ideal of feminism. It is a common belief that feminism is a movement of women and men are not allowed into it which is rather a narrow definition. In fact, feminism is not concerned with a limited group of people to benefit their demands, rather it wants to eliminate social injustice, works in favour of the oppressed. Lisa Tuttle defines feminism thus: "the term feminism, taken from the Latin word 'femina' (woman), originally meant having the qualities of females. It originated in the perception that there is something wrong with the treatment of the females by the society."[2] The feminists attempt to analyze the reasons, dimensions of women's oppression, and the remedies. Feminism incorporates both a principle of equal rights for woman (the organized movement to attain women's rights) and philosophy of social renovation aiming to create a world for women beyond uncomplicated social equality. But feminism must distinguish for itself between women's rights and women's emancipation. Coming to the "Feminist" like feminism, there is not a single definition of feminist since feminists have many differing affinities—of sexual preference, class and race. In short, a feminist is a woman who recognizes herself, and is recognized by others, as a feminist, as the one who has the awareness and knowledge of women's oppression, and has a recognition of women's differences and commonalities. Some feminists argue for a classification that is future oriented—that a feminist must have a notion of social change.

Some sources say that Viking women were the first feminists. Broka Aubur, one of Iceland's legendary Viking heroines, attacked her unfaithful husband with a sword ten centuries ago and defied social tradition by wearing trousers. Another Icelandic woman, Gudrid Porbjamadottir, helped lead the third Viking expedition to America early in the 11th century and gave birth to the first European child on the new continent. Since the origin of the American civilization, women were assigned a subordinate role within the family irrespective of wealth or talent and were denied the political and civil rights enjoyed by men; the feminine world was basically alienated from the masculine world. By 1870, American women challenged this restrictive view of family. Higher education gave women their most important opportunity to reject the traditional claims of male-female distinctions. During 1870s, Mrion Talbot and her mother Emily Talbot persuaded the Harvard University premises to open the doors for women.

Dr. Edward Clarke, a former medical school professor and a Harvard overseer, opined that higher education would destroy women's health, beauty and reproductive ability which the Talbot mother and daughter proved false with research and survey. This seems to be the first recorded attempts of the feminists to challenge male supremacy. Sam Shephard has said "The real mystery of American life lies between men, not between men and women."[3] "Women's movement and thinking has emanated from the urgency of the age,"[3] says Helen Cixous, one of the pioneering feminists in France. Her writings challenge the male hegemony that exists in opposition to the prevailing ideology. She says, "When I started writing I instinctively felt an ethical obligation towards women and decided to take up cudgels on behalf of them. When I say 'women' I'm speaking of women in their inevitable struggle against conventional man; and of a universal women subject who must bring women to their senses and to their meaning in history...we don't need to be a part of men, we stand as entities by ourselves."[3] She warns against the danger of confusing the sex of the author with the sex of the writing a man or a woman produces.

In an essay entitled "Women and Fiction" (1929), Virginia Woolf speculated on the new colours and shadows in women's writing after the English woman was transformed from a weak, fluctuating, vague character to a voter, wage-earner, a responsible citizen. Woolf considered that the relations of the new woman with the society will not only be emotional but also intellectual and political. She described the woman's world of cooking, child bearing as intangible, vague, anonymous, as if that were a dark country, which could be compared to Mary Wollstonecraft's view in *Vindication of the Rights of Women* (1722) that women were immured in their families, groping in the dark. The second wave feminists were just the followers defining women's oppression as her imprisonment in the bourgeois household as a mother and unpaid servant. "First-wave/second-wave feminism" has been a long tradition of writers and thinkers who have criticized the position of women in western societies, but not until the nineteenth century did that critique inspire a mass movement. Between approximately 1880 and 1920, and beginning again in the 1960s, questions of women's social, economic and political rights generated substantial popular support and public discussion, initially in Europe, North America, Australia and New Zealand and then, in the twentieth century on all continents. Although the term feminism did not come into popular use until the 1910s, commentators since have termed the two movements 'first' and 'second-wave' feminism, likening the ebb and flow of the movements' mass appeal to that of a cresting wave. The origins of nineteenth-century feminism lie in the changes that altered western societies in the early part of the twentieth century. Foremost was industrialization which undermined household production and established a hierarchy between the male-dominated public sphere and the female-dominated private one. At the same time, liberal-democratic ideologies, socialism, evangelical Protestant Christianity, and social reform movements, especially abolitionism and temperance, propelled a wide spectrum of women to challenge their exclusion from the public realm. The relative importance of each factor depended on the specific national or even regional circumstances, as historian Chiristine Bolt has observed, the story of first-wave feminism 'is one of national distinctiveness within an international cause'. Feminist criticism is just one aspect of the Cultural Revolution in America in 1960s. In 1970s that was categorized as Black feminist criticism, Lesbian feminist criticism with woman as the reader as well as woman as the writer. Some such books are Alice Jordine's *Gynesis: Configurations of Woman and Modernity* (1985), Noami Schor's *Reading in Detail: Aesthetics and the Feminine* (1987), Tania Modeleski's *Study of Hitchcock: The Women Who Knew Too Much* (1988) and Elaine Showalter's *Towards a Feminist Poetics* (1979), where she coins a new world, 'gynocritics', making women conscious of "only what men have thought women should be".[4]

Feminism has been classified under certain categories keeping in view its characteristics and dimensions. "Liberal feminism" refers to the tradition defined by John Stuart Mill in his book, *The Subjugation of Women*. It argues in favour of the basic liberty of women to determine their social role and to walk equal to man. "Liberal Feminism" confers upon the state the duty to ensure that every individual, both man and woman, has got the right to engage himself/herself in the competition to gain his/her self-interest. The state must ensure and enforce equality of opportunity. Liberal Feminism is the theory of individual freedom for women. Liberal feminism is one of the main streams of feminist political and social theory and has the most long-term history. Liberal feminism argues for individual fulfillment free from the strictures of highly defined sex roles. It limits itself to reformism, seeking to improve the status of women within the system but not fundamentally contesting either the system's operation or its authenticity. Contemporary liberal feminists espouse women's rights in terms of welfare needs, worldwide education, and health services. For example, liberal critics point to unfair employment practices rather than attacking the society as a whole. The "Classical Marxist Feminism" states that women's oppression is a result of our larger socio-economic system. Man's traditional responsibility to provide woman with the means of living makes him look down upon her. Women's traditional position excludes her from participating in public production, confines her only to domestic works in the private world of the family. Thus, even if she takes maximum responsibility of the family, still she is not recognized by the society. This domestic slavery of the wife can come to an end only under socialism, in the Marxist feminists' view. Because now the state will undertake food preparation, childcare, nursery and other major female activities within the sphere of public production by providing public sector services like childcare centres, hotels, hospitals, etc. specially for women. After this, man will no longer be the bourgeois and woman the proletariat. To the feminists, a woman should be provided with her basic rights in her own individual world. Elizabeth Cady Stanton has written, "In discussing the rights of woman, we are to consider first what belongs to her as an individual is a world of her own, the arbiter of her own destiny, an imaginary Robinson Crusoe, with his woman...on a solitary island."[5] "Radical Feminism" is a rather recent concept that argues in favour of the sexual liberty of women. The different forms of social oppression upon women are basically the outcome of the sexual oppression. Woman is generally accepted as the weaker sex, the second sex. It is a neo-Freudian theory; Fred believed that "The crucial problem of modern life is sexuality."[6] The heart of women's oppression is her role as a child bearer and rearer. Writers as Ti Grace, and Alkinson and Shulamith Firestone do not believe that woman's oppression consists in her lack of political or civil rights. Neither do they support Marxists who classify women in the society in a lower class. Rather, the radical feminists require a biological revolution for women, a liberation from fundamental inequalities in sex through developed technology and artificial reproduction. The prototype role of woman as a child production machine should be challenged, renovated by the state making her equal with the male. "The situation of a woman is that she—a free and autonomous being like all creatures—nevertheless finds herself living in a world, where men compel her to assume the status of the other."[7] Radical feminism argues that woman's oppression comes from her categorization as an inferior class. Radical feminism aims to destroy this sex-class system. What makes this feminism radical is that it focuses on the roots of male domination and claims this all forms of oppression are extensions of male superiority. Radical feminism argues that patriarchy is the defining characteristic of our society. The other central hypothesis of radical feminism is the belief that the personal is political and that woman-centeredness can be the basis of an upcoming society. "Cultural feminism" is an approach to feminism thinking and action which claims that either by nature and/or through nurture, women have developed what society refers to as 'feminine' or 'female' characteristics. This set of characteristics, say cultural feminists, is to be compared and contrasted with the set of 'masculine' or 'male' characteristics which men have developed, also through nature and/or nurture. Cultural feminists fault western thought for its tendency to privilege 'male' ways of being, thinking, and doing over 'female' ones. Specifically, they argue that the traits typically associated with men—'independence, autonomy, intellect, will, wariness, hierarchy, domination, culture, transcendence, product, asceticism, war and death'—are no better, and perhaps worse, than the traits typically associated with women—'interdependence, community, connection, sharing, emotion, body, trust, absence of hierarchy, nature, immanence, process, joy, peace and life.' "Existentialist feminism" draws inspiration from existentialists including Beauvoir, Merleau-Ponty, and Sartre. They see women's and men's lives as concretely situated and highlight concepts like freedom, interpersonal relations, and experience of lived body. They value the competence for fundamental change, but recognize that various factors limit it, such as self-deception, and anxiety raised by change and self-responsibility.

Feminism as a theory has very recently given rise to a new area in criticism, known as "Feminist Literary Criticism". The motto of this literary criticism is to search for underlying, powerful female tradition in literature. The feminist literary critics attempt to uncover and interpret women's writing from a symbolic point of view and to rediscover the lost works of women in the past. They aim at interpreting the works of the male writers from a feminist standpoint and to distinguish between the politics, style and language of the male and female writers. Feminist theory is a locale of writing which represents a critical and original contribution to current thinking. With increasing acts of physical belligerence towards women, there is an even greater need for feminist psychoanalytic theory which investigates sexual distinctiveness. Unique to feminist hypothesis is its insistence on the inextricable link between theory and practice and between the communal and private. Theory and experience have a very singular relationship within feminism encapsulated in its slogan 'the personal in political'. Certain terms in contemporary theory are used to sum up what appear to be the key experiences of women. Among these are 'work', 'family', 'patriarchy', 'sexuality'. These concepts reflect feminism's effort to reveal nucleus social processes and to find what constantly reappears in various guises in the itinerary of women's account. An elementary goal of feminist theory is to comprehend women's oppression in terms of race, sex, class and sexual preference and how to revolutionize it. Feminist theory reveals the magnitude of women's individual and collective experiences and their struggles. It analyses how sexual divergence is constructed within any intellectual and common word and builds accounts of experiences from these differences.

Feminism will always need an agenda within which it can travel around diversity. Feminist theory represents that prospective for a broader politics. Its vision and forms of practice constitute a major break with traditional definitions. The issues of feminist theory—"ecological feminism", "pacifism", "anti-pornography", "Third World affairs", and "sexuality debates"—all focus on women's specificity grounded in the sexual division of labour and reproduction. Most reservations are really misgivings about traditional theory and not about feminism. As Edward Said and others argue, the cult of this theory reduces continuation to elements in a self-confirming, intellectual maneuver. Feminist theory, on the other hand, enables women to recognize their interests and standing as historical agents. Feminism actively refuses the arrogant mystification involved in traditional theory which is often incomprehensible or abstract and has a inclination for losing contact with the world. Traditional theories have been applied in ways that make it complicated to understand women's involvement in social life. Feminist theory is instantaneous, and urgently about the world of women.

As the goals of the women's movement diversified, so too did its ideological underpinnings. Liberal ideals of political and educational equality, along with socialist principles of redistributing economic wealth, remained influential, but by the end of the nineteenth century, the rhetoric of maternalism was being deployed with increasing frequency. Maternal, also called domestic or social, feminism celebrated women's superior morality as the justification for female participation in public affairs and for improved state services for mothers and children. Although some non-European women used similar rhetoric, maternalism often relied upon radicalized images and arguments to marshal support and to legitimate white women's special 'civilizing' role in reform and missionary work. The fledging women's right movement that emerged in the 1850s through 1870s advocated a single sexual standard for men and women, (primarily within marriage), dress reform, equal property and other legal rights, and higher education for women, especially in professions such as medicine and law. With the movement's dramatic growth after 1880, concerns over the conditions and wages of working-class women gained prominence, as did a revitalized interest in temperance and a new commitment to social purity—protecting women from sexual 'vice'. In the process, feminism became allied with numerous other social reform movements. By 1900, ideological differences were over-shadowed by the growing agreement amongst activities that success on key legal, educational and economic issues could not be gained without grater political leverage, and thus the vote emerged as a unifying objective for feminists of all persuasions and in many nations.

Adrienne Rich is an American poet and critic who, in "Of Woman Born" (1976), "On Lies, Secrets and Silence" (1980), creates a feminist theory which she calls her 'Re-vision' or rewriting of patriarchal customs. The term refers to a new feminist perspective which could link women's culture to the realities of our past and existing history. Rich uses the technique in her own work to mix study and personal experience. Making a major contribution to feminism with her accounts of education, sexual politics, reproduction and ethnic identity, Rich argues that the English language and the intellectual tradition have been used as weapons of colonialisation and describes how a woman's university and female-identified education could provide a substitute to this tradition. Rich rediscovers the concept of motherhood by distinguishing between a patriarchal institutionalization of motherhood and the joy and experience of motherhood. Similarly, Rich redefined the concept of 'lesbian' and greatly expanded the boundaries of lesbian history and experience by distinguishing the historical existence of lesbian from lesbian ethnicity and Jewish identity. In all her writings, and in her gynocentric view of world history, Rich creates a new tradition of feminist scholarship. In this regard, some typical and very important phrases related to feminism, coined by Rich and other feminists, may be discussed in detail.

If we go on to give a historical sketch of feminist theories, we have to discuss the origins of the 'second wave'. British feminist Juliet Mitchell characterizes feminism as "an ideological offspring of certain economic and social conditions."[8] Its radicalism reflects the fact that it comes to prominence at points of decisive change and envisages it with an imagination that goes beyond it. One of Freud's most articulate pre-second wave feminist critics is Simone de Beauvoir, whose observation, "one is not born, but rather becomes a woman",[8] gives subsequent analyses of patriarchally constituted psychological and sexual femininity. Feminism itself, feminist film theory, feminist epistemology, the body, gender, feminist history, queer theory, women's studies, black feminism, Chicano feminism, feminist theology—these are just some of the entries whose very headwords give evidence to the mark that feminist theory and practice have made on the shape and content of academic curricula.

"Anarchist feminism" is a theory that female subordination is determined as much by a system of sexual and familial relationships as by State controls, and that legal change cannot in itself provide equality without full psychological autonomy. Anarchist feminism would eliminate all social restraints and replace these with decentralized, organic communities of women. Early feminist anarchists, for example, Emma Goldman and Voltarinine de Cleyre, believed that communal attitudes would grow organically into sexual and psychological freedom. Anarchist feminists argue that the State and patriarchy are twin irregularities. To obliterate the State is to destroy the major instrument of institutionalized patriarchy; to abolish patriarchy is to put an end to the State. This theory is more *avant-garde* than radical feminism because it believes that any State is always illicit. Perhaps for this rationale, many feminist science fiction writers are anarchists. Anarchist feminists also believe that the means used to revolutionize the society must be the models of the future society in themselves. Therefore, women's cooperatives and consciousness-raising groups can make a more momentous social and ideological input than their numbers or financial status might entail. "Anarchist feminism" refers to the inspiration feminists have gained from the concept of anarchy from the Greek word, literally, non-rule. The foremother of anarchist feminism, Emma Goldman (1869-1940), opined that political ideas were meaningless unless they were acted on, and she was arrested numerous times for speaking out and advocating such action. As a nihilist, she knew that men and women are oppressed by authoritarian social structures, but she also saw that women are oppressed specifically as women. The convergence of feminist concerns with anarchism meant that no mere reform of hierarchical institutions would be adequate to the task of allowing women to live full lives. Thus, she spoke out against women's suffrage because she saw it as merely a way to gain women's cooperation in the maintenance of an essentially unchanged organization. Goldman was outstanding because she was able to draw one theory without being lured by it; while inspired by communism and anarchism, she insisted that their appliance should be elastic and adaptable, resisting any urge toward rigidity, uniformity, or essentialism.

"Abolitionist Feminism" is one of the main theories of nineteenth-century feminism. It takes the view that woman's subjugation and liberation paralleled the struggle for Black liberation from slavery. The nineteenth-century faction to eliminate slavery in the USA preceded, and provided strategies for the development of feminism. The notion of *alienation* is vital to feminist theory. Women's alienation has so many different elements and the feminists argue that a new theoretical framework can be used, but it must go past Marxism. It must connect women's intimidation in the home, in culture and in sexuality, with our knowledge in wage labour. Even within wage labour, the sexualisation of women's work and the sexual persecution of women generate a gender-specific form of women's isolation. Socialist and Marxist feminists consent that the first stride is to eliminate the sexual allotment of labour in every area of life because while alienation reduces the woman to an appliance of labour within industry, it reduces the woman to an instrument for man's sexual contentment within the family. Women are alienated from skill and scholarship, which presents a male-biased model of human nature and collective reality. These forms are interrelated. For example, the form taken by woman's sexual estrangement results in an even more damaging alienation from her intellectual capacities. In addition, women's participation in male-dominated opinionated activity might also be described as alienated.

The term "Body Politics" refers both to physical power relations and to the resistance against all forms of tortuous violence against women. Nancy M. Henley argues that the body language of existing culture is inherently sexist. Other feminists use the commencement of body politics to illustrate aggression against women embedded in other controlling and domineering relations like class and imperialism, as well as in the patriarchal institutions of family, medicine or education. Feminists writing about body politics share one main theme that there is the doggedness on the human essence of women, on our dignity, integrity and purity as human beings and a denunciation of women's objectification.

Under "Christian feminism", the feminist theories of Christianity fall into three categories: those that challenge the theological view of women and the androcentricity of customary theology; those that challenge the theological laws that bar women from ordination; those that weigh up the church as an organization and aim to promote the certified status of woman in the church. Feminist theologians clash the recurrent use of masculine terms to refer to God or the Holy Ghost. In research about the descriptions of women in the church and in Christian history, theologians reveal that there are only two images of women—the transgressor (Eve) or the virgin (Mary), which includes motherhood and obedience. They argue that this dualism, by creating a sense of the other, is inherently racist, sexist and could lead to the destruction of the planet. Feminist Christians are not antichristian but argue instead that Christianity has excluded transcendental biblical themes in favor of anti-women images.

"Domestic labor" is the way in which women regenerate labour power for capitalism by servicing the domicile and socializing their families. The scrutiny of domestic labour is a central hub of feminist theory has been the domestic labour dispute, in which feminist ideas confront the political concepts and theoretical positions of the traditional left. The domestic labour debate was initiated in 1969 by Margaret Benston in *The Political Economy of Women*. She drew awareness to the fact that housework must be taken seriously in many analyses of the workings of the economy, and not relegated to a marginal or non-existent status. Housework could be recognized both as productive labour and, simultaneously, as a locale of exploitation and a source for capital growth. At the centre of the debate is the issue of whether Marx's theory of value could be applied to domestic labour or not. It is only within capitalism that men are able to exclude and marginalize household labour.

"Escritoire feminine" is the term for women's writing in French feminist theory. It describes how women's writing is a specific dissertation closer to the body and to emotions both of which are repressed by the social treaty. Writing and literature are crucial areas because literature reveals the introverted, the clandestine and unsaid and, in a force of the imagination, can be a space of aspiration and pleasure. Most feminists are actively creating a new women's language while concurrently critiquing the old one. "Black feminism" is related to the theory of Black-defined women's struggles. Black feminism has built on a tradition of leftist activism, adapting models of socialist feminism. Initially, Black feminism argued that meaningful change in a social order, which represses both men and women could be accomplished by building a federation between women of colour and progressive movements. Black feminists like Barbara Smith, Audre Lorde, Gloria I. Joseph, Gloria Hull or Alice Walker have created theories which meet the needs of Black women by helping Black women to stimulate issues that they perceive to have direct impact on the overall value of life. Black feminist theory examines the margin of sisterhood with white feminists in order to transact fully with the contradictions intrinsic in gender, race and class within the context of a racist society. Black feminists argue that all feminist theories must grasp imperialism and challenge it.

"Essentialism" refers to the succinct in unique female nature. Feminists defy assumptions that women are essentially weaker, whether biologically, emotionally, than men since these assumptions underline misogyny and favoritism against women. For example, feminist historians show how discrimination against women in medicine and science is often based on a mythical essentialism. Alternatively, radical feminism believes that there are essential feminine modes of perception which can communicate female creativity and culture. This sometimes leads radical feminism to idealization which often underlies essentialist views of women. For example, women are described as "finer pacifist beings"[8] by some peace groups. But it is impossible to distinguish between 'authentic' and 'obligatory' feminine essentials. All feminists recognize that this theory should be thoroughly genderised and that women do have preoccupations which are essentially female—for example motherhood and female bonding—even if all women do not wish to mother or to affiliate with other women.

"Female consciousness" defines women's recognition of how a particular class, culture and historical period create definitions of female. Female consciousness is not necessarily feminist but is an unconscious feminism, particularly when it occurs in women's groups. Female consciousness promotes a shared vision embodying fundamental opinionated implications that feminist theory needs to address. "Female ethic" has three main features. It includes a critique of notion and a principle that female thinking is more tangible. It stresses that the values of compassion, nurturance and care are values of women. It stresses too that choices are in reality the hassle of situations. "Female eunuch" is a phrase coined by Germaine Greer in her book of the same name to describe the 'castration' of women by aspects of patriarchy such as 'romantic love' and by male antagonism. Greer used de Beauvoir's concept of woman in order tc squabble that women's providence is to befall deformed and incapacitated by the disparaging action of male domination in existing society which deprives women of getting in touch with peripheral reality. Greer suggests that its significance is to make women inner-directed. "Sexism" is a phrase to define a social relationship in which males denigrate females. Contemporary feminism argues that sexist social beliefs and practices not only limit the activities of women, but are an impertinent way of making distinctions between the sexes, because they are not founded on evidence. A sizeable body of feminist research has documented sexism in the media. For example, it criticizes the use of sex-role stereotyping where women are always mothers and household workers. Feminist psychoanalysis argues that sexism stems from the configuration of gender identity as well as from contemporary culture.

"Sisterhood", sometimes called *sorority,* includes the idea and experience of female bonding, and the self-affirmation and identity discovered in a woman-centered vision and definition of womanhood. Because sisterhood is based on a clear awareness that all women, irrespective of class, race, or nation have a common problem—patriarchy—the term which is an important part of contemporary feminism. Radical feminism argues sisterhood is not at all symmetrical with brotherhood or male comradeship. Sisterhood has at its core the affirmation of freedom and is radically self-affirming. There are other definitions of sisterhood, for example Catherine Beecher's idea of separate spheres for women. Sisterhood is also implied in the maternalists' affirmation and celebration of the unique qualities of female experience as well as in Mary Daly's vision of women-centered separatism. Bell Hooks and other Black feminists prefer the term 'solidarity' to sisterhood because sisterhood implies the erasing of difference. They argue that political solidarity must be the main feminist agenda. "Spiritual feminism", sometimes called "myth feminism", is a growing area of feminist theory. The ecology of myth described by critics such as Carol Christ, Mary Daly and Charlene Spretnak involves the construction of cultural archetypes of power useful to women and psychological tools which can facilitate women to articulate desire through symbols and rituals. Defining "Jewish feminism" is difficult for feminists both because the language available to describe Jews as a racial group is insufficient. Characterizing Jewish feminism as a narrow version of identity politics has margins because anti-Semitism is not only an attack on identity, nor does it only affect Jewish women. Women stand in a particular relationship to Jewish culture. Adrienne Rich points out how Jewish women suffer a double disadvantage by being both a target of biological determinism and also invisible in Jewish history.

"Gay liberation" is a movement (which began in America in the late 1960s) for political, social and cultural rights for homosexual men and women. Critics argue that the women's movement shares with gay liberation a common goal: a society free from defining and categorizing people by virtue of gender and/or sexual inclination. "Lesbian feminism" is rather epigrammatic that women-identified women, committed together for political, sexual and economic support, provide an alternative model to male/female relations which lesbians see as tyrannical. The theorists Charlotte Bunch, Ti-Grace Atkinson, Adrienne Rich argue that lesbian feminism involves both a sexual preference and a political preference because it rejects male definitions of women's lives. In statements like "feminism is the theory, lesbianism is the practice"[9] the Furies and others made lesbian feminism a primary force in a radical women's culture. Lesbian feminism attacks both the institution and the ideology of heterosexuality as being the centre of patriarchy. Radical lesbians were the first lesbian feminists to suggest that the concept lesbian should be reconstructed, but theories of lesbian feminism differ in their prominence on sexual or on political goals.

Feminist theory defines *rape* as an act and a social institution which perpetuates patriarchal domination and which is based on sadism, rather than specifically as a crime of violence. This definition is a major contribution to social theory. Feminist analysis proves that rape is the consistent conclusion of sexism. It is one of the most alarming forms of social duress because rape is a steady reminder to all women of their susceptible and vulnerable condition. Radical feminists like Susan Brownmiller, Susan Griffin and Andrea Dworkin, argue that patriarchy legitimizes rape by defining rape as 'normal'. Under patriarchy, not only are women defined as sexual objects but men are thought to have 'drives' towards heterosexual intercourse. Because patriarchal culture defines women as being sexually passive and receptive. Adrienne Rich suggests that rape is one of the main means of reinforcing enforced heterosexuality. Consciousness raising groups reveal that women's understanding of rape is not an isolated individual event but a symptom of a society-wide structure of power and powerlessness. Currently, feminist theory takes the observation that rape is a political act of terror against an exploited group.

Since the origin of humanity, male domination has been an accepted fact. Genesis symbolizes this by depicting Eve as made from a "Supernumerary bone of Adam".[10] Aristotle believed "a female is a female by virtue of certain lack of qualities: We should regard the female nature as afflicted with a natural defectiveness."[9] Plato thanked god that he was created a man, not a woman. St. Thomas considered a woman to be an "imperfect man", an "incidental being"[9]. St. Augustine declared, "Woman is a creature neither decisive nor constant." The morning prayers of the Jews, "Blessed be God...that He did not make me a woman", reflect the status of a woman as compared to a man. In the Bible it has been written that both Adam and Eve ate the forbidden fruit, both faced the fall. But God distinguished between their punishments. Adam was condemned to labour, and it is the male toil that results in the building of the civilization. Eve was relegated to the inferior, vulnerable, sexual status, as God said to her, "In sorrow thou shalt bring troth children. And thy desire shall be to the husband. And he shall rule over thee."[10] "Femminism" which means men in feminism was introduced in a ground-breaking compilation edited by Alice Jardine and Paul Smith (1987) and refers to the rethinking of masculinity by male academics who have begun to absorb aspects of feminist politics and theory into their thinking, sometimes to the extent that they assert themselves feminists. While some of these male feminists have limited themselves to an admission of the complicity of men in perpetuating patriarchy and beg women to understand that not all men are oppressors, others explore what it means to be a man and the practices and discourses which shape masculinity in various social, cultural and historical contexts. At its best, 'femmenism' situates the study of masculinity in a gender/power framework, linking it to relations of power between men and women as well as among men. "Androcentrism" means male centeredness, which is the assessment set of our prevailing customs based on male norms. Charlotte Perkins Gilman first used this term to draw attention to male favoritism. Any explanation which characterizes aspects of women's lives as nonstandard is andocentric. "Androcentrism" affects the hypothesis, not only because universities and research institutions are largely male domains but more subtly in the preference of areas of research, research policies, theoretical concepts and research methods. Feminist literature establishes the idea that artistic creativity is a masculine quality. "Phallocentric" is a term in feminist theory used to describe the way the society regards the phallus or penis as a symbol of power, and believes that attributes of masculinity are the norm for cultural definitions. The phallocentric fallacy in disciplines is the assumption that the term 'person' stands for male and therefore women's experience has made no contribution to disciplinary methods or content. This perspective—also sometimes known as androcentric—makes women unknowable. Some feminists argue that phallocentricism is a source of women's oppression in education.

The main goal of feminism is to redefine, and change this age-old dogma by discovering the subtle causes of woman's subjugation. It is a way to making the entire culture conscious of the natural rights of women relating to unequal labour, unequal pay for equal work, marriage and divorce laws that make man the supreme authority, economic independence, division of labour inside the family, to think a woman's income as extra rather than a support, and then to introduce reforms in the traditional social structures. Feminism conceives of a utopian world free of male privilege, chauvinism, hierarchy, authority. It is a movement to bring about a sociopolitical change to condemn the subordination of any sex, to rebalance the social, economic, political power between man and woman. It raises a voice against man's claim to define what is good for a woman and what is not keeping in view his own selfish motives. Feminists believe woman to be a mature decision maker. Protesting against the social institutions that denied women any other identity except that which they acquired through their men—that of a daughter, sister, wife, mother. Feminists like Mary Wollstonecraft, John Stuart Mill, and Elizabeth Cady Stanton dreamt of a world which guaranteed individual identity to a woman. In India there are many female writers/poets like Amrita Pritam, Meena Alexander, Mamata Kalia, Kamala Das, Anita Desai, Shashi Deshpande, Mrinal Pandey, Deepti Khandelwal and many more in whose writings a voice for woman's identity can be assessed. Feminists intend to deconstruct all the indefinite identities of women opposing the binary oppositions between the male and the female. The society has cut a straight line between good and bad, black and white, dark and light, man and woman—feminism is a movement against this distinction, this binary opposition.

NOTES

1. Sushila Singh, Ed. *Feminism: Theory, Criticism, Analysis.* Delhi, Pencraft International, 1997, p. 22.
2. *Ibid.*, p. 30.
3. *Ibid.*, p. 101.
4. Quoted in *Asian Age.* February 7, 1997, p. 21.
5. *Ibid.*
6. *Eighty Years and More: Reminiscences 1815-1897.* New York: The Fisher Unwin, 1898, p. 89.
7. *The Dialectic of Sex: The Case for Feminist Revolution.* New York: Batam Books, 1970, p. 31.
8. Simone de Beauvoir. *The Second Sex;* New York: Penguin Books, 1984.
9. Jardine, A. and Smith, P. (eds) *Men in Feminism.* New York and London; Routledge, 1987.
10. *The Holy Bible, The Old Testament*, Book I.

Spaces, Gender, and Healing in Alice Walker's *The Color Purple* (1982) and Mariama Bâ's *So Long a Letter* (1981)

2

Emmanuel N. Ngwang

Alice Walker's *The Color Purple* (1982) and Senegalese Mariama Bâ's *So Long a Letter* (1981) seem to have a very uncommon connection. Not only are they centered on the struggles of two female protagonists of color to find a voice for themselves and finally become liberated from the clutches of male slavery, they have to make a very succinct and powerful statement about spaces, gender and healing. Both novels are prefaced on the concept of two female characters who grow together under very difficult conditions which force one to go away from home in an attempt to find meaning for herself and thereby creating a medium of healing for the main characters. Secondly, the protagonists write to the characters who have gone away as a way of staying in touch and searching for continuity. In Walker's *The Color Purple*, Nettie (an American) goes to Africa with missionary friends to avert the fate Celie suffers. She, thus, provides her sister Celie, who is left behind with the man who has raped her and fathered her two children, an opportunity to come to terms with her weaknesses and to regain her strength. In *So Long a Letter*, Aissatou's going away to the United States gives Ramatoulaye (an African) a clearer perspective of her options and her emotional survival. She has the space to reconstruct her live through writing her experiences and impressions to Aissatou, trying to figure out how to survive.

In fact, Alice Walker shares common grounds with her African counterpart in at least five main domains: (1) common experiences of female marginalization; (2) marginalization inherent in the racist nature of their country; (3) the women's self-definition in a discriminatory society is indeed double jeopardy; (4) both novels share a common narrative method: the epistolary (letter) form which; (5) both use as distance/space for healing; and finally (6) both send the other main character on some sort of exile: Walker to Africa and Mariama Bâ to the United States. In both novels, a sister or female friend's going away to another continent (Aissatou to the United States and Nettie to Africa) creates space and, at the same time, this space acts as therapy for the sister left behind. This seems to suggest, in the issue of female characters, that spaces (as in distance) are a necessary accompaniment to self-fulfillment and gratification. In fact, the spaces create room for mental, physical, and psychological healing in both novels.

I intend to focus on the roles of Aissatou and Nettie who are secondary characters of both novels and to show how this shift in perspective complements the themes of healing that have so often been approached only from Ramatoulaye's and Celie's perspectives. In fact, each of them presents the *raison d'être* of each novel because they are the immediate causes of the letters that are written: though Celie also writes to God, her main focus is Nettie to whom she writes more letters and in Ramatoulaye's situation, it is to Aissatou that she writes so long a letter. These characters become empowered through writing (Silber 2003).

Distance in *So Long a Letter* and *The Color Purple*

According to Pauline Ada Uwakweh, "as many African and Diasporan women have shown in their fiction, the dilemma of choice-making for the female is linked to her social marginalization. The most notable fact in their creative works is the limited options to self-definition open to women generally" (47). Uwakweh goes further to assert that women are faced with the social problems of the limitations of motherhood and the limited options available to women, and the expectations from the communities with respect to predetermined and clearly defined female roles and responsibilities. Consequently, the females find it increasing difficult, if not insoluble to "define their individuality and assert their freedom for equal opportunities as their male counterparts" (47). She then offers women's militancy, gained through involvement in war and revolutionary movements as a new option to motherhood, one that is self-affirming. However, I would like to assert that in *The Color Purple* and *So Long a Letter*, Alice Walker and Mariama Bâ respectively portray that the African and African-American woman does not necessarily have to consider motherhood and marriage as limitations, but rather as sources of strength.

It is as if Alice Walker and Mariama Bâ decided to exchange characters and to compare the effects of this exchange on the characters who stay behind: Celie in *The Color Purple* and Aissatou in *So Long a Letter*. Although the characters are separated by choice, we cannot fail to note that the going away of each character is a temporary solution to the abuse and humiliations they have encountered in their respective societies: Aissatou and Nettie in West Africa and Ramatoulaye and Celie in the United States of America. However, I would like to look not at the departed sister or friend but at the one who stays behind, the one who has no choice but to confront the demons at home and to win this battle on the home front, for, they are the true heroes. The two sets of sisters' lives developed in parallel: they lived in the same house, went to the same schools and experienced the same tragedies. Thus, Ramatoulaye reminisces these special moments in her letter to Aissatou thus:

> Our lives developed in parallel. We experienced the tiffs and reconciliation of married life. In our different ways, we suffered the social constraints and the heavy burden of custom. (19)

In *The Color Purple*, Celie has often put her life on the line for Nettie, her junior sister. In fact, she asked their father "to take me instead of Nettie" (7). Both of them went through the torment and frustration of living with a father who was abusive to their mother as well as to them. In fact, Celie confesses about the rape she suffered from her stepfather who kept on eyeing her junior sister "I see him looking at my little sister. She scared. But I say I'll take care of you. With God help" (3). Both of them live in environments that are totally controlled by men whose greatest delight is sexual gratification. In fact, the first sets of letters to

God in *The Color Purple* are a confession and depiction of the horrible and unbearable conditions under which the two sisters lived. This explains why Nettie's initial letters to Celie refer back to when they had to fight for each other: "But God, I miss you, Celie. I think about the time you laid yourself down for me. I love you with all my heart" (127). Nettie indeed refers to the first move towards liberation and the healing process—creating a distance and space between the abused and the abuser:

"You've got to fight and get away from Albert. He ain't no good" (126). Nettie's first sense of victory and healing comes from having fought Albert away: "Well, I started to fight him, and with God's help, I hurt him bad enough to make me let me alone" (126). In her second letter to Celie, Nettie refers to meeting a couple Corrine and Samuel and their little girl Olivia and boy Adam, "sanctified religious and very good" who bring out from her a spirit of unity, love and peace: "they always try to include me in everything they do, so I don't feel so left out and alone" (127). Nettie finally has gotten the "room" (space) she needed to find herself and peace of mind.

The two sets of sisters started their live battle on the same level plane and together. Separating them is like separating twins to see the effect of the environment on each of them. However, the home battle could not have been won without a concomitant challenge sustained from the outside by the departed sister. The creation of this space between the one that goes away and the other that remains behind leads to and is primarily responsible for this healing. The girl/woman that remains behind sees herself initially as abandoned and doomed, but the escape of her sister from this doomed environment gives her the strength to fight her own battle if only to prove to her departed sister that she too can achieve something. Her life becomes a continuous battle of achieving some measure of independence and selfhood to be dispatched to her sister in the next letter. Each letter writing session becomes a session of self-examination and analysis, a measurement and an assessment of her achievements. She needs to continue to fight and to achieve great things to have something reasonable to report to her distanced sister and friend. This justifies why Emmanuel Obiechana in *Feminine Perspectives in*

Selected African Novels characterizes the letter as having "a tonal mixture between a personal complaint, an introspection, a feminine tract and a lecture" (36). To me, it is the therapeutic effect embedded in the "introspection" of this letter on Aissatou that is of great significance. Had it remained at the level of personal complaints or feminine tract and lecture, the letter would not have carried the weight it does. It is the healing values of the writing that have changed Aissatou and Ramatoulaye from the almost defeated women at the beginning of the *So Long a Letter* to the somewhat liberated women who await the ultimate re-union at the end of the novel with a lot of expectations. It resonates with the biblical parables of the talents whereby the servants have to give account of their investments or stewardship to the master who had entrusted them with various talents according to their abilities (Matthew 25: 14-30).

Though Mariama Bâ might not have considered this parable in conceiving her novel, one cannot avoid this parallel built on the principle of accountability. Ramatoulaye knows very well that her friend and sister-in-arms will return to Senegal, and that this return will be a period of reckoning. Towards the end of the novel, Ramatoulaye sees the so-called restrictions and constraints of marriage and children now in a different light. Though Obiechina prescribes divorce or the termination of a relationship which has become full of taint and pain as the way out for "a true feminist" (39), Ramatoulaye adumbrates and communicates it to her sister differently, and I tend to subscribe to this new view: she cannot undo what has been done. Instead, she would transform a hopeless situation into a hopeful one:

> I am one of those who can realize themselves fully and bloom when they form part of a couple. Even though I understand your stand, even though I respect the choice of liberated women, I have never conceived of happiness outside marriage. (55-56)

Ramatoulaye understands the dilemma of the African woman who is brought up to practice her predestined role of motherhood in marriage, and she thus sees marriage as a fulfillment of her womanhood, not as bondage.

Ramatoulaye is perplexed by what is going on around her. But what she needs more than anything else is a personal healing, not the preserving of the culture or the tradition of the bowl and stability of the family (Merri-Johnson 243). The family simply gives her a greater reason to heal, to accept the present dispensation, which would give here a better sense of self. Consequently, *So Long a Letter* is not novel about society, but rather a novel about Ramtoulaye. When Ramatoulaye wakes up, she is not thinking about what traditional values or aspects she is breaking or preserving, but how she will get through the day without destroying that sense of herself. Ramatoulaye does not choose the African community as framework to work within it to create a more habitable space for women. But she is born into it and her choices are limited. But Aissatou's departure to the US creates space and gives Ramatoulaye the first opportunity to see the weaknesses in men:

> For Mawdo, and through him, all men remained an enigma to me. Your departure had truly shaken him. His sadness was evident. When he spoke to you, the inflexions in his voice hardened. But his disillusioned air, the bitter criticisms of his home, his wife, which railed at everything, did not in the least prevent the periodic swelling of young Nabou's belly. (33)

Mawdo becomes an embodiment of the male principal which can only find temporary gratification in and through sex. He sees in Aissatou's flight to the US a lost opportunity to gratify his manhood, which he now performs unceasingly and with a lot of vengeance on his new wife.

Towards the end of the novels, Aissatou and Ramatoulaye prepare to meet, to reunite in Senegal Africa, while Celie and Nettie prepare to reunite in the USA. In each case, the challenge is not in the meeting but the challenge lies in the reckoning that will take place. The two groups have been physically separated for a considerable length of time (Aissatou and Ramatoulaye & Celie and Nettie). In Walker's *The Color Purple*, the separation of Celie and Nettie creates a void that Celie attempts to fill with Mr.—, Shug and other friends, but none of her friends can replace Nettie. Apart from Shug, who is technically present yet not related to her, Celie finds space in the departure of Nettie to adumbrate and articulate her sense of womanliness and consciousness in communication with a distant God and sister who are physically not present to see her. However, Celie has to be honest to both recipients because God is omniscient and will not forgive her for lying and she will have to give account of her past to Nettie whenever they meet. Celie thus develops a positive feminine image and feminine voice as she learns to become the central unifying subject of her destiny. She can stand her grounds before Albert and other male folk who all along have used the women like slaves. In her letter to Nettie, she now has the courage to philosophize about men and women: "Dear Nettie/ Well, you know whenever there's a man, there's trouble" (200). This is an integral part and parcel of Celie's new identity, her new voice which came out of the need to forge a life forward without her sister. Indeed, she used to live in the shadow of Nettie and with Nettie gone now, she needs to assert her own individuality by coming out of her shell of shame and fear. Her lessons in self-worth come from distance: in her and from her letters to God and Nettie where neither is like god in human form. Both Nettie and God complement each other here as they both function as catalysts in Celie's ultimate search for her identity.

In fact, Nettie's going away to Africa creates room for Shug to come into Celie's life to teach Celie how to regain her worth as a woman. Though Shug introduces another dimension of sexual orientation, there is no denying that Celie accepts or is inclined to it because Nettie, who has always served as her moral barometer is no longer there and cannot impede her new lifestyle. In this light, Nettie then becomes the metaphorical as well as real distance which, removed from her, assumes almost the posture of a distant God and a healing process, as this writing becomes a process of self-examination, self-evaluation, and growth. The result of this spatial arrangement encouraged Martha Cobb to acknowledge that:

> Finally, amidst all the cruelty and degradation, life takes on a new meaning for Celie, which she communicates to the

God to whom she still writes letters and to her sister Nettie, whom she finally sees again, after many years, when the missionaries come home from Africa. (199-200)

Indeed, distance and space have emboldened Nettie to fight off Albert, who dogs her on her way to meet the missionaries: "Well, I started to fight him, and with God's help, I hurt him bad enough to make him let me alone. But he was some mad" (126). For the first time, Nettie confronts the abusive Albert because Celie is no longer there to intercede or take the blows. Spaces have given her the courage to stand up to Albert, and she has to pass the lesson on to Celie: "You've got to fight and get away from Albert. He ain't no good" (126). These are positions taken after Nettie has created space between herself and the sister and each of them has to face her crucible alone: they both understand that when all is said and done, survival is a personal, private and individualistic struggle.

In fact, Nettie comes to equate God with distance and with Nettie. This is succinctly stated in her complaint to Nettie about the silence that non-communication has created between them:

> I remember one time you said your life made you feel so ashamed you couldn't even talk about it to God, you had to write it, bad as you thought your writing was. Well, now I know what you meant. And whether God will read the letters or no, I know you will go on writing them; which is guidance enough for me. Anyway, when I don't write you I feel as bad as I do when I don't pray, locked up in myself and choking on my own heart. I am so lonely, Celie. (130)

Later on, Nettie confesses that her separation to Africa has taught her to grow intellectually:

> I hadn't realized I was so ignorant, Celie. The little I knew about my own self wouldn't have filled a thimble! And to think Miss Beasley always said I was the smartest child she ever taught! But one thing I do thank her for, for teaching me to learn for myself, by reading and studying and writing a clear hand. And for keeping alive in me somehow the desire to know. So when Corrine and Samuel asked me to if I would come with them and help them build a school

> in the middle of Africa, I said yes. But only if they would teach me everything they knew to make me useful as a missionary and someone they would not be ashamed to call a friend. They agreed to this condition, and my real education began at that time. (132)

For once, Nettie sees herself doing something useful and helpful to humanity. This could only be possible away from a society that has continued to degrade her and reduce her services to slavery. She now sees herself as a missionary, a leader, and a pioneer in Christian charity; in addition to building the school, Nettie can share genuine love for Corinne and Samuel's children. She boastfully asserts, "And now 'God' has sent me to watch over them, to protect and cherish them. To lavish all the love I feel for you on them. It is a miracle, isn't it? And no doubt impossible for you to believe. But on the other hand, if you can believe I am in Africa, and I am, you can believe anything" (133). The emphasis here is on the transformation that Africa (distance and space) has effected on Nettie. There is no doubt that Nettie would hardly have realized and utilized these gifts had she remained in America, where she whined and pined under the yoke of sexual abuses, discrimination, and male-subjugation. The freedom experienced in Africa and the trust that has developed between her and her American companions have combined to bring out these humane qualities that lay buried in her tormented sub-conscious mind. Consequently, she is confessing that anything is possible in Africa, the land of freedom and possibilities. In fact, these miraculous realizations stand in opposition to Eugene O'Neill's *The Emperor Jones* wherein the main character, a runaway New York black convict Brutus Jones disintegrates into beasts and voodoo worshipper and finds humiliation and death on the banks of the River Congo. Indeed, Nettie finds rejuvenation and redemption, some sort of healing in Africa while the male character in *The Emperor Jones* is deprived of such redemptive values.

Like in the New Testament parables of the talents and the sewer, each group will present what they have each acquired in terms of growth and healing. Nettie has aged considerably and Celie displays her own acquisitions: Albert and Shrug, her house, shop, and newly acquired freedom. Nettie is now "dumpty...with grey hair in plaits cross on top her head" (286). She brings Adam and his wife Tashia. Nettie who had been away in Africa does not look and feel much better than Celie who had remained at home. In fact, Celie has acquired a greater degree of independence with a trade and some business establishments than her sister has. She has actually healed. She can now relax after dinner and dream big dreams:

> Me and [Albert] and Shug sitting out on the porch after dinner. Talking. Not talking. Rocking and fanning flies. Shug mentions she does'nt want to sing in public any more—well, maybe a night or two at Harpo's.... I talk about Henrietta Sofia, My garden and the store. How things going generally. So much in the habit of sewing something I stitch up a bunch of scraps, try to see what I can make. The weather cool for the last June, and sitting on the porch with Albert and Shug feel real pleasant (my emphasis). Next week be the fourth of July and us plan a big family reunion outdoors here at my house. (285)

From the above, it is very evident that Celie has grown remarkably. She has moved from self-doubt to confidence, from dependence on others to independence, from serving to being served. She can even afford to employ a white woman to work in her shop. She, therefore, has not only acquired economic and personal success but also she has acquired the peace that comes with spiritual healing. This is so important because she has progressed to this level of achievement by herself and in the absence of Nettie.

On Aissatou's and Ramatoulaye's part, this re-union is highly anticipated. In her last letter to Aissatou, Ramatoulaye contemplates:

> So then, I will see you tomorrow in a tailored suit or a long dress? I've taken a bet with Daba: a tailored suit. Used to living far away, you will want—again, I have taken a bet with Daba—table, plate, chair, fork. More convenient, you will say. But I will not let you have your way. I will spread out a mat. On it there will be the big, steaming bowl into

> which you will have to accept that other hands dip beneath the shell that has hardened you over the years (my emphasis) beneath your skeptical pout, your easy carriage, perhaps I will feel you vibrate. I would so much like to hear you check or encourage my eagerness, just as before, and, as before, to see you take part in the search for a new way. I have warned you already, I have not given up wanting to refashion my life.
>
> Despite everything—disappointments and humiliations—hope still lives on within me. It is from the dirty and nauseating humus that the green plant sprouts into life, and I can feel new buds springing up in me (89).

Ramatoulaye indeed ends her letter saying, "the word 'happiness' does indeed have meaning, doesn't it?" The spirit of joy, rebirth and continuity summarized in the concluding paragraphs of Ramatoulaye's letter to Aissatou in preparation for their re-union is symptomatic of the healing that has gone on in Ramatoulaye. The above excerpt draws an exciting comparison between life in Senegal, Africa and life in the USA. They contrast in dressing habits and the concept of sharing as a sign of love. Both characters have been physically separated but they remain one in spirit and in truth. They both vibrate underneath their skin, and they will act as check and balances for each other: Ramatoulaye to check Aissatou's foreign ways and the Aissatou to check Ramatoulaye's "eagerness" and search for the "new way" (89). Ramatoulaye has evolved to one of the modern mothers who favor "forbidden games;" however, to this lesson she adds that her daughters be aware of their bodies emphasizing the sublime significance of the sexual acts, as an expression of love. Ramatoulaye goes even further to philosophize on the importance of control in sex:

> It is through self-control, his ability to reason, to choose, his power of attachment, that the individual distinguishes himself from the animal. Each woman makes of her life what she wants. A profligate life for a woman is incompatible with morality. What does some one gain from pleasures? Early ageing, debasement, no doubt about it. (87)

The spring of this philosophizing originates in Ramatoulaye's growth, a spiritual healing which has come from her separation in death from her husband and secondly, a physical separation from her dear friend, who is in the United States.

The direction of separation also plays a significant part: the fact that her friend goes to America, which, in the African mind, stands for freedom, education, wealth and advanced ideas, puts a greater burden on Ramatoulaye who must prove herself up to par with her friend. She hence takes a very aggressively defensive posture to prove her worth. And in doing so, she seems to have gained more from this separation, this distancing from her bosom friend Aissatou, whose gains would be measured in terms of Western education and ways than in the hard knocks of life. In *The Color Purple* there is an almost irony twist to the novel: death, in fact, becomes the long awaited space for financial healing that Celie has been waiting for. The death of their stepfather Alphonso reveals the true ownership of the huge house. Daisy is honest enough to call Celie and tell her about the house:

> Your step daddy been dead over a week.... When us went to town to hear the will read yesterday, you could have knock me over with a feather. Your real daddy owned the land and the house and the store. He left it to your mama. When your mama died, it passed on to you and your sister Nettie. I don't know why Alphonso never told you that. (244-45)

Therefore, Celie writes to Nettie in Africa that they now have a house and that Nettie can now come home because they now have a home. The underlying understanding here is that house and home are synonymous, standing for love, freedom, and spatial healing. Alphonso's death creates a vacuum (space) which now gives room for the burgeoning of love for Celie, Shug, and Nettie and her children. Indeed, at this point, Celie bridges Africa and the United States of America as he builds an imaginary gastronomic bridge, reaching over to Africa for physical healing and nourishment:

> The only thing keep me alive is watching Henrietta fight for her life. And boy can fight. Every time she have an attack she

> scream enough to wake the dead. Us do what you say the people do in Africa. Us feed her yams every single day. Just our luck she hate yams and she not too polite to let us know. Everybody for miles around try to come up with yam dishes that don't taste like yams. Us git plates of yam eggs, yam chitlins, yam goat. And soup. (252)

Unfortunately, it is this "yam" that Henrietta hates which is the chief food and crop in Africa. The Olonga's of Africa have inadvertently substituted yams with canned and powdered goods, thereby destroying their defense against malaria and the control of chronic blood disease for thousand and thousand of years: "left without a sufficient supply of yams, the people—what's left of them—are sickening and dying at an alarming rate" (256). This is indeed time for Nettie and her missionary family to return to the United States, because Nettie fears for their health, especially for the children's health. This obsession with Africa is a further measure of this search for distance, especially the meaningful distance that will inevitably bring with it healing and a forgetting of the trauma of growing up in America. In the end, Celie longs for the company of Nettie, because the news of the apparent death of Nettie has made her more lonesome: "I sit here in this big house by myself trying to sew, but what good is sewing gon do? What good is anything? Being alive begin to seem like a awful strain" (255).

The Day of Reckoning

As Nettie prepares to meet Celie after thirty years, the former contemplates what time and distance have done to her sister: will she still be alive, will she "still have Tashi's honest and open spirit," or "will years of childbearing and abuse from Mr.—have destroyed it?" The answer to these questions resides in and is born of a resilience that Samuel has encouraged in Nettie, "who advises me not to worry, to trust in God, and to have faith in the sturdiness of my sister's soul" (257). Indeed, this is a new Nettie and a new God, a God of hope, faith and clear assurance. In fact, it is a new Nettie who has come to embrace a new concept of God:

> God is different to us now, after all these years in Africa. More spirit than ever before, and more internal. Most people

> think he has to look like something or someone—a roofleaf or Christ—but we don't. And not being tied to what God looks like, frees us. (257)

This assertion is the ultimate expression of spiritual healing and redemption. It is the spirit of the born-again believer whose rebirth has been tested by time and distance. Nettie's journey to Africa, therefore, becomes a spiritual pilgrimage of sorts. She is returning to America as a missionary, and she will, with Samuel "found a new church in our community that has no idols in it whatsoever, in which each person's spirit is enough to seek God directly, his belief that this is possible strengthened by us as people who also believe" (257). It is ironic that Nettie returns from the supposedly "dark continent" with a new vision, an epiphany to shock the enlightened first class society. However, it is a truth born out of conviction and a closeness to nature, an Edenic past made up of the "very African independence of opinion and outspokenness, also extreme self-centeredness" (258) where color had no role to play in relationships. In this regard, therefore, Nettie sees Africa far more developed and advanced in human values and virtue than the discrimination-ridden and daughter-rapping America of her past. Indeed, Adam does not want to return to America; he is missing and is presumed to have escaped to the Olinkas. For, has Nettie not questioned "how the children will manage the [American] hostility towards them, having grown up here [in Africa]?" (258). It is, therefore, very obvious that the scale of values are tilting towards Africa rather than America and that this separation has been a much desired and welcome separation that brought with it profound moral, spiritual, physical, and material healing. These considerations lead to some sort of permanence or rather youthfulness when Celie anticipates the imminent meeting with Nettie:

> I feel a little peculiar round the children. For one thing, they grown. And I see they think me and Nettie and Shug and Albert and Samuel and Harpo and Sofia and Jack and Odessa real old and don't know much what going on. But I don't think us feel old at all. And us so happy. Matter of fact, I think this the youngest us ever felt. (288)

The Color Purple is concluded on the above note, feeling and joy. We cannot help but join in this grand celebration of what is now new: the old have become new and young. This is a moment of spiritual transformation that transcends and overcomes any other moods that preceded and led to it. This is a moment of celebration, a moment of renewal, and a day of euphoria and celebration.

On Aissatou's and Ramatoulaye's part, the atmosphere is rife with similar moods of expectation, albeit sober and mature. In her final communiqué to Aissatou, Ramatoulaye reminisces and rehearses what she will tell her friend. She is determined to prevail in her philosophical change of mind. She is now a worker and has asked for more leave time to spend with her friend:

> I reflect. My new turn of mind is hardly surprising to you. I cannot help unburdening myself to you. I might as well sum it up now. I am not indifferent to the irreversible currents of women's liberation that are lashing the world. This commotion that is shaking up every aspect of our lives reveals and illustrates our abilities.
>
> My heart rejoices each time a woman emerges from the shadows. I know that the field of out gains is unstable, the retention of conquests difficult: social constraints are ever-present, and male egoism resists. (88)

However, Ramatoulaye concludes by advocating precisely the tonic Celie proposes at the end of *The Color Purple*—a new type of love:

> My reflections determine my attitude to the problems of life. ...I remain persuaded of the inevitable and necessary complementarity of man and woman. Love, imperfect as it may be in its content and expression, remains the natural link between these two beings. To love one another! If only each partner could move sincerely towards the other! If only each could melt into the other! If only each would accept the other's successes and failures! If each would only praise the other's qualities instead of listing his faults! If only each could correct bad habits without harping on about them! If only each could penetrate the other's most secret haunts to

> forestall failure and be a support while tending to the evils that are repressed!
>
> The success of the family is born of a couple's harmony, as the harmony of multiple instruments creates a pleasant symphony. The nation is made up of all the families, rich or poor, united or separated.... The success of a nation therefore depends inevitably on the family. (88-89)

This spirit of hope and liberation was born out of the need for Ramatoulaye to remain strong and independent in society that was overwhelmingly oppressive and patriarchal in beliefs and practices. Consequently, she has transformed her despised and disfavored position of subservient and servitude to one of victory and mental liberation. In fact, she ends the letter to Aissatou in the most optimistic and liberated tone:

> I warn you already. I have not given up wanting to refashion my life. Despite everything—disappointments and humiliations–hope still leaves on within me. It is from the dirty and nauseating humus that the green plant sprouts into life, and I can feel new buds springing up in me (my emphasis). The word 'happiness' does indeed have meaning, doesn't it? I shall go out in search of it. (89)

Like Celie at the end of *The Color Purple*, Ramatoulaye has finally come to terms with her life, with her surroundings, and with life in general. Both of them believe in the new God of love, a love that brings and gives hope. Their separations from respective sister/friend have truly taught each of them the meaning of love. Their ultimate re-union brings out the best in each of the four characters, especially the left-at-home characters Ramatoulaye and Celie respectively. The two sets of women have finally found the friendship that enables them to find and express their profound sense of personal truth. They have created relationships that are intimate, free of hierarchy, based on shared values, experience, and deep affection. Incidentally, this new-found security and long-standing feelings of unconditional love for the family are born out of the experiences of separation and space. Ramatoulaye can now speak her mind because she has grown wiser and matured in modern ways.

Writing to God and to Nettie was only possible in the spaces and distance created by the physical absences of both God and Nettie. In fact, Donna Winchell subscribes this idea when she maintains that, "in writing to God she [Celie] is writing the part of her personality growing progressively stronger until she is able to acknowledge the God within herself and demand due respect" (89). In addition to looking up to God for help, Celie finds solace in other women as a way out of male abuse and oppression. According to Mae G. Henderson, "the women in the novel form a vast network of communal relationships in which female bonding is the dominant connecting link" (Bloom 76). In *So Long a Letter*, Aissatou and Ramatoulaye have created a powerful bond through distance and space which has kept each of them going. Their constant communications through letter writing has empowered them to resist the intolerable limitations and the unyielding circumstances of male domination. While these sets of characters gain prominence and liberation through writing, Kate Chopin's Edna Pontellier finds peace in suicide, which Dara Kinnison could not identify if such an act was cowardice, irresponsibility or "a conscious assertion of strength and autonomy" (24). The two pairs of sisters/friends can now devote their energies not to their abusive husbands, but to the development of their individual abilities. They are the proverbial birds that must soar above the level plain of traditional prejudice, male domination, sexual abuses, and self-pity. They have all used spaces and distances to heal and they are proud to communicate the process through and in their letters. When in the analysis Chopin's Ednar Pointellier Kinnison states that the female character in a male dominated society has only two options: the reward of complete self-sacrifice versus the reproof of female self-assertion (Kinnison 22). Kennison was too hasty in passing her judgment. In fact, Celia and Nettie in the United States and Aissatou and Ramatoulaye in Senegal, Africa have proven beyond doubt that the female characters have a third option: freedom, self-realization, and happiness as they relate to the world and to each other.

WORKS CITED

Bâ, Mariama. *So Long a Letter*. Trans. Modupé Bodé-Thomas. London: Heinemann Educational Publishers, 1981.

Bloom, Harold. *Alice Walker*. New York: Chelsea House Publishing, 1989.

Cobb, K. Martha. "Images of Black Women in New World Literature." *Women in African and the African Diaspora*. Eds. Rosalyn Terborg-Penn, Sharon Harley, and Andrea Benton Rushing. Washington, D.C.: Howard University Press, 1987: 197-209.

Johnson, Merri Lisa. "Ramatoulaye's Letter: Cross-cultural Reading Strategies & the Criticism of Mariama Bâ's *So Long a Letter*." *Postcolonial Perspectives on Women from Africa, the Caribbean, and the U.S.* Ed. Martin Japtok. Trenton, NJ: African World Press, Inc., 2003: 229-48.

Kelly, Ernice B. "Paths to Liberation in Alice Walker's *The Color Purple* (1982)."

Women in Literature: Reading through the Lens of Gender. Eds. Jerilyn Fisher and Ellen S. Silber. Westport, Connecticut: Greenwood Press, 2003: 75-78.

Kinnison, Dara. "Female Resistance to Gender Conformity in Kate Chopin's *The Awakening* (1899)." *Women in Literature: Reading though the Lens of Gender*. Eds. Jerilyn Fisher and Ellen S. Silber. Westport, Conn: Greenwood Press, 2003: 22-25.

Obiechina, Emmanuel. "Feminine Perspectives in Selected African Novels." *Nwanyibu: Womanbeing & African Literature*. Ed Phanuel A. Egejuru and Ketu H. Katrak. Trenton, NJ: African World Press, Inc., 1997: 32-46.

O'Neill, Eugene. (1920). *The Emperor Jones* New York: New York University Press, 1961.

Silber, Ellen S. "Empowerment through Writing in Mariama Bâ's *So Long a Letter*." *Women in Literature: Reading through the Lens of Gender*. Eds. Jerilyn Fisher and Ellen S. Silber. Westport, Conn.: Greenwood Press, 2003.

Uwakweh, Pauline Ada. "Female Choices: The Militant Option in Buchi Emecheta's *Destination Biafra* and Alice Walker's *Meridian*." *Nwanyibu: Womanbeing & African Literature*. Eds. Phanuel A. Egejuru and Ketu H. Ketrak. Trenton, NJ: African World Press, Inc., 1997: 47-59.

Walker, Alice. *The Color Purple*. New York: Washington Square Press, 1982.

Winchell, Donna. *Alice Walker*. New York: Twayne Publishers, 1992.

Traditionalizing Christianity in Kenjo Jumbam's *The White Man of God*[1]

3

Ernest L. Veyu

Deep down of the Nso man, as evidenced in Kenjo Jumbam's *The White Man of God*, the traditional worship system and Christianity, whether Catholic, Presbyterian or Baptist are the same, and point to the same end. They may differ in the method, but never in essence from his indigenous worship system. Consequently, Christianity and tradition co-habit in a relationship of mutual inclusiveness. The coming of Christianity occasions a crisis, but which is quickly resolved by incorporating Christianity into the Nso man's traditional worship system.

In all of the text, not a single Nso person abandons the traditional worship system in favour of Christianity. The methods of Christianity and the white man who brings it are both foreign, but in essence, Christianity is seen as another form of worship of the God the Nso man has always known.

In this paper, we seek to demonstrate that the Nso traditional worship system is very strong and deeply ingrained in the Nso man to the extent that Christianity, which has often been celebrated as working against many a traditional worship set-up, does not have deep in-roots into and does not affect the fundamentals of the Nso belief system. The two systems differ, but do so in ways that afford a fair level of compatibility. We further look at the text as mirroring in actual terms what one finds in present day Nso Christianity.

A. Nso Traditional Religious System *versus* Christianity: Divergence

The two belief systems do not agree principally in the notions of God and hell. Christianity teaches that a sinner dies straight into hell; a place of eternal suffering in a lake that burns with fire and sulphur. Faced with this, Yaya uncompromisingly declares that the new religion:

> Has impossible laws and its God is cruel. It is only the God of the white man who puts a man in hell-fire and lets him burn there like wood, never dying but crying there everyday for ever and ever while God never lifts up an eye of mercy to him. What cruelty to imagine of a God! (33)

In like manner, Tansa, in what is both the voice of Jumbam[2] and the Nso man in general says, "But strange, very strange that God should treat human beings worse than man. ...Man is the soil of the earth plus God's breath. And yet, when the soul parts from the body and the earth welcomes the body, God casts the soul into eternal flames! God!" (151).

Traditionally, God is not a God of judgement and punishment; "Whoever heard that God who is the final hope of man put him into eternal flames? How can God, being God, do that?" (37). Traditionally, there is no day when the dead shall appear before a judgement seat for their fate to be decided, as it is believed by Christians. The defaulter in the things traditionally and morally considered as unlawful only makes his upward move at death a slower exercise than that of the person who has not much violated the laws. Furthermore, unlike in Christianity where one could be worse off at death, every dead person, by traditional conception, is in every way better than the living.

> Death in the traditional setting consequently approximates what Cirlot describes in terms of liberation: "Death is a supreme state of liberation. In the positive sense then, this enigma symbolises the transformation of all things, the progress of evolution, dematerialization". (78) The dead are also believed to possess something of deity, and are nearer God: "That is why if you have a problem you must solicit your ancestors to plead to God for you," says Yaya.

The traditional set-up accepts polygamy, but the church does not. Fonjo is asked to put away the other two wives before his wife, Dubila, is baptised. To him, this is incomprehensible, scandalous and wicked beyond telling: "Whoever heard such a thing? Is this white man merely wicked!...To tell a man to put away the mothers of his children!...I shall have to see the Fon. These are the things that spoil the country" (52). The church on the other hand, "permits a man to marry only one wife, and a woman, one husband. They must remain faithful to each other until death" (88).

Atem Wilson Ebot in "Language and Action in Kenjo Jumbam's Prose Narratives" says, "Jumbam, as it were, consistently portrays the inhabitants of his native Nso country as a dynamic and ingenious people with a deep sense of communal awareness." This communal sense of belonging is a Christian principle, but cuts through the Christian notion in that the Christians are not to be unequally yoked with unbelievers" (I Corinthians 6:14). But the Nso man in *The Whiteman of God* is unable to make a difference with his blood brothers on the basis of Christian beliefs. Christian, catechumen or pagan are in the traditional sense of the word, brothers. This is most likely why less rigid Father Cosmos is generally loved and even made into a Fai by the Fon.

One other differencing element has to do with the meaning of sin. As far as Christian teaching is concerned, by choosing to sin, the sinner hates God. Traditionally, it is inconceivable that anyone could hate God. One may, "do the things God does not like but that is not the same as hating him" (54). In the traditional sense of the word, the sinner's hope lies in God, to whom he cries out for mercy if he gets into trouble because of his sin.

In about the same line of thinking, it is inconceivable that persons who have suffered or been punished because of sin committed should be punished a second time by God in hell. If it so happens that in this life they do not receive punishment for sins committed, "God punishes them in the spirit world. But they don't suffer forever" (54). This notion contradicts the Christian notion of eternal damnation for the sinner who dies in sin.

B. Nso Traditional Religious System *versus* Christianity: Convergence

The Nso traditional system and Christianity both recognize a single supreme God. But while Christianity is rigid about the non-existence of the gods, the traditional community acknowledges their presence and reveres them. It is common belief in *The White Man of God* that the traditional sacrifices by those in authority like the Fon, the Fais and Sheys are offered to the supreme God. Consequently, whether a person relates to God traditionally, through church worship or both, is really nothing the matter.

The traditional creation story relates very closely to the Christian version. In both stories, there is a supreme God whose work or word brought the world and all its elements into being. All the plants and animals that exist are credited to Him. The first created man and woman are Leng (Adam) and Njing (Eve) in the traditional and Christian versions. Both versions make provision for a heaven (Up) and an earth (Down), where the heaven (God's home) is in every way better and the ultimate hope and strive of the living. Yaya says the following about God and the creation:

> When God made the world, he divided it into two parts, the Up, where he lives, and the Down, where we are. Up where he lives you find such good things as the sun, the moon and the stars which give us light at different periods of the day, and the rain which falls on our crops at will. Down where we live he lets all types of crops grow and gives us animals for our use.... On the surface, you find all living things, men, animals, birds, insects, plants and so on. Below the surface is the place for things lower than those at the surface, worms, and dead things. If I die now my body becomes too low for the surface of the earth. When our body is put in the earth your breath begins its upward journey to God. Its speed depends on your life on the surface of the earth, the better, the faster, even the slowest is better than us on earth because he is already on the way Up. (37)

Both worship systems employ the services of a priest who is believed to be ahead of the ordinary man and woman in spiritual matters. The priests, traditional and Christian, are both regarded as fulfilling a divine vocation, to which they have been specially called. Shey Fonki is the family priest of Mborn, working under the supervision of the Fai, who has been specially appointed and ordained by the Fon. In *The White Man of God* we read that, "every Fai sacrifices for his family and guards the family against evil spirits. That is why the Fon elects one member of the family to be a Fai" (103). In like manner, there is Big Fadda and Father Cosmos (commonly called Small Fadda), who have equally been ordained and assigned to officiate on behalf of the Catholic Church; a Christian family.

Both systems operate a shrine system. The regular sacrifices are made in the different shrines of the different Fais and on special occasions like the cleansing ceremony done on Dinni and Biy Wirba. The alter from where the Christian priest officiates, and the confessionary are shrines. These shrines, both traditional and Christian are held sacred and believed to be sites of divine presence. They are normally restricted to the common man.

Ritual[3] is a common medium for intercourse between the priests and God, (or the gods in some traditional ceremonies). During the expiation of the crime between Dinni and Biy Wirdin, the ritual runs as follows: "The shit that sticks on the finger from the anus must realise that it was never meant for the finger. It must be sent back to where shit is meant to be.... 'Go! Go to where you came from!'" (73). In like manner, the Catholic "Hail Mary", the "Our Father" and chorus responses during Mass are ritualistic in nature.

In both systems, water is used as a tool for cleansing. After the expiation ceremony on Dinni and Biy Wirbah, Fai sprinkles what Lavran calls the pagan blessing water on the feet and hands of Dinni and Biy Wirbah and on the hands and feet of Shey Fonki. Then he invites everyone to receive the family blessing. This particular cleansing is meant to ward off any curse, perchance, from those who participated in the ceremony. In like manner, Christian water baptism is believed to cleanse from sin.

We get this notion from Paulina who says, "Baptism washes away everything" (41).

Both worship systems have a history of ancestral links. In Yaya's understanding, prayer is begging God through one's ancestors. Her major problem with Christianity is that the white man leads Christians to pray through his own ancestors as though it were impossible to do the same through one's own black ancestors. Her fear is that those who are taking the white man's ancestors too seriously may cause their own black ancestors to turn their backs on them, with the risk that the ancestors of the white man may not recognize them. Her question is:

> Do you believe that if you knocked on the grave of a white man and he raised his head and saw a black face he would listen to you? He would just run away. He wouldn't even understand what you were saying if he listened. He would ask you to go to your own people. (32)

In the traditional belief system, there is life after death, just as it is with Christianity. Whereas the dead in the traditional notion are in every way better than the living, Christianity teaches that one could be worse off at death or much better depending on whether he goes to heaven or to hell. The central thing, however, is that death is not an annihilation experience. The dead continue to live and commune with the living. Christianity believes that the dying go to meet the living, but that full communion with them is only possible at death, except the persons are saints. In *The White Man of God*, Yaya's one quest is to be able to meet her late husband when she dies. This, in a sense equates to the Catholic notion of the "Communion of the Saints" (J.F. Sollier).

The notion of the family is fundamental to traditional beliefs and to Christianity. A father heads the home, just as a father, called priest, is at the head of the Christian family; the church. The Christian God is equally seen in terms of the family. He is a heavenly Father. In the same manner as Tansa is brother to Maria, Beri and Lavran, fellow Christians are brothers and sisters in Christ, and expected to love one another as themselves.

C. Nso Christianity: Assimilation and Peculiarities

From a reading of Jumbam's *The White Man of God*, it is hard to say with precision, which aspects of the Nso traditional belief system have been drastically altered by the coming of Christianity. Annie Gigiano thinks that this is because, "the indigenous culture is so vital and socially cohesive." In my opinion, Christianity came to form an appendage of the people's strong belief system, not to alter it. It would not be an exaggeration to say that Christianity does not add to the spirituality of the Nso man. He is already a very spiritual person. It is not from the white man that he learns prayer, absolution, worship and the like.

In a sense, the Nso man goes to Christianity for its social advantages and not for its spiritual value. For example, Lalav's arguments in favour of Christianity run as follows: "I have shown you that this new way is the right one. You can see what the new religion is doing for our people. You have to see the white man working where I go to deliver these children. They are doing all that for God" (32). Furthermore, there are the schools, the jobs and better hygienic conditions—which are all social factors. Yet in the pursuit of these things, Yaya warns:

> A partridge with a brood of chickens once led them into a farm because she saw a lot of maize there. She refused to listen to the advice of her elders. She wouldn't refuse the children such nice maize, so she led them there and fell into a trap. She screamed and asked the chicks to run for shelter. "Away! Away!" she cried. The chicks ran for shelter under her wings and the farmer came and that was the end. (33)

Christian names are deformed to carry something of Lamso,[4] at least in the pronunciation; Felix becomes Feliy, Lucas becomes Lucar, and Cosmas becomes Cosima to name a few. The point to be made here is that there is no effort to learn the white man's pronunciation of these names. Rather, the effort is to appropriate and localise these names. At the time of her baptism, one of Yaya's reservations lies in the requirement to take a Christian name at Baptism. She fears that if she does, her late husband may not recognise her by a Christian name when they meet in the world of the dead.

A number of issues are peculiar to Nso Christianity as depicted in *The White Man of God*. In the first place, Nso Christianity is an all-community affair. When the white man of God is coming, it is not the affair of the Christians alone: "The church was packed full of Christians and catechumens from Jakiri, Mensai, Ronkar, Vekovi, Sov, and the mission stations in Nkar" (43). The Catechist's announcement on how the white man of God will be received run thus:

> On the Wailun which falls on Tuesday, every Christian, man and woman, boy and girl and every catechumen should come to the motor road near the Tsemkan river. Invite all your relatives who are not Christians. Samba leaders should bring their dancing instruments. The Chong women should come with all their dancing equipment. The procession will be led by the women's dances. The white man of God will follow them and the men's Samba will follow after him. (45)

The Samba[5] and the Chong[6] are not Christian groupings. But Christianity as practiced in Nso has incorporated them into the functioning of the church. They have as much weight in the social organisation of the church as does the choir. In the case at hand, there is the church house, and in the churchyard, there is a house for the Chong and one for the Samba. This is a pagan introduction into the church. When the white man of God arrives in Nkar, "the catechist took the samba drum and gave it a rippling beat that set all hearts thumping" (47).

The Nso man, whether Christian, catechumen or pagan participates in traditional sacrifices. Tansa and all the others who go to church seem to be operating under a gravitational pull that lures them to the site of sacrifices. In the death celebration of Fai Mission, every body is present, Christians and pagans alike. Actually, while the jujus are still out displaying, no one goes to Church, although it is church time and Big Fadda shouts at them to that effect. In the next Mass, he complains as follows:

> Most of you went to confession and several of you were baptized. And yet you all swept away to the palace soon afterwards to drink and dance pagan dances and bow down to pagan jujus.... Are you Christians or Christian-

> pagans?... When the jujus came you knelt or bowed down before them. You as Christians! You honour jujus more. (59)

The Nso Christian as portrayed by Jumbam, believes in the power of the juju, and bows to it. When the Wan-mabuh comes, although Feliy is with the priest, he squats as do all the rest. It is firmly believed that not to bow amounts to a curse, and that the cursed person would have to spend enormously in traditional sacrifices for a cure to be obtained, whether he or she is Christian or not.

The Fon makes Father Cosmos into a Fai. When he dies, all the Christians, in conjunction with the pagans and the palace jujus, celebrate his death in the traditional manner. The jujus come out as they would come out for the death of every other Fai. Since it is the Fai from the church who dies, the catechist wears the mask of the principal juju on that fateful day. Irrespective of his role in the church and the preaching he has been trained to do, he does not cut away from his traditional practices. He belongs to the family of Christians, but he also belongs to the palace family.

The Shigwalah, the Wan-mabuh, the Kibaranko all dance and come up to the Catholic Mission premises during the death celebration of Fai Mission, Father Cosmos. There is no division between the holy and unholy, in the church's sense of the word, in people's minds. The church and the priests may think it unholy, but not a single Nso man thinks in this manner (42-143).

When Tansa, as a Christian, goes for the traditional sacrifice, Yaya says:

> What that child did was perfectly correct. Do you know what drew that child to the place of the sacrifice? You cannot break away from the past like that and live. You cannot. Hear me, if the Fai does not include you and your children and their father in his sacrifices, you cannot live. You are all well because he is good and conscientious in his duty and sacrifices for the whole family including you; do you hear what I am saying? (31-32)

The Nso Christian also believes in the traditional healing method and in the power of talismans. When sufficient milk does not flow from Lalav's breasts after the birth of the twins, "Ngoran the medicine man came with his bag of medicine and sat in mama's house. I called papa and we all sat and watched" (125). When Father Cosmos is sick, the Fon sends a medicine man:

> One day Ta'adom came to the Mission carrying his bag of medicines, an antelope's horn marked with white and red lines, a fan of feathers of assorted colours and half a gourd containing some liquid. Approaching the father's house he dipped his fan into the liquid and sprinkled it all about him. (135-36)

The Christians are later to blame Big Fadda bitterly for refusing to let Ta'adom, whose practise is judged by the priest as unchristian, to treat Father Cosmos of his fever. Nso Christianity is such as would turn to sources judged unchristian by the church, provided they relieve a desperate situation.

In *The White Man of God*, a to-the-letter application of the truths of Christianity is subject to general ridicule. When Tansa does not steal kolanuts, because he is sticking to what Big Fadda said in church, he is blamed in the end. Paulina must be baptized but finds no problem in going to prostitute in Bamenda in order to obtain the baptismal fees. She believes that even if she prostitutes, Christian baptism will wash away all her sins (41). Tom steals a watch from Fadda's table when he goes to pay his church contribution (57). A talisman could be used if needed. For example, in the Christian tug of war, Andreas from Kimakong uses a layas.[7] To this Lavran exclaims, "Well, imagine a Christian like him wearing a belt full of layas and bringing them to the mission! Is that not testing the power of his laya against God's?" (83). Simply put, Christianity and sin are not mutually exclusive in the Christianity of *The White Man of God*.

There comes a time when Big Fadda confesses that he came to bring Christ to the people, but has discovered that they are not ready for Him: "You are not ready for Christ even on Easter day! You cannot have God and juju; you have preferred juju to

God and so I must go back" (35). Deep down of the people, they have not rejected God. The problem is with the white man who thinks that God and the juju are mutually exclusive. To the Nso Christian, both parties should be appeased because, just as the white man's God could throw you to hell, the power of the juju could hurt you.

From the example of the life lived by the priests, with the exception of Father Cosmos, the Nso man is not convinced that one should take the white man's religion too seriously. The kicking of Lucar's mother in church by the priest, the sexual immorality of Big Fadda with Lucy, coupled with the unchristian solitude he maintains, prompts the people to conclude that the "White man of God was a wicked man" (61).

Irrespective of the fact that Sunday is already a Christian worship day, there is still the traditional Sunday when no one goes to the farm. It is the day the Fai goes out to sacrifice for the entire land. The Christians normally do not violate this day. They recognize it and believe in the need to observe it for the spiritual well-being of the land. They believe that non-observance of this sacred day could bring disaster to the land. Whichever way God may be pleased, either through tradition or the church, it should be done.

Even if the traditional sacrifices and the observance of the traditional sacred days are satanic, the general opinion is that one must be careful because, "When God condemned Satan to hell he did not take away his power and so Satan remains very powerful" (146). Furthermore, Tansa's father, a regular Christian, and leading person of the church in Mborn warns that:

> There is magic and there are herbs that have wonderful power. If you have not studied them, people can use them to harm you. Mere herbs mixed in certain proportions can work wonders. These are facts which the white man of God did not know. You don't read such things in books. They are things of this land and those who worship the land can do them. (146)

The ordinary Christian, therefore, believes that Christianity has only a part of the truth, which must be completed from tradition. The Christianity in Nso consequently co-habits with the traditional system. Kenjo Jumbam seems to stand to the opinion that traditional worship systems and Christianity are mutually inclusive.

At the time one closes the pages of the novel, the argument is not settled, but the insinuation is that although Christianity is good, there is certainly a power in tradition that ought not to be tempered with. Faced with what happens to Big Fadda when he unmasks the juju, Maria cogitates as follows: "Things like this make one wonder whether Satan is more powerful than God. How can God's own messenger see the juju and fall down dead or half dead?" (148).

D. Nso Christianity Beyond *The White Man of God*

Kenjo Jumbam's novel is generally acclaimed as autobiography, and a number of the incidences in the text are commonly discussed among the Nso people till date. His description of the setting, and places such as Shisong, Meluf, Jakiri and the rest are very accurate. Observably, the novel is a near exact representation of the Christianity and traditional practices in Nso.

As stated in the novel, the present day Catholic Church building in Nso almost inevitably stands side by side with the Samba meeting place for the men, and the Chong meeting place for the women. Nso Catholic Christians have continued to uphold and revere their tradition, and believe in the power of traditional sacrifices and in the divine endowment of both traditional and Christian priesthoods.

As in *The White Man of God*, Christianity and traditional practices are mutually inclusive in Nso. A Christian who wears the juju mask, as does Pa. Mitiu may be frowned at, but not excommunicated, because such is tacitly permissible. Watch a juju display today, and you find the same squatting in honour of it, by Christian and non-Christian alike. Unlike the fears of Yaya in the novel, the conflict phase between tradition and Christianity has settled down unto a peaceful co-existence.

This peaceful co-existence has recently been cemented by the Pope's message on Ecclesia in Africa. In the talk given in Yaoundé, on 14th September 1995, during the Feast of the Triumph of the Cross, one of the issues decided upon was on the enculturation[8] of the church in Africa:

> Inculturation includes two dimensions: on the one hand, "the intimate transformation of authentic cultural values through their integration in Christianity" and, on the other, "the insertion of Christianity in the various human cultures". (87) The Synod considers inculturation an urgent priority in the life of the particular Churches, for a firm rooting of the Gospel in Africa. (88)

In essence, the challenge of enculturation consists in ensuring that the followers of Christ assimilate the Gospel message, while remaining faithful to all authentic African values. Here then is a step ahead in the marriage of Christianity and fundamental traditional Nso practices. It is a case of traditionalising Christianity or, Christianising tradition. It becomes a form of Christianity, robbed of the strict Biblical and Roman Catholic forms; a brand of its own.

WORKS CITED

Bjornson, Richard. *The African Quest for Freedom and Identity: Cameroon Writing and the National Experience*. Bloomfield and Indianapolis: Indiana University Press, 1991.

Cirlot, J.E. *A Dictionary of Symbols*. New York: Pengamon Press, 1965.

Ebot, Wilson Atem. *Language and Action in Kenjo Jumbam's Prose Narratives*. Oracle. http://www2.univ-reunion.fr/~ageof/text/74c21e88-282.html. 29/12/2006.

Gigiano, Annie. *The White Man of God* http://www.oulitnet.co.za/africanlib/jumbam.asp, 14/01/2008.

John Paul II, *Ecclesia in Africa*, http://www.vatican.va/holy_father/john_paul_ii/apost_exhortations/documents/hf_jp-ii_exh_14091995_ecclesia-in-africa_en.html. 20/12/2006.

Jumbam, Kenjo. *The White Man of God*. London: Heinemann, 1972.

Larson, Charles. *The Emergence of the African Fiction*. London: Macmillan, 1978.

Mbiti, John S. *African Religions and Philosophy*. London: Heinemann Educational Books, 1975.

Sollier, J.F. "In memory of Sister Ignatia," *The Catholic Encyclopedia, Volume IV*. New York: Robert Appleton Company, 1908, http://www.newadvent.org/cathen/04171a.htm, 14th January 2008.

NOTES

1. "The best known post 1972 novel written by an Anglophone Cameroonian...about the relevance of traditional and modern values to life in contemporary Africa" (Bjornson 402).
2. Jumbam often switches from direct authorial commentary to making comments that involve the whole community. Larson calls such statements the, "lyrical centre" or "collective consciousness" (Larson 22).
3. Ritual is, "a set form of carrying out a religious action or ceremony. It is a means of communicating something of religious significance through words, symbols and actions (Mbiti 83).
4. The language of the Nso people.
5. The Samba is the Banso men's war group. It is danced with spears and cutlasses, accompanied by military chanting. The dance is a show of physical strength and dexterity in brandishing and clanging spears and cutlasses.
6. The Chong on the other hand is the female counterpart of the Samba. Common lore holds that it is a most sacred and occultist group, whose occultism beats that of the Samba.
7. A pagan charm or talisman believed to tap from the power of Satan to the aid of the one in possession of it. In the tug of war, the people of Kimakong only lose to those of Mensai when their laya is discovered and taken away. They have been stripped from the source of their power.
8. The Synod Fathers interpret inculturation as "a process that includes the whole of Christian existence—theology, liturgy, customs, structures—without compromising what is of divine right and the great discipline of the Church."

Exquisite Depiction of Cultural Sensitivities in Doris Lessing

4

Devika

Writers, the product of their age and culture, invariably reflect the richness of the culture through their stories, background and characters. The way they react to the situations, the way they deal with people, the way they stand in relation to their family and friends and the way they evolve in relation to themselves are ample signs of their cultural proclivity, though not a bigoted one. Apparently, the seeming alikeness of human beings is all encompassing and true too in relation to humanity, but beyond that or may be within an inner circle, as the representative of their culture, they stand related to smaller and individual groups. Jung's (quoted by Vevaina 1996: 31) observation regarding the all-embracing chain of connectivity seems an apt one, "the psyche is not individual, but is derived from the nation, from the collectivity, from humanity even. In some way or other we are part of a single all-embracing psyche, a single 'greatest man', the homo maximus, to quote Swedenborg." However, equally elevating is another aspect of it. Nowhere restricted or narrowed down in humanity, people reflect a point of view to bigger issues also which are enriched by the fertility of their private faiths and myths. The bigger issues remain the same, retain the same intensity and demand the same dedication or challenge, but the perceptions vary because of one binding, that is, culture.

Writers, all over the world, individually and uniquely fertile with their own cultures, in fact provide a singular view of life; the distinct appeal nurtures their cultural flavour if it is properly backed by universal elements. Over-emphasized or restricted and deliberate projection of cultural flavour instantly takes away the grandness of credibility. Mary Jane Edwards seems to strike the right chord when she opines, "A writer cannot be a good internationalist and a good nationalist without being a regionalist, for it seems essential that the creative writer has a strong sense of his own time and place (Denham 1980: xvii). No wonder, the natural and effortless blending of cultural streaks with bigger and relevant issues yields a fruitful consequence. The incidents, the spontaneous responses of the characters to the situations may strike unusual to the readers of other culture at first, but if the writer attempts to hide or overshadow his/her culture, s/he would be merely cheating the readers of the real pleasure of reading.

Writers, through their works, familiarize people with the richness of their culture and its complexities; the intention never works to draw attention to their culture but the small or big issues in the lives of their characters. Surprisingly, this adds to the opulence of already fascinating aspects of humanity. Some issues are very prominently highlighted in the works of one author, but surprisingly those issues are completely missing from the works of another author, for the selection, collection and execution of issues is largely guided by cultural aspects. Same relationships elicit different responses, families hold varying places, and the importance of society and self also keeps changing because of the cultural sparks. Discussing the role of a writer in society, Atwood remarks that the writer "tends to concentrate more on life, not as it ought to be, but as it is, as the writer feels it, experiences it. Writers are eye witnesses, I-witnesses." (Singh 1994: 16) Like Atwood, Doris Lessing also highlights the individual variations of her culture.

Deliberate attempt to reflect the culture always seems to take away the grandness of it but if it fuses well with the situation and characters, it coruscates an alluring and irresistible charm. Minute details about British culture of twentieth century get disclosed in Doris Lessing's works, which even otherwise retain a powerful projection of some of the issues directly related to feminism. An analysis of the undercurrent of these cultural aspects perfectly bedecks the powerful storylines. When the works are read, the problems in those specific situations by those characters reveal much about their culture at that time and the subtle shift in their culture and their acceptance, rejection or protest against it. Not only that they also reflect the differences very acutely if characters are put face to face with the people of other culture.

In Britain, after Second World War, dissent and decadence flourished in profusion. However, this growing dissent in society helped in establishing a critical and influential tradition of social realism. There was a discernible shift from the highlights of the better educated affluent minority to the concerns and problems of ordinary people. Since nothing seemed stable in life, evasive inwardness and nostalgia resulted in resentment and anger. Young people rejected politics and consumerism in favour of spirituality and enlightenment but never shedding the feeling of hollowness. Somehow, the situation changed with the passage of time. "Expansion of higher knowledge encouraged many young people to think critically about politics and society" (Christopher 1999: 8). In addition, material affluence increased their self-confidence and prodded them to move ahead and find meaning in their lives. Delicate shifts keep enriching beliefs and habits. Noticing the difference between mid-twentieth and late-twentieth century, Doris Lessing has this to say in an interview with Dwight Gamer:

> You know, people that didn't smoke, it was quite extraordinary. People were quite apologetic, "I'm sorry, but I don't smoke." And the drinking! We drank! And that's gone completely, because if I ask people around now, less and less alcohol gets consumed all the time. Whereas if I had a party, let's say, in the '50s, enormous amounts were drunk as a matter of course. (Gamer 1997)

Perpetual alterations do take place but things do not transform completely; the undercurrent, even with changes, remains more or less the same. Primarily, the British are "uninhibited, tolerant, exhibitionist, passionate, aggressive, sentimentalist, hospitable and friendly people" (Else 2003: 65). Many British people hold strong views and these normally lie beneath the surface, but not that far below. They abhor the idea of flouting their convictions but the slight amount of challenge could trigger them to instant and strong reaction. For them, the order is sacrosanct; codes of courtesies and formalities are prevalent and exercised also. In fact, its absence makes the whole scenario look very flabby but whatever is apparent at the visible level might be surprisingly deceptive too. Display of these formalities is neither preferred nor publicized but the adherence is loyal and sincere.

Characters engrossed in personal, professional and social exchange unconsciously take extra care to adhere to the accepted and expected rules of conduct. Even for small things the decorum is maintained, as is clear from the situation when Anna and her boyfriend in *The Golden Notebook* say sorry to each other, "He apologised for not telephoning; she apologised for not being dressed" (Lessing 1977: 627). Unlike manners, money receives passive acceptance. Though money exercises an important place in life, it is never blown out of proportion. British people may be rich but no conscious efforts are made to flaunt their accumulated wealth. They don't put too much emphasis on money for "(s)ignificant section of people had money to spend on an alternative" (Christopher 1999: 8). Absence of the dire need for fulfilling the primary need relegates money to the secondary level, merely a means to get the things done.

In *The Golden Notebook*, Doris highlights the attitude of English people towards money, "By English standards they were all rich. In England people are rich as they don't talk about money. An atmosphere of money all the time, anxious money, with these American people" (471). A contrast between two cultures is intensely clear through these words; English people assume money to be a great commodity but the emphasis is never on the hungry and craving possession for it. Not only the money but its influence also exercises its power in different ways the moment there is a change of culture. However, it speaks its own language with reference to individual personalities. It rarely comes directly in picture and it never gets importance to the extent of being hub of anything; though money is required, life is not altered for the same. Absence or presence of money neither spoils nor improves their relationships. Even Richards, who is very money-minded and ambitious, keeps it at the back of the talk. There is no display as such and it never becomes the main focus of the things. Richard does not feel comfortable with his wives and he marries thrice but without any trace of money.

In *The Summer before the Dark*, Kate and her husband plan to move to a small house not because they have less money but because they have other reasons. Their relationship as husband and wife is never affected by monetary concerns. Treading on the same line, Anna Wulf's life is never steered astray because of money. She gets money from the royalty of her books. Though it is never in abundance yet it does not change her decision not to sell her novel when they want her to change the contents of her work. The idea does not appeal to her and she refuses the agreement despite repeated requests. Money never gets prominence to affect her relationships with her divorced husband, friends or one-night lovers. The distinction for holding the money is not primarily for males as is the case with Indian culture, where money and its importance is meant and understood only by the males.

Another aspect that is utterly different from other cultures is the relationship males and females share in terms of physical abuse. Concept of female liberation follows in relation to the existing trend of her place. In fact, after Second World War the "most significant advance was in the position of females" (Christopher 1999: 6). They are not bruised and physically abused, something very prominent or at least not absent in the works of Indian, African-American and Canadian writers. In the other societies, women may be intelligent, economically independent and mature, but in their relation to males they take subservient position and males are free to exercise their physical power over these females as and when they desire. They are treated as mere commodities to be used, abused and discarded as per their mood swings, considerably volatile all the time. Their smartness, intelligence, talent and skills are scoffed at liberally or suppressed loyally.

In Britain, females may not be intelligent, economically independent or mature but wife-beating as such is not a part of their culture. Husbands are treated as merely human beings not as the focal point of their life or demigods. Women are neither contented to serve their husbands like slaves nor do they deify them; rather they are treated as normal human beings with no special gifts. Doris Lessing is one such writer who keeps the hallucination of male superiority away. Alistair Davies (2000: 3), in the introduction to his book *British Culture of the Postwar: An Introduction to Literature and Society*, says, "Women writers appeared—notably Doris Lessing and Margaret Drabble—who devoted themselves to the...distinctive insights of women." Doris Lessing's females are independent beings, if they lack something Doris Lessing allows them to make mistakes, learn from their mistakes and move ahead as enlightened beings, nowhere banking solely on males. In *The Golden Notebook*, Anna and Molly are nowhere beaten by their husbands. In *The Summer before the Dark*, Kate is nowhere physically bruised by her husband. Physical torture does not take place, for it is not a part of their socio-cultural life.

Male-female relationship or specifically husband-wife relationship is also different. Males do not cherish privileged predominance and the females cherish their own authority, not purely dominated by males. Husbands are not meant for guiding and instructing the wives about the handling of affairs; wives take their own decisions regarding economic and professional matters. Nowhere, they are looked down upon by male counterparts; their capabilities are never doubted or scoffed at. Richards does discuss things with Anna and Molly, when he is concerned about his son. When Kate takes up the job of an interpreter, the husband is neither jealous of her nor does he take the decision on her part. She is advised about the perspective and then the rest is left with her to decide on her own. It does not matter much whether she remains inside the house or goes out for a job. In fact, he suggests the name of his wife for the job. Marriage is there on the cards but it is not the ultimate goal of relationship. Marriage, divorce and fornication are not serious affairs. In marriage, undiluted dedication, reverence and complete surrender are neither expected nor fulfilled. Kate in *The Summer before the Dark* is one such lady who has no expectations from her husband; When Kate is away from home she does think of her husband but she does not miss him. The intensity is not as acute as in Indian scenario and females are not mere tools meant to serve and please husbands.

Marriage is also not a sacred institution to provide fulfillment, instead "(m)arriage had had a load heaped on it which it could not sustain" (Lessing 1975: 62). Kate and her husband have been aware of this and accordingly "they had been right in making sure they did not expect too much from each other, or from marriage" (63). Domestic unhappiness has crept in and divorces have ensued in abundance. That's why in *The Golden Notebook*, Richard, Anna, Molly and Marion don't expect wonders from their marriages. Anna, Molly and Richard walk out of the institution of marriage as soon as it starts appearing to be a burden to them but another marriage is never out of question. Services of psychiatrists and marriage counselors are liberally sought. Richards marries three times and Molly also plans to get married again. Though the desire to have a steady relationship exists, it does not mean the end of the world if it does not get fulfilled. They have the liberty to walk out of relationships sans much propaganda. Nevertheless, her heroines are highly intelligent ladies who despite being aware of reality willfully choose to stay in relations. A stage of reality is portrayed where complexity and fragmentation are perceived as both necessary and inevitable.

Another distinguished feature of marriage is that the relationship the couples share is too flimsy because after marriage fidelity is not something very strictly adhered to. Sexual liberation is taken as an individual right and these excursions are allowed in happy married lives also. There is a "more relaxed attitude towards sexuality" (Christopher 1999: 4). Women enjoyed sex as much as men; discontent and adultery were common. Kate in *The Summer before the Dark* does take care of her husband and his needs but she does not mind sleeping with another man when she goes out for a tour. Shifting of male partners is not a transgression; Anna Wulf, switches over to any and every male who comes in her life, though she has got married and has had a daughter. Anna wants fulfilment with the help of a male but when she senses an intrusion, she never hesitates to put him at bay.

Sporadic excursions in sexual arena may not be considered uncommon; sex is nowhere considered something sacred culminating in the realization of wedded bliss. It can take place when something is to be done and when nothing is there to be done, then sex must go on. It is strangely deprived of love as well as hatred and strongly infused with indifference. This mechanical activity dominates, brutally brushing aside even the fulfilment of a basic need. Nonchalant indulgence makes it just a physical activity to be accomplished. Anna Wulf, the lady who does not wish to compromise, is too liberal in her attitude to sex. Whenever a man comes in her life, she sleeps with him though she derives neither enjoyment nor satisfaction out of it. Both Anna and Molly remain interested in men with a curiosity as if there are so few good ones left that it is necessary to hunt them amid the ruins. Both, in a wry and pleasing way, are frank about their sexuality; both are ready to have affairs when their emotions are stirred. Males are expected to make them feel complete and when one fails them they switch over to another one. In fact, they don't shun males completely but when emotional desires are stirred, efforts are made to bask in the company of males. Since they are not serious about males, they don't mind having affairs.

Personal space is sacredly preserved; anything or anybody that intrudes is discarded. Females prefer to lead a life where they may remain free women; sometimes they pay too heavy a price for their freedom, but they prefer not to be fettered by relationships. When Kate fails to have the sufficient place to move around, she feels smothered. To give herself enough breathing space, she rids herself of her accepted garb, something too prominently flaunted by Anna. Her efforts are not as bold as that of Anna but she does make try at her own level. Efforts are small but they do exist and the desire and intention are not overflowing but smoldering somewhere in her. They understand that they have to pay a heavy price for being free creatures but they do give it a try. Irving Howe (1979: 113) in his article

"Doris Lessing: No Compromise, No Happiness" talks about the desire to retain the freedom, "At the very least, Anna Wulf is someone who has measured the price for being what she chooses to be—'a free woman,' she would say with pride and irony—and who is prepared, no matter how much she groans, to pay it."

In *The Golden Notebook*, though Anna and Molly pay heavy price yet they prefer to cling to her saving difference. They demand from their men the completion of their being and claim that they provide those elements of strength and assurance which they, as women cannot. Anna, as a representative, wants in her men "both intimacy and power, closeness and self-sufficiency, hereness and thereness. Modernist in sensibility, she is traditional in her desires. And no matter what she must settle for at a given moment, she does not delude herself; she will not compromise with the idea of compromise" (Howe 1979: 115). Irving Howe clarifies further that not only the desire to retain the freedom but also the spirit to stand by that choice does prevail. Anna Wulf and her old friend Molly understand perfectly well that modern women do face difficulties when they choose one or another role of freedom. But they do not fall back upon their charm, wit or headaches. All females try hard to preserve their independence, which means not a refusal of relationships but a hard decision not to bamboozle themselves, when they do take up second-raters and even more, keep a strict watch, mostly within themselves, against the mediocre, the resigned, and the merely comfortable.

In the end, Kate wants to go home to her husband, Molly does think of marriage and Anna after coming out of the disastrous affair with the American keeps pushing ahead when she decides to go into Labour Party work and probably to take up a job as a marriage counselor. They remain loyal to that refusal to compromise which has bound the two women in friendship. They share ruthless honesty about relations they have with males in their lives making them more detached and objective in their relations. Kate and her friend never give a false picture of their conditions and whenever Anna and Molly meet they repeatedly talk about their personal relations but always with muted irony and impatience. They are alternately open and guarded, sometimes wounding but usually honest. No efforts are attempted to make the scenario appear serene and soothing.

Honesty is highly valued. If they are unhappy, they do not hesitate to accept it and if they are happy in casual flirtations, they do not feel ashamed. Pretensions are neither made nor appreciated. When conversations between Anna and Molly recur, one turns to them with delight of encountering something real and fresh. They stand in sharp contrast to Atwood's heroines who prefer hiding behind the mask they put on and which becomes an integral part of their personalities. Lessing's heroines remain away from simulations, as they firmly believe in candid confessions about the reality. They may be hurt, they may be losers but tampering with reality is not allowed by their conscience. They discuss their failures in love, their problems as divorced women with children to raise, their disillusionments as former communists who would still like to needle the Establishment, their ability to talk with the passionless and apolitical young, their contempt for the new gentility of intellectual London, and their difficulties in coping with the disillusionment of self-sufficient women concept.

When the protagonists want to realize an internal self, independent of social forces, they often end up inventing multiple and conflicting subject positions. Sometimes they perceive themselves as simply a feminine figure waiting for a man to call their selves into being. This contradiction between the desire to find themselves as well as to be created by men leads to self-divisiveness in their perception of themselves. Although they are initially seduced by the romantic discourse to actively take up a gendered position in a type of narrative that can be loosely described as woman needing a man for fulfillment they can hardly ignore their other self that is essentially anti-romantic in nature. Their personalities are highly fragmented; their sharp knowledge of self does not allow delusion of any kind and their intellectual honesty makes them accept that many diverse personalities are struggling to co-exist within them. Their experiences fail to satisfy them and the longing to integrate these disparate parts remains.

Kate though willy-nilly has adjusted herself according to the accepted norms yet feels uncomfortable as the desire to follow her own instincts persists. In the end, though not too rebellious, she wants to shed the nonchalant acceptance of something that does not suit her temperament. Nowhere does she make an attempt to tamper with the reality; not even when she is brutally treated by her kids. The same discomfiture is visible in Anna Wulf also who, like Lessing, strives for ruthless honesty as she aims to free herself from the chaos, emotional numbness, and hypocrisy afflicting her generation. They may be battered by the affairs of life but they are tough-minded and face every difficulty with determined grit. They are concerned not only with themselves but with those things also over which they have little control. Lessing's heroines suffer because of the social upheavals also as visible from the case of Anna for Lessing grasps the connection between Anna Wulf's neuroses and the public disorders of the day. The feminine element does not become a self-contained universe of being; it sprawls beyond its immediate setting. Anna Wulf, a mature intellectual woman and a writer with sophisticated mind, sharp tongue and an abundance of emotional troubles, is "sufficiently representative of a certain kind of modem woman to persuade us that her troubles have relevance beyond their immediate setting; she has also an intelligence keen enough to support the public combativeness and personal introspectiveness that Miss Lessing has given her" (Howe 1979: 113).

The tussle between social and personal is very strong, as when they pay too much attention to themselves, then the society ignores them and when society accepts them then it is at the cost of their personal freedom. This leads to disintegration in her characters; the degree may vary drastically but there is no escape from this erosion. Some prefer to cling to social norms but the leading ladies feel fidgety about it and they do try to have personal fulfilments discarding some or all of the social norms. Efforts are made and prices are paid for being the axis. There is no fear of social stigma; they hardly care whether people know about them or not. Social system is not stringent and social approval is hardly cared for. They are open about their relationships and society also does not pay too much attention.

In fact, "a fit of collective indifference" (Ward 2001: 3) lulls the social concern. Though social acceptance for relationships is not required, the desire to improve the social standards prevails; people make conscious efforts to improve the scenario. When they notice nil difference, they become disappointed. The desire to break away from the society is too strong but it never materializes. Most breakdowns in women are known to take place when extraneous factors like familial responsibilities do not make the kinds of demands they once did "with children having grown independent, leading to a feeling of superfluity and unwantedness in the female psyche. Kate in *Summer before the Dark* goes through a similar experience" (Kumar 2001: 60-61).

There is guilt in Lessing's response to motherhood too. This experience is not a rewarding one but a constricting and peripheral experience; mothers are either bent under the duress of guilt or they are blessed with disinterest. Mother remains as an individual not as a mother; expectations set her as a servant who takes care of everybody by sacrificing her interests but unlike Indian scenario this mother-child relationship is not maintained. Mother is given her due space and if she finds motherhood too burdensome then she is also given the liberty to move out of it, take a break or even discard it. In British culture, when children are grown up, parents, especially mother feels unwanted, for their needs can be fulfilled elsewhere: "Mother was an uncertain quantity. She was like an old nurse who had given her years to the family and must now be put up with" (91). Kate openly admits being maltreated by her children and also refers to psychological void in her life. She calls her kids monsters that thrive on her sap and they have enervated her of her energies to pay attention to her own likings. When her kids shout at her she feels like crying and compares herself to a stray cat that is simply worthless.

Parent-child relationship is detached; children prefer to be independent as soon as possible. Hostels are preferred to homes because children exercise more liberty there. Home is a place to be regularly visited. Needs and desires of children are nowhere monitored by parents only. The concern about the wellbeing of parents is not of the children. Parents have to look after themselves. Kate's kids use her as a commodity who is there to cater to their needs. On the same line, Anna prefers her daughter to stay at home but the baby girl prefers hostel to school because the concept of family or parents is different for her. A joint family where grandparents and grandchildren share the same home is rare because younger generation requires more and more space for themselves. "For children like Janet the fabric of security is woven, not of grandparents, cousins, a settled home; but that friends telephone everyday, and certain words are spoken" (257). The concept of joint families is weak in occidental world. Intricate patterns of relationships don't create much problem. Kate, her husband and her kids are mentioned but there is no reference to the relatives. Similarly Anna, Molly, her husband and their kids are mentioned but no reference is there of the elder generation.

There is no space for the parents of the elder generation. Parents don't have much control over children and separate lodging is required for them to lead a life of their own. And as soon as they are grown up to take care of themselves, they prefer to lead an independent life. Parents, instead of enjoying the company of their children, know it well that they have to stay alone now. Kate and her husband know it perfectly well: "... she and her husband had recently been saying that now the children would soon be altogether grown-up, it might be time to start thinking of getting themselves something smaller? A flat? They could buy a house in the country and share it with friends—perhaps the Finchleys" (12). Apparent sense of detachment is not untoward because it is prevalent there. The close-knit bond that makes parents and children inseparable or interdependent is not a part of their culture. Their culture and society have seen, accepted and practiced decently distanced relationships. They behave this way because their culture does not object to it. Culture, indubitably, is a determinant of human behaviour. Doris Lessing's works, with a touch of subjectivity, display an impressive array of mores that are deftly dented by cultural sparks.

To reprise, the apparent influence and the subtle exercise of the accustomed ambience, invariably colour the mindset as well as the reaction of the beings. Though, there are certain elements that refuse to be bound by any lines and prefer to remain universally ubiquitous, yet there are certain elements that take pleasure in being specific to the region and people they belong to. The way people are similar yet so singularly individual is also true of their manners which give them the specialties that set them apart from the rest. The observation does not come in contrast until it is placed against a different backdrop, the moment it differs, the contrast gets highlighted. Doris Lessing is also acknowledged for being a great feminist who prefers to celebrate the womanhood of females, yet inadvertently she discloses the cultural individualities of the characters. The problems, the reactions, the thinking process, the dressing sense and the issues are specifically bound by her culture. However, her indulgence and preference are very specific, but her appeal is not restricted because though she banks on her indigenous elements, she speaks to all as a human being, an essentially universal quality, strong enough to sweep readers off their feet. No wonder, her charisma works very prominently even with those who are alien to her native roots.

WORKS CITED

Christopher, David. *British Culture: An Introduction*. London: Routledge, 1999.

Davies, Alistair, ed. *British Culture of the Postwar: An Introduction to Literature and Society*. London: Routledge, 2000.

Denham, Paul and Mary Jane Edwards, ed. *Canadian Literature in the 70's*. Toronto: Holt, Rinehart and Winston, 1980.

Else, David. *Lonely Planet Britain*. 5th ed. 1995. London: Lonely Planet, 2003.

Garner, Dwight. "The Salon Interview: Doris Lessing." *Salon.com* 11 Nov. 1997. 25 June 2005 http://www.salon.com/books/feature/1997/11/cov_si_11lessing.html

Howe, Irving. *Celebrations and Attacks: Thirty Years of Literary and Cultural Commentary*. New York: Horizon Press, 1979.

Kumar, Alka. *Doris Lessing: Journey in Evolution*. 1st ed. New Delhi: Books Plus, 2001.

Lessing, Doris. *The Golden Notebook*. 1972. New ed. London: Granada Publishing House, 1977. All the quotes from this novel are from the edition cited here.

Lessing, Doris. *The Summer before the Dark*. 1973. Middlesex: Penguin Books Ltd., 1975. All the quotes from this novel are from the edition cited here.

Singh, Sunaina. *The Novels of Margaret Atwood and Anita Desai: A Comparative Study in Feminist Perspectives*. New Delhi: Creative Books, 1994.

Vevaina, Coomi S. *Re/Membering Selves: Alienation and Survival in the Novels of Margaret Atwood and Margaret Laurence*. New Delhi: Creative Books, 1996.

Ward, Stuart, ed. *British Culture and the End of Empire*. New York: Manchester University Press, 2001.

The Poetry of Kamala Das: A Study in Radical Feminism

5

Purnendu Chatterjee

The first use of the word 'feminist' can be traced back to a French medical book that was published in 1871. The term was then used to "describe a cessation in development of the sexual organs and characteristics in male patients, who were perceived as thus suffering from 'feminization' of their bodies."[1] With the passage of time, the term 'feminist' underwent a sea-change in its meaning. Biologists, psychologists, psychoanalysts and sociologist defined the concept of feminism from various points of view. It can be said very loosely that a feminist is a person who sees the gender systems currently in operation as structured by a basic binary opposition—masculine/feminine—in which the masculine is always privileged over the feminine and that this privileging has had the direct effect of enabling men to occupy positions of social power more often than women. But, such a concept of feminism does not take into account the fact that all feminists do not accept the binary opposition. For instance, Jane Scott advocates that feminists must deconstruct the binary opposition:

> Instead of framing analyses and strategies as if such binary pairs were timeless and true.... Instead of remaining within the terms of existing political discourse, we need to subject those terms to critical examination.[2]

So, it is well-nigh impossible to give an all-comprehensive definition of feminism. But the progress of feminism and the different modifications of feminist thought down the ages may be traced with greater aplomb than arriving at a definition of feminism. Women have been questioning their inferior status demanding redress of their lot long before Mary Wollstonecraft published *A Vindication of the Rights of Women* in 1792. But, Wollstonecraft's book has obvious historical importance as being the first book of its kind. Wollstonecraft voiced the need for women's right to education, economic independence and self-respect. Virginia Woolf in *A Room of One's Own* (1921) showed how domestic duties took away from women the time and means to earn their livelihood and gave rise to mental anguish. She, however, broke a new ground in feminist thought by pointing out that the artistic mind is androgynous and in the mind of the artist the male anima and the female animus harmonized to form a balanced personality. Woolf went one step further in *Three Guineas* (1938) when she questioned the need for a feminist movement after women have won their economic rights. Elaine Showlater in *A Literature of Their Own* (1977) spoke of three stages of feminist movement: "first feminine (1840-1880), where women wrote to equal men and internalized male assumptions about femaleness; second feminist (1880-1920), where women protested against patriarchy and advocated their own values; and last female (1920ff), where women turned inward and tried to discover themselves and develop a sense of their own identity."[3]

I

The French feminists, unlike their Anglo-American sisters, were more concerned with the issues of women's subjectivity, "women's language, women's time and women's sexuality."[4] Julia Kristeva, Luce Irigaray and Monique Wittig voiced their protests against the psychoanalytical views of Freud and Lacan who, with their concept of "female penis envy", looked upon woman as a sort of deformed man. Influenced by Michel Focault and Jacques Derrida, the French feminists were rooted in the body. They advocated the notion of *ecriture feminine* and suggested that women should write through their own bodies.

In India, the feminists protest against the dominance of patriarchy and the stereotyping of women's role in society. The Indian feminists often take help of the tenets of Marxism in presenting their views for ameliorating the lots of women in society. One of the significant works of the Indian feminists is their effort to develop a canon of women's writing. The Herculean efforts of S. Tharu and K. Lalita in compiling a two volume anthology, *Women Writing in India* (1991-93) deserve special mention.

The different stages of feminist movement have given rise to different schools of feminist thought. For the present, I shall briefly consider Radical Feminism.

Radical Feminism provides the bulwark of theoretical thought in feminism. It provides an important foundation for the rest of feminist flavours. Seen by many as the undesirable element of feminism, radical feminism is in reality the breeding ground for many of the ideas arising from feminism; ideas which were shaped and moulded in various ways by other branches of feminism. Radical feminism is centered on the necessity to question gender roles. It questions why women must adopt certain roles based on their biology, just as it questions why men adopt certain other roles based on theirs. Radical feminism attempts to draw lines between biologically-determined and culturally-determined behaviour in order to free both men and women as much as possible from their previous narrow gender role.

II

Kamala Das broke free from the metaphysical and romantic traditions and created a poetry that centered round the *self*. In *My Story* she pointed out:

> A poet's *raw material* is not stone or clay, it is her personality.[5] (italics mine)

This statement implies that she does not accept Eliot's distinction between the man who suffers and the mind that creates. Her poetic creations are rooted in her personality that becomes its "raw material". It must, however, be realized that the personality of the poet is a "raw material" and in no way a finished piece of poetry. The "raw materials" undergo aesthetic transmutations before they are presented as poetic wholes. Facts and fantasy, experience and imagination are inseparably mingled in her works, thereby creating a sort of Magic Realism. But, unfortunately, often her poetry has been interpreted as a true reflection of her personality and this has resulted in unleashing a battery of trenchant criticism against her self and her writings.

Kamala Das was married at the tender age of 16 to an insensitive homosexual who was fourteen years older to her. She entered the domain of marriage with high hopes of obtaining love, warmth and comfort. The poet herself candidly and honestly states her expectations from her husband:

> I had expected him to be all that I wanted my father to be, and my mother. I wanted conversation, companionship and warmth. Sex was far from thoughts.[6]

Reality, however, falsified her expectations. Frustrated and embittered, she devoted herself to the service of the literary Muse. She had been an exemplary mother and wife, caring for the home and hearth and using her literary talent to ameliorate the financial stringency of her family. In moments of creation she transcended the mundane realities and her protean creative self spoke in million different voices. It is through her poetry that she resurrects herself and makes a bold quest for identity. The search for identity by the woman writer has been aptly explained by Linda Anderson :

> The myth of self which recent theorists have questioned may not be present for her in the same way; it is more difficult for her to believe in a self that can exist before writing, a self that is unified and continuous. Autobiography may self-consciously exist for her—an alternate place for identification. This means that there may be a greater formal awareness in her writing, an emphasis on the self-reflexiveness of writing, the idea of the self as written.[7]

The first person personal pronoun "I", that is strewn over her poetic canvas, represent the various poetic personae and also becomes the nucleus of her poetry. The several poetic persona that stalk through the world of her love poems in her first three anthologies, *Summer in Calcutta* (1965), *The Descendants* (1967) and *The Old Playhouse and Other Poems* (1973), are very different from her autobiographical self. It is in the poems about her ancestry, the poems that express her melioriostic vision, the poems concerning self-introspection and in the poems addressed to Allah, that her poetic self and autobiographical self merge. Sharada Iyer has shown the difference between the autobiographical self and the poetic self in Kamala Das:

> The former (autobiographical self) occupies a safe position accepted and esteemed by society..., while her counterpart (poetic self) haunts the fringes of human intercourse.[8]

The poet's fragmented self generates a kind of ambivalence that underlies the entire oeuvre of Das's poetry. Indeed, any attempt to recreate her life from her love poems would not only be futile but also throw up monstrously distorted images of the poet's personality.

III

Kamala Das's poetry is a critique of the patriarchal hegemony that gave women a subaltern status. Patriarchy teaches women to be ashamed of their bodies. Das's candid statement about the female body is a form of protest against patriarchal domination. In "Death is so Mediocre", the persona deliberately indulges in a detailed description of the female body:

> Vulgarities of the final rites are not
> Quite right, the slow unwrapping of the carcass,
>
> The many paltry, human details that must disgust
> The esthete, the flabby thigh, the breasts that sag
> The surgery scar.[9]

The protest against the codes of a patriarchal society is inherent in these lines. The "human details" shock the traditional male sensibility and by bestowing these details to a corpse the poet tweaks the nose of patriarchal codes.

In "The Old Playhouse", one of the most anthologized poems of Kamala Das, the persona shows her revulsion of male dominance. The male figure in the poem has squeezed out the inherent qualities of the persona.

> You planned to tame a swallow, to hold her
> In the long summer of your love so that she would forget
> Not the raw seasons alone, and the homes left behind, but

Also her nature, the urge to fly and the endless
Pathways of the sky.[10]

The swallow is not only tamed, but also made to forget that she could fly. The spatial image in the expression "endless/ Pathways of the sky", by contrast, implies the restricted compass that is allowed to the persona. The image of the "swallow" in the quoted lines and the image of the "room", mentioned later in the poem, together imply painful imprisonment of the feminine psyche and an utter betrayal of expectation. Sunanda P. Chavan gives a brilliant rendition of the relation between the two images.

> The crucial images of "swallow" and "room" concretize the tension between the ideal, and the experience of love. The image of "swallow" with its "urge to fly" defines the feminine psyche's desire for freedom, while the image of "room", with its artificial lights and windows always shut, projects the nature of his love which prevented natural growth of her personality.[11]

The images centering around the body help to heighten the persona sense of disgust:

... You were pleased
With my body's response, its weather, its usual shallow
Convulsions. You dribbled spittle into my mouth, you poured

Yourself into every nook and cranny, you embalmed
My poor lust with your bitter-sweet juices.[12]

It is the "body's response" that satisfies the male and he does not need to peep beyond the body. It is obvious that the male can only initiate and satisfy the "skin's lazy hungers" ("The Freaks"). The lustful advances of the male disgusts the persona, but she can do nothing to ameliorate her lot. The patriarchal society would not allow her to break away from the traditional set-up. She must "fit in/...belong" ("An Introduction"). The ultimate result is that she becomes a role-player.

I was taught to break saccharine into your tea and
To offer at the right moment the vitamins.[13]

Her daily work is chalked out by the patriarchal society and whether she wills or no, she must perform the roles assigned to her. In "The Suicide", the persona describes the different roles that she has to play:

I must pose,
I must pretend,
I must act the role
of happy woman,
happy wife.
I must keep the right distance
between me and the high.
I must keep the right distance
Between me and the low.[14]

The verbs "pose", "pretend", "act" show that the activities undergone by the persona are imposed upon her. Her personal choices of association is pre-ordained, she must follow a set of social codes in order to make relationships. She has to perform her part, just as a clown in a circus goes through the routine histrionics. In the poem "Substitutes" the poet, indeed, compares the persona to a clown.

It will be all right when I learn
To paint my mouth like a clown's.
It will be all right if I put up my hair
Stand near my husband to make a proud pair.[15]

Such role-playing is soul quenching and it results in a loss of identity. In the hands of the patriarchal gods, the persona is transformed from a live human being into a puppet, a clown. She does not have a free choice even in matters pertaining to her social appearance. The repetition of the phrase "It will be all right" reflect a desperate effort of the persona to come to terms with the norms prescribed by the society. S.C. Harrex succinctly points out:

> Many of Kamala Das's poems epitomise the dilemma of the modern woman who attempts to free herself, sexually and domestically, from role bondage sanctioned by the past.[16]

Indeed, the patriarchal gods can perform greater feats than the mythological Pygmalion. While Pygmalion brought to life the stone statue of Galatea, the patriarchal gods can turn a "swallow" into "a bird of stone" ("The Stone Age"). The inevitable corollary of such an existence, under a ruthlessly constrictive culture, is a dwarfing of individual identity.

> .... Cowering
> Beneath your monstrous ego I ate the magic loaf and
> Became a dwarf. I lost my will and reason, to all your
> Questions I mumbled incoherent replies.[17]

The word "monstrous" carries with it the double implications of power and evil. On its own, the male ego is not as potent as the persona feels. Its colossal proportion is only apparent. The male ego appears titanic because the patriarchal set-up has transformed the female into a pigmy. With the possibility of becoming, to put it in Auden's words, an "unknown citizen" the only hope of escape from a total annihilation of personality lies in a complete annihilation of existence.

> For, love is Narcissus at the water's edge, haunted
> By its own lonely face, and yet it must see at last
> An end, a pure, total freedom, it must will the mirrors
> To shatter and the kind night to erase the water.[18]

The persona's ideal of love, like Narcissus's ideal, is doomed to failure. The word "night", with its characteristic of darkness, implies death which is mysterious, and hence, dark. This death is "kind" because it releases the persona from a miserable existence. The phrase "erase the water" implies, that through death, the persona would escape the compulsion to keep ruminating all the time of her own lonely face and the desolation which it represented.

The poet's desire to eschew an "average/Identity" ("The Siesta") and live life to the full is fleshed out in the poem "Spoiling the Name". The poem boils down to the simple notion that a name is made for a particular individual, not an individual for a name. The name is described as a "medal, undeservingly/ Gained" because the poet had no hand in naming herself, she was given a name by somebody else. So, she cannot sacrifice all the celebrations of life on the altar of a superfluous object called "name" and any proposal contrary to this end appears foolish to her.

.... You ask of
Me a silly thing. Carry
This gift of a name like a corpse and
Totter beneath its weight
And perhaps even fall.... I who love
This gift of life more than all![19]

The comparison of a corpse to a name is, definitely, a conceit. The conceit suggests that a name curses the poet with a death-in-life existence. It is like a heavy load holding back the poet from taking part in the celebration of life.

The intense suffering and pain felt in living a life within an andocentric, constrictive culture finds moving expression in 'The Stone Age'. The poet uses the devices of irony and contrast to describe the predicament of the persona:

Fond husband, ancient settler in the mind
Old fat spider, weaving webs of bewilderment,
Be kind. You turn me into a bird of stone, a granite
Dove, you build round me a shabby drawing room,
And stroke my pitted face absentmindedly while
You read. With loud talk you bruise my pre-morning sleep,
You stick a finger into my dreaming eye.[20]

The expressions "ancient settler" and "old fat spider" reflect the scorn that the persona bears for her husband and the feeling of hatred is further heightened by the skilful use of the adjective "fond". Through the juxtaposition of opposites, bird (living)—stone (non-living) and granite (non-living)—dove (living), the persona brings out the misery of her own life. The careless attitude of the husband is revealed in the manner in which he strokes her face. The use of the verb "stroke" is unusual. It adds a ring of harshness to the husband's gesture. And the fact that he does not even look at her, his eyes are riveted to the book, while stroking her face not only reflect the insensitivity of the male figure, but also reveal the intense humiliation of the female persona. The imagery in "you stick a finger into my dreaming eye" conveys a sense of intense suffering. The contrast inherent in the imagery heightens the intensity of pain. As Anisur Rahman puts it:

Obviously, the poet relies on the poetic strategy of contrast
to accentuate the effect of pain.[21]

The cruelty meted out to women by the feudal, patriarchal society is the stuff of the poem "Honour".

Honour was a plant my ancestors watered
In the day, a palm to mark their future pyres, at night their serfs
Let them take to bed little nieces, and pregnancy
A puzzle to the young toys, later thrown into wells and ponds
From which they rose like lotuses and water lilies each with
A bruise on her throat and a bulge below her naval.[22]

It takes heroic courage to write in this fashion. It is not surprising that Das was ostracized.

Suffering and humiliated, fallen on the thorns of life and bleeding, the persona seeks a way out of such a persecuted and tortured existence. But her attempt is doomed to fail.

When you leave, I drive my blue battered car
Along the bluer sea. I run up the forty
Noisy steps to knock at another's door.
Through peepholes, the neighbours watch, hey watch me come
And go like rain. Ask me, everybody, ask me
What he sees in me, ask me why he is called a lion,
A libertine, ask me the flavour of his
Mouth, ask me why his hand sways like a hooded snake
Before it clasps my pubis.[23]

The "sea" gives her peace. But, this peace is temporary. The man, to whom she has turned, the "lion", hurts and humiliates her with his lustful advances. The hosts of erotic images in the last three lines reflect the brutality of sex and the horror that such brutality brings in its trail.

The persona craves for a love that would give her the highest form of happiness, without hurting and humiliating her. Sunanda P. Chavan aptly comments:

> The beloved yearns for the kind of love which will be a spiritual experience involving meaningful sexual relationship without the loss of her own identity.[24]

But, her attempts to enjoy such a blissful love prove to be abortive, both within and outside the ambit of marriage. The love she had from the male personae is like a shadow, without any substance. Such love only breeds a sense of negation which in its turn breeds more negation, till life is turned into an arid waste of frustration.

.... For years I have run from one
gossamer lane to another, I am
now my own captive.[25]

With the prospect of finding sexual-spiritual fulfillment shrinking back in embarrassment, the poet ridicules and castigates the institution of marriage. In the poem "Composition", she advices married couples:

Turn your home into a merry
dog-house,
marriage is meant to be all this
anyway,
being arranged in
most humorous heaven.[26]

The traditional and romantic concept of marriage as leading to a sweet and happy home is subverted by the expression "dog-house" and we cannot fail to notice the mischievous twinkle in the poet's eyes as she writes the adjective "humorous".

In "The Conflagration", she questions the concept of marital happiness:

Woman, is this happiness, this lying buried
Beneath a man? It's time to come alive,
The world extends a lot beyond his six-foot frame.[27]

Here is the radical feminist in Kamala Das. She questions the traditional concept of happiness in marriage and urges women to break free from patriarchal domination. The expression "six-foot frame", by contrast, implies the vast world that resides outside the domain of a home that is dominated by the husband.

The poet not only castigates the institution of marriage, but also questions gender roles. The distinction between the male and the female is blurred in the poem, "The Doubt".

When a man is dead, or a woman,
We call the corpse not he
Or she but it. Does it
Not mean that we believe
That only the souls have sex and that
Sex is invisible?
Then the question is, who
Who the man, who the girl,
All sex-accessories being no
Indication. Is she
A male who with frail hands
Clasps me to her breast, while
The silence in her sickroom, turning
Eloquent, accuses
Me of ingratitude?
And, is he female who
After love, smoothes out the bed sheets with
Finicky hands and plucks
From pillows strands of hair?
...... How well I can see him
After a murder, conscientiously
Tidy up the scene, wash
The bloodstains under
Faucet, bury the knife.......
And, what am I in sex who shuttles
Obsessively from his
Stabs to recovery
In her small silent room?[28]

The poem follows an argumentative pattern to give expression to the poet's thoughts. In the first six lines of the poem, the poet shows that bodies have no gender as the dead bodies which are without soul takes the neuter pronoun "it" while living human beings who have soul within their bodies are addtressed as "he" or "she". This argument leads to the conclusion that souls have gender and since the soul is "invisible", so is the sex of a person. This is syllogism at its brilliant best.

The poet, like the radical feminists, questions the traditional concept of gender. Kristeva, Cixous and Irigaray, the champions of radical feminist movement, pointed out that there is no such thing as Woman, because womanhood is not a homogeneous concept. The radical feminists suggest that gender is extrinsic, and hence, its coordinates are changeable: whom society refers as men may be women and *vice versa*. Shormistha Panja sums up the views of the radical feminist, Julia Kristeva, on the issue of gender:

> Kristeva...thinks femaleness is a matter of choices, a choice between the semiotic of the mother and the symbolic of the father and not something intrinsic; it is a question of positionality, not essences. When subjectivity itself is questionable, what indeed is a woman?[29]

This is Das's *raison d'être* in the poem. The last seven lines with its images of violence, murder and bloodshed reveal the poet's horror of sex.

NOTES

1. Jane Freedman. *Feminism* (Delhi, 2002), p. 2.
2. Quoted in Jane Freedman. *Feminism* (Delhi, 2002), p. 23.
3. Shormistha Panja, (ed.) *Critical Theory Textual Application* (Delhi, 2002), p. 60.
4. *Ibid.*, p. 65.
5. Kamala Das. *My Story* (Kottayam, 2004), p. 124.
6. *Ibid.*, p. 69.
7. Linda Anderson. "At the Threshold of the Self: Woman and Autobiography", *Women's Writing: A Theory*, ed. Moira Montieth (Sussex, 1986), p. 59-60. Also quoted in N.V. Raveendran, *The Aesthetics of Sensuality: A Stylistic Study of the Poetry of Kamala Das* (New Delhi, 2000), p. 44.
8. Sharada Iyer. "Split-self in the poetry of Kamala Das", *Kamala Das: A Critical Spectrum*, ed. Rajeshwar Mittapalli and Pier Paolo Piciucco (New Delhi, 2001), p. 114.
9. Kamala Das. *Collected Poems* Vol. I (Trivandrum, 1984), p. 55.
10. Kamala Das. *The Old Playhouse and Other Poems* (Madras, 1973), p. 1.

11. Sunanda P. Chavan. *The Fair Voice* (Delhi, 1984), p. 63.
12. *Op. cit.* 10
13. *Op. cit.* 12.
14. Kamala Das. *The Descendants* (Calcutta, 1991), p. 8.
15. *Op. cit.* 14.
16. S.C. Harrex. 'The Strange Case of Matthew Arnold in a Sari: An Introduction to Kamala Das', *Kamala Das—A Selection with Essays on Her Work*, (eds.) S.C. Harrex and Vincent O' Sullivan (Adelaide, 1986), p. 163.
17. *Op. cit.* 13.
18. *Op. cit.* 17.
19. Kamala Das. *Summer in Calcutta* (Kottayam, 2004), p. 27.
20. Kamala Das. *The Old Playhouse and Other Poems* (Madras, 1973), p. 51.
21. Anisur Rahaman. *Expressive Form in the Poetry of Kamala Das* (New Delhi, 1981), p. 21.
22. Kamala Das. *Collected Poems* Vol. I (Trivandrum, 1984), p. 47.
23. *Op. cit.* 20.
24. *Op.cit.* 11.
25. Kamala Das. *The Descendants* (Calcutta, 1991), p. 23.
26. *Ibid.*, p. 40.
27. *Ibid.*, p. 26.
28. Board of Editors. *An Anthology of Indian English Poetry* (New Delhi, 2002), p. 56.
29. Shormistha Panja, (ed.) *Critical Theory Textual Application* (Delhi, 2002), p. 97.

The Reactive Expatriate

6

Alessandro Monti

I will consider three novels dealing with troubled issues of failed migration and perturbed growing into foreign location. Although very different in scope and background, the fiction I am going to speak of (*Transmission* by Hari Kunzru, 2004; *Tourism* by Nirpal Singh Dhalival, 2006; *The Reluctant Fundamentalist* by Mohsin Hamid, 2007) may suggest a homogeneous continuum. All of them concern a contemporary passage from East to West, with a disappearance and a cruel return respectively in *Transmission* and in *The Reluctant Fundamentalist* whereas, the more mundane *Tourism* focuses on the miscegenating lost heritage of a second-generation expatriate. However, all these texts load quite dramatically uncouth geographies mapping interstitial belonging as a major factor of isolation and alienity. No doubt that *Transmission* deploys a more traditional approach, given how the "on the bench" life of the computer geek Arjun Metha updates to me the dreary clandestine life led in the sixties by the Eastern community of workers in *Emigré Journeys* (2000) by Abdullah Hussein. Both novels emphasise invisibility, or the temporary and flexible presence of the migrant/expatriate in terms of marginality and episodic nomadism in the sites and roles of work.

As a matter of fact *Transmission* moves on the fringes of imagined reality outside history, in a rather extravagant way that percolates into a revengeful myth disrupting the authoritative and authoritarian network of worldwide communication, by means of Bollywood extreme romance and the picaresque disappearance of the telematic hero. A similar return to hostile and belligerent nothingness may be claimed by the reluctant terrorist, one which exchanges a difficult assimilation with the ambiguous posture of the Muslim fundamentalist withdrawing out of a possible metissage with Western influence. Thus, the interstitial belonging of such migrants not deferring to a pacified or pacifying frame of mind, whose growing into Western relocation must be perceived in bleak terms of truncated experience, yields finally to acts of extreme resistance.

The institutional seclusion to which Eastern migrants have been historically doomed when entering, but not joining at all, the Western world (if we consider the British Southalls or Brick Lanes, not to mention the French "cités" or the dreary suburbs everywhere) becomes in *Transmission* and in *The Reluctant Fundamentalist* a conclusive move of escape beyond the ambiguous borders of hybridised marginality. Both characters in the two novels step over and across migration, so as to claim the revengeful repossession of a belonging previously lost.

In the latter novel the interstitial movement of ambiguous behaviour in-between friendly visibility and horrible invisibility features sharp intimations of metaphysical disguise, akin to the game of spies and murder of colonial representation. As a matter of fact, the backward movement from West to East, after a previous passage of migration, concerning the repentant protagonist of *The Reluctant Fundamentalist* inverts the paradigm of regained Western identity formerly advocated by Kim in Kipling and claimed as such by the military agencies within colonial powers. The event of migration to the West generates a spatial void, the confused consciousness of the migrant, whose ontological state of tension (both in terms of inner and outer space) should be viewed as analogous to the colonial clash for possession and hegemony of a coterminous territory. Indeed, terrorism is the heir to the "Great Game" in nineteenth-century Central and South Asia, of course not in sheer terms of real political strategy, but in the focus of the manifold urges to safe hybridisation opposing the unauthorised claims to subversive presence.

To make matters worse, the autodiegetic events are narrated through the narrational Victorian device of the high-strung "dramatic monologue", a strategy of argumentative literary communication in which the listener constitutes a passive and quasi-silent presence in front of the persona who speaks. This unflexible one-way discourse allows a strong effect of distancing on the part of the implied author, if we consider how Robert Browning manipulates the discursive technique of the "dramatic monologue", as in the "Last Duchess" for instance, so as to represent critically an exotic location, whose stigma of reproach and alien cultural belonging are evoked through its own spoken words, thus engendering a consequent rhetoric of unconscious but self-revealing blame. In the novel by Hamid East speaks through its own voice but the melliflous tone concealing however murderous intents is inscribed into a Western mode of language, whose ultimate type recalls racial figurations of Asian untrustfulness and betrayal. Contemporary chronicle seems to be conclusively entrapped within an undialogic logos of external anatomy of the Eastern mind and of belligerent relationships excluding mutual comprehension.

In *The Reluctant Fundamentalist* there is neither way of escape, except through violence, nor possible interactive communication between the two worlds. Vice versa the title *Transmission* of the novel by Hari Kunzru evokes postmodern and globalising myths, or perhaps urban legends in updated language, of resistential sabotage. However, the exploited migrant kept "on the bench" becomes an all-world icon for the folk-insignia of opposing power. It is highly ironical that the destructive thrust against computer age (and its post-colonial anthropology of checked and impeded movements of unwelcome migrancy) should rely on the massification of values nurtured by Bollywood cinema. The unreal person of an Indian female star is turned into a disruptive password against the planned checking out of unwanted migrants from the European core of comfortable identity and selective identification. By adopting Bollywood glamour as a victorious tool for global guerrilla Kunzru deconstrues the Western normative text whose regulative system of computerised archives impose patterns of hegemonic control upon the lives and movements of people which are considered to be in an external subaltern position and role. *Transmission* and *The Reluctant Fundamentalist* beget two different hypotheses of devolutionary chaos, the former by defusing as useless the data banks and the computer system that regulate order and economy in the Western World, the latter by moving on the dangerous and unstable edge of mimic discursive appropriation.

The Westernising strategies of narration adopted by the author are fully mirrored by his character Changez, whose attitude when moving inside the American upper class is one of exterior similarity of manners. Beyond these shallow but anguished acts of postcolonial mimicry one should detect the tearing stream of continuous inner argumentation and painful confrontation: a self-questioning of roots and heritage, of birth and relocation. This absence in presence, or perhaps a double absence, makes an outside of Changez, albeit his prestigious location within American society. It would be difficult to trace out the unstable border between the successful expatriate and the ethnic dropout. However, as I told before, one cannot compare his split frame of mind with the lapses in nostalgia that are recurrent in a few short stories by Bharati Mukherjee. It could be more similar the parenthetical stance deployed by the second-generation British Nirpal Singh Dhaliwal in *Tourism*. His character Bhupinder, whose hyphenated "deshi" identity recognises him as a Punjabi Sikh, is caught in a half-way upward move from inferior migrant suburb to ethnically mixed British high middle class. Drink, sex and women in huge quantities and numbers are his commitment in life, in a sort of self-destructuve reaction against his sense of loss and uprooting. Neither a British nor an Indian, Bhupinder stands lonely as a postmodern "étranger", a tourist through life, as he says. Thus, the title *Tourism* should be interpreted as a synonym for a life without belonging.

The sense of postcolonial void of which V.S. Naipaul speaks seems to have engulfed the protagonist, a devoluted mimic man in London, one who has given up before trying. Dhalival impresses a new and utterly cathacrestic turn to typical postcolonial malaise and uprooting. Extensive and repetitive sex is perhaps the one feature he adds to the discourse of estrangement introduced by V.S. Naipaul. It is highly debatable if sexual galore in his novel might just reflect contemporary mundane chronicle in British high life (so as to constitute a naughty correlative for the Gucci or Armani items of high fashion that crowd the migrant stories by Divakaruni) or might possibly indicate an everlasting condition of "taedium vitae". To understand better the meaning which is implied in the representation of such transgressive way of life, one could take into account the "deshi" filmic comedy Namastey London (2007), in which a handful of second-generation migrants, either Hindus or Muslims, are seen sowing dutifully their too wild oats. However, repentance is just behind the corner, through the agency of a rustic Punjabi boy that rescues the un-Indian migrant heroine out of a posh marriage within high British society. It would be a valuable asset to compare the redeeming return to healthy and arcadic "deshi" life in the film with the discovery of his fatherhood on the part of the runaway protagonist in *Tourism*—the incipit of a return back home and presumably to a new life, according to the call of duty for a householder, so strong in Indian culture. Identity lost and regained, one would say, given how the previous cynicism and refusal to engage in any serious purpose gives way to a Bollywood-style ending.

This truncated continuity in the thematic thread reinstates the usual trudging on towards domestic comedy or tragedy that we find in the novel (or romance) concerning the life of the Indian expatriate. One is led back again to Jumpha Lahiri (*Interpreter of Maladies*, 1999) or even to Bharati Mukherjee, if one also considers the dark side of the question (the novel *Wife*, 1975, in particular). In any case, the three novels I have been dealing with introduce a return to uncompromising reactive type–by means of typical Bollywood extravaganza in *Transmission* (a fairy-tale in the computer age), by refusing assimilation and coexistence in *The Reluctant Fundamentalist* (a treatise on ambiguity in intercultural relationships) and finally in the sublime pathos of fatherhood in *Tourism*, so as to transform a tale of alienation into a possibly mawkish Punjabi elegy.

The Reluctant Fundamentalist does not elude the confrontation with traumatic history, that is the crumbling down of the Twin Towers. In a highly metaphoric way, this turning-point event crystallises de facto the stubborn opposition to Western hegemony in everyday personal life practised by the expatriate character. His attitude does not defuse the time-honoured fictional stereotype of regressive return to type in the migrant persona, such as outlined in a handful of pioneer short stories by Bharati Mukherjee. *The Reluctant Fundamentalist* shares with the fecal expatriate of "Nostalgia" or with the Kali-obsessed man of "A Father"[1] a constant uneasiness with the too easy ways of Western life and the sexual behaviour they imply. However, something has changed since the seventies, mainly in the purview of reactive violence an expatriate is allowed to, isolation is no more individual, or simply unideologically expressed, but leads to organised terrorism. This reversal of perspectives downgrades the struggle for hegemony from the would-be pacified and fertile fields of cultural assimilation to the barren and violence-swept lands of military imposition.

If one reads *The Reluctant Fundamentalist* in the light of an inner disease gnawing rather cruelly at the mind of the lonely migrant, one who radically translates his life in the Western world as an uninterrupted sequence of antagonistic tension, one should understand as well the Twin Towers as the consequence of mnestic heritage in the mind of the character, rather than a starting point laying bare his psychic devolution. The cathacrestic return passage of the character from West to East should be more correctly viewed as part of a balanced movement back to the ideological chaos of postcolonial nationhood. The same pattern of epistemological confusion makes havoc in *Transmission* of the Western authorised network of selective global information. In this novel, Bollywood unrealistic romance is the key that deregulates the communicative hegemony of the West and instructs at the same time counter-myths of resistance and refusal within the Western walls. As a side effect one has to face a fracture, in the subcontinental ethos of "deshi" values, between Muslim fundamentalism and the subversive exaggeration of the maieutic powers a "lila" has. As a matter of fact the cinematic body of the actress (one in-between reality and illusion) can be easily equated to the suspended body of the migrant, such as depicted in *Transmission*, before and afterwards his disappearance: an event that makes a spectacle, and message as well, of his imposed marginalisation. *Tourism* moves the picaresque perspective of residual, from the perennial nomadism for survival of the migrant kept "on the bench" to the perspective of a continental "Grand Tour" masquerading as a flight in search of an impossible answer. The call of the archaic that instructs the return home of the Muslim expatriate lays bare his inability to cope with the Western world and its ways of life. It arises out of an excess of unbearable tension that goes beyond the mere fright for what is initially unknown and reaches to the archana phobia of fundamentalism. It also goes beyond the partition of the hybridised self, no more the "cannibal serving at a table", of the colonial imagination, but the cannibal eating bodies.

NOTE

1. Both short stories are collected in *Darkness*, 1985.

Demarcating a Marginalized Lineage: Reading *Robinson Crusoe* through *Roxana* and into *Foe*

7

Natalie Wall

J.M. Coetzee's *Foe* is easily read as a rewriting of Daniel Defoe's *Robinson Crusoe*. Crusoe is still Cruso, despite the loss of his "e." Friday is still Friday, despite his loss of tongue. These are easy correspondences to make, simple and complete unto themselves. So the only question to be asked is: who is Susan Barton? She narrates *Foe* from beginning to end (correct, I assert that Susan Barton narrates even the problematic/enigmatic ending to the novel) and exists not in the male-focused island tale of *Robinson Crusoe*. Instead, she is found in the pages of another novel by Defoe, that of *Roxana*. So, here I posit that *Foe* is not only a rewriting of *Robinson Crusoe*, but a writing-back to this source-text through the narrative of *Roxana*. Why, you ask? I say, because Coetzee is creating a space of feminized marginality in his effort to undermine his (and Defoe's) male-centered authorial authority in their treatment of the colonial victim, Friday. Friday and Susan maintain, throughout the novel, a liminal relationship whereby Friday's silence frames Susan's guilty chatter and Susan's narration frames Friday's mutilated marginalization. The two are both Other, the same in difference while maintaining a strict demarcation of Susan's privilege and Friday's enslavement. While Susan is Friday and Friday is Susan, the two are also, irrevocably, separate.

In her 1987 article "Post-Colonial Literatures and Counter-discourse," Helen Tiffin examines the potential anti-hegemonic literary power of *writing-back*. In her first coining of the term "counter-discourse", Tiffin describes the process as "dynamic, not static: it does not seek to subvert the dominant with a view to taking its place, but to, in Wilson Harris's formulation, evolve textual strategies which continually 'consume' their 'own biases' at the same time as they expose and erode those of the dominant discourse" (18). Here, Tiffin analyzes the ways in which counter-discourse can be used as a subtle tool of deconstruction, not to ignore the canonical imperial works that came before, but to incorporate the colonial author into a postcolonial world and, therefore, reinvent the work in a self-reflexive moment of critical investigation. Counter-discourse offers the chance to challenge naturalized notions of hegemonic conventions through a subversive incorporation of the master's tools. Furthermore, Tiffin claims that:

> these subversive manoeuvres, rather than the construction of the *essentially* national or regional, are what are characteristic of post-colonial texts, as the subversive is characteristic of post-colonial discourse in general. Post-colonial literatures/cultures are thus constituted in counter-discursive rather than homologous practices, and they offer 'fields' of counter-discursive strategies to the dominant discourse. (18)

Counter-discourse then becomes the central tenet in postcolonial theory; the strategically empowered starting point from which analysis can best be made. This point, however, is not fixed. Counter-discourse takes many forms and moves in any direction. It is this fluidity of motion that lends postcolonial works their poignancy, standing apart from the stagnancy of the imperial canon, as post-modern texts of meta-discourse.

Looking at the applicatory power of writing-back, it becomes obvious that it is the potential that exists between the texts that lends the discourse its heterogeneous homogeneity. Reading the way that colonialism and postcolonialism inform one another allows for a reinterpretation of text which relies on a dialectic of converging voices. In his book, *Culture and Imperialism*, Edward Said sees counter-discourse as a means to read contrapuntally, in a synthesis of divergent subject positions. "The main idea is that even as we must fully comprehend the pastness of the past, there is no just way in which the past can be quarantined from the present. Past and present inform each other, each implies the other and...each co-exists with the other" (Said 4). Here, Said invokes the true spirit of counter-discourse as the means to connect two texts to each other; it is not a writing-against, but a dialogic of complementary voices that inform each other. Postcolonial theory is not moving away from its colonial roots, but, instead, moving towards and against the hierarchical normalizations that make up the canonical discourse, in the effort to undermine the hegemonic conventions within that discourse. Looking at ideas of contrapuntuality, Said says:

> I shall consider the ways in which a reconsidered or revised notion of how a post-imperial intellectual attitude might expand the overlapping community between metropolitan and formerly colonized societies. By looking at the different experiences contrapuntally, as making up a set of what I call intertwined and overlapping histories, I shall try to formulate an alternative both to a politics of blame and to the even more destructive politics of confrontation and hostility. (Said 18)

So, a contrapuntal reading relies on a foundationally layered set of histories that always already exist consistently and enigmatically in a state of continual flux. Counter-discourse becomes magnetized both positively and negatively within itself, always already repulsing and attracting simultaneously.

In J.M. Coetzee's *Foe* there exists an interstice through which a contestatory dialogue is established between it and its well-known predecessor, Daniel DeFoe's *Robinson Crusoe*. This interstice is Defoe's other novel *Roxana*. Coetzee challenges the conventionality of writing-back by offering a third text in his counter-discourse; *Roxana* becomes the novel that allows *Foe* to speak to *Robinson Crusoe*. It is the quest of Susan Barton, in seeking herself as her own author, which enables a disjunctive space of meeting and identification. Meeting and identification in *Foe* and *Roxana* are the means to break through a patriarchal objectivity into a feminist subjectivity, achieved by the intense self-recognition of the authors of their own problematic male gaze. In her article "Coetzee's *Foe*: Reading Defoe's *Crusoe/Roxana*," Gayatri Spivak looks at the problematic relationship between a counter-discursive text and its privileged author; she says that "in the face of *this* question, deconstruction might propose a double-gesture: Begin where you are; but, when in search of absolute justifications, remember that the margin as such is wholly other" (157). As a woman-oriented text, intruding on the colonial expectations set up by *Robinson Crusoe*, *Roxana* allows for a reinterpretative moment of persistent marginality in *Foe*. Looking at the ways in which *Foe*, *Robinson Crusoe*, and *Roxana* merge together to create a symbiosis of counter-discursive thought, Spivak also says that "it is as if the margins of bound books are themselves dissolved into a general textuality. Coetzee makes the final episode of Defoe's novel *Roxana* flow into this citation of *Robinson Crusoe*. Coetzee's Susan Barton is also Defoe's Roxana, whose first name is Susan (163). The moments in *Foe* that are unsubstantiated in *Robinson Crusoe* can be found in *Roxana*. The three narratives move together to paint a mosaic of thought, all carefully planned by Coetzee to reflect the de-essentialization of previous colonial standards in a (now) postcolonial world. Susan Barton's authority as female narrator moves against the naturalized patriarchal hegemonic order that *Crusoe* represents, and allows for a dialectic between the questing of the matriarchal lineage and the colonial imperative behind the patriarchal impulse. *Foe:*

> reopens two English texts in which the early eighteenth century tried to constitute to marginality: Daniel Defoe's *Robinson Crusoe* (1719) and *Roxana* (1724). In *Crusoe*, the white man marginalized in the forest encounters Friday the savage in the margin. In *Roxana*, the individualist female infiltrates nascent bourgeois society. In Coetzee's novel, a double-gesture is performed. In the narrative, Roxana begins her construction of the marginal where she is; but when her project approaches fulfillment, the text steps in and reminds us that Friday is in the margin as such, wholly other. (Spivak 157)

Femininity becomes the discursive potential of *Foe*, as it enables Coetzee to use a marginalized voice to express sentiments of sympathy without reinforcing a hierarchical appropriation of subjectivity, but it also complicates the novel as it reflects the colonial complicity of the white, English woman.

Though Susan Barton narrates *Foe*, it is Friday (as speechless and decentered) who truly occupies the counter-discursive space as the symbol of colonial victimization. Friday is mutilated. His tongue has been removed and he has been castrated. It is Friday, as neither woman nor man that allows for a full investigation of the role that Susan Barton plays in this text as counter to *Robinson Crusoe* and *Roxana*. Friday has no language, he is illiterate and dispossessed. It is this decentering of Friday, from home and society, which allows Coetzee to implicate authorship as a means of negating voice in the effort to stage a just portrayal of the position of marginality. In his essay "*Foe's* Defoe and la Jeune Née: Establishing a Metaphorical Referent for the Elided Female Voice," Peter Morgan looks at the position of the feminine voice in Coetzee's *Foe*, as representative of an imperial marginal complicity. Morgan sees Susan's narrative as a pathway towards an understanding of colonial objectification; he says that "Friday's partially elided narrative presents an image in absentia of the state Susan is seeking to conceptualize (although it is of course important not to see Friday merely as the psychological double of Susan, but to see both Friday and Susan, and Friday/Susan as the text/s of imperialism)" (91). Susan Barton is writing back, through the allegory of Friday's emasculation, to marginalization as a hierarchical tool of differential privilege. It is the space between slave and wife that enables a confrontation of ideas regarding *partnership*; the space occupied by the body of the Other. Looking at the potential discursivity between Friday and Susan, Morgan reminds us that "the postcolonial task and the discourse of ecriture feminine share, then, the need for a similarly dramatic revision of history, a 'political strategy, designed to redress the wrongs of culture through a revalidation of the rights of nature,' and a rewriting of literature" (Morgan 84). Friday's mutilation sits akin to Susan Barton's naturally mutilated flesh (woman as incomplete man) and allows for an integrity of mutual colonial manifestation. It is this hybrid space between slave and woman that allows for a new conception of marginality:

a comprehensive marginality that occupies all space outside of privilege. In this way, the narrative of Susan Barton works to disavow Friday's silence, while simultaneously respecting the representational boundaries of Coetzee's own hierarchically privileged voice.

Narration and voice are the vehicles through which Coetzee moves between the avowed objectivity of Friday and the ambiguous subjectivity of Susan Barton. Where Friday is unarguably the victim of Cruso (and colonialism itself), Susan Barton exists as a subject with potential. Susan exists in the world; she has the ability to make changes, or to change herself. Susan's first-person narrative marks her, her voice is our own, we exist both within and apart from her (and she us). Susan is no victim, she is the author and creator of our tale; "the question of and search for metaphor therefore becomes the all-encompassing economy of *Foe*, a rewriting of Daniel Defoe's *Robinson Crusoe*, in which Susan Barton is cast away on Crusoe's island and struggles to realize an imaginative space of her own under his tyrannical rule" (Morgan 82). By giving the one control over the entire narrative and the other no voice at all, *Foe* moves back and forth between a conception of symbiotic marginality and complicated hierarchical differentials. In the opening to *Roxana*, Defoe creates an exaggerated distance between his author, narrator, and subject. He says:

> The History of this Beautiful Lady, is to speak for itself: If it is not as Beautiful as the Lady herself is reported to be; if it is not as diverting as the Reader can desire, and much more than he can reasonably expect; and if all the most diverting Parts of it are not adapted to the Instruction and Improvement of the Reader, the Relator says, it must be from the Defect of his Performance; dressing up the Story in worse Cloaths than the Lady, whose Words he speaks, prepar'd it for the World. (1)

Defoe challenges his own narrative by inserting his own pseudo-voice over that of Roxana's, thereby both disempowering the woman while simultaneously drawing attention to her authorial treatment. In this way, Defoe has already set up the framework in which Coetzee moves; a preamble that draws attention to notions of authorship and creative narratology, which allows for an examination of the space between a writer and his/her subject.

In her article "Women's Words: A Reading of J.M. Coetzee's Women Narrators," Sue Kossew examines the manner in which Coetzee's female narrators situate Coetzee's novels "between feminist and postcolonial discourse" (12) as a means of drawing attention to the disparity of his own privileged position and the marginalized positioning of his postcolonial narratives. Coetzee reinforces a sympathetic community of readers by resisting the urge to conflate subject positions: of himself, his characters, or his readers. He is conscientious in his devotion to exhibiting disparate notions of narrative; narratives that rely on a critical audience. Kossew says that "rather than suggesting that Coetzee's use of women narrators is an assertion of appropriating male authorship…it may be more productive to examine carefully the position his women narrators occupy, as both colonized and colonizing" (Kossew 13). Susan Barton is desperate for Foe to write her story; she thinks to herself "here I wait for you to appear, or for the book to be written that will set me free of Cruso and Friday" (Coetzee 66). The unwritten narrative that Susan Barton wants Foe to create exists within a space of authorial potential, a space that exists as the result of authorial authority. Her desire is quickly undermined when she begins to consider Friday's story as complementary to her own (and completely unattainable). She says that "to tell my story and be silent on Friday's tongue is no better than offering a book for sale with pages in it quietly left empty. Yet the only tongue that can tell Friday's secret is the tongue he has lost" (Coetzee 67). She goes on to interrogate Friday on the history of his lost tongue through visually rendered potentialities, asking him to point to "the truth." Susan Barton's search for the manner in which Friday lost his tongue is frustrated by her realization of a narrative subjectivity that is culturally situated. She says:

> Might the picture itself not confuse him? (For, examining it anew, I recognized with chagrin that it might also be taken to show Cruso as a beneficent father putting a lump of fish into the mouth of child Friday.) And how did he understand

> my gesture of putting out my tongue at him? What if, among the cannibals of Africa, putting out the tongue has the same meaning as offering the lips has amongst us? (Coetzee 69)

Susan Barton is a conflicted collusion of attitudes that represent narrative subjectivities within a postcolonial world; she demands a self-reflexivity while simultaneously criticizing complicity of mass marginalization. Coetzee's Susan is frustrated with herself, Friday, and the set of circumstances that have brought them together. Susan wants no part of Friday, but she feels responsible for him. This responsibility to the oppressed is echoed in Coetzee's (and to a lesser degree, Defoe's) treatment of Susan's narrative. Privilege weighs heavily on all three. When Susan continues her thoughts with the words "might you not then flush with shame when a woman puts out her tongue and you have no tongue with which to respond?" (69), she is (unconsciously) drawing attention to Friday's inability to prove his own maleness. Friday is impotent in the face of Susan, her use of language, and her sexuality.

In *Foe*, "the white woman narrator is represented as being as complicit as Defoe in colonizing the Other [...] and her text is over-ridden (over-written?) in the final section (which seeks to release Friday's voice in a non-colonising way) just as it was 'written out' by Defoe" (Kossew 17). Roxana spends the novel claiming a power over herself and her life. Her eventual heinous criminality and subsequent downfall disproves her declaration of independence. It is this method of storytelling that moves *Foe* into a new discursive space of ambiguity; Coetzee does not replace Friday's voice with that of Susan Barton, but, instead, uses the interstitial location between Friday's silence and Susan Barton's narrative as the means to complicate marginalized positions of subjectivity.

The juxtaposition of Susan's own narration with Defoe's appropriation of the female voice and Coetzee's attempt to find an authorial 'middle ground' enable Coetzee to explore the complexities of authorship, authority and narration, in which his own authorship is included. Here again the narrating voice of the woman colonizer provides a vehicle for ambivalence, as

Susan is caught between her colonized and colonizing selves (Kossew 17).

In the end, both Susan and Crusoe are creating Friday's silence by making it a part of their own narrative. Defoe's Crusoe does this by enslaving Friday and recreating an island colon in the vein of his English peers. Coetzee's Susan silences Friday by insisting on the narrative of her own guilt, rather than focusing on the ways that Friday chooses to communicate. There is tension between the overt narrative of Susan and the inaudible language of Friday. It is this ambivalence which empowers Friday, as the postcolonial presence within the text, in its subversive manipulation of the narrative impetus and its positioning of marginalized voices within a counter-discursive novel.

The manner with which Coetzee treats gender and marginalization in *Foe* relies strictly on the ways that each of these are conceived in his source texts: *Robinson Crusoe* and *Roxana*. Where Defoe uses a strategy of race/gender conflation to examine the plight of the eighteenth century woman through the trope of slavery, Coetzee moves past this simplification towards a space where marginalization has an acknowledged symmetry without a strict equation (between racism and sexism). Morgan examines this space in relation to gender associations in *Robinson Crusoe*:

> Of course, Susan Barton does not appear in Daniel Defoe's novel. In fact, excepting their appearance dictated more or less by dramatic necessity and even then in extremely minor roles (Robinson must have a mother, after all), no women do. Friday is the closest thing the story to a traditional 'feminine' role model, appearing as he does as a sort of male domestic, passive and grateful, simple and devoted. (Morgan 85)

Friday, as feminized domestic, assumes the role of *wife* to Crusoe's *husband*. He becomes, in this idyllic world of white male colonial empowerment, the help-meet to Crusoe's originating Adam. Rather than wishing for a wife, on a remote and lonely island in the middle of the Caribbean, Crusoe designs to acquire a slave as his lifelong companion. As he watches Friday's escape from his captors, Crusoe thinks to himself that "it came now very warmly upon my thoughts, and indeed irresistibly, that now was my time to get me a servant, and perhaps a companion or assistant; and that I was called plainly by Providence to save this poor creature's life" (206). Friday is clearly gendered female in *Robinson Crusoe*, his status as racialized slave equivalent to the position of the sexualized and contemporary wife, according to Defoe. This becomes even clearer in Defoe's portrayal of the disempowered Roxana, as a character who desires freedom from male tyranny by claiming male authority of action. In her attempt to gain agency within the framework of her own destiny, Roxana says:

> I knew no Reason the Men had to engross the whole liberty of the Race, and make the Women, not-withstanding any disparity of Fortune, be subject to Laws of Marriage, of their own making; that it was my Misfortune to be a Woman, but I was resolv'd it shou'd not be made worse by the Sex; and seeing Liberty seem'd to be the Men's Property, I wou'd be a Man-Woman; for as I was born free, I wou'd die so. (171)

Here, Roxana reinforces the conflation of marginalization, as it results from being *othered* as an object of the periphery. This equation of race/gender is typical of Defoe, as a narrative tactic of examining the ways in which the two inform one another. Race and gender prejudices become equalized under the wider umbrella of non-conformation to the naturalized norm of the white male.

When Coetzee writes-back to *Robinson Crusoe*, through *Roxana*, he enacts a new method of interpreting the relationship between race and gender. Working from the premise that Defoe has established, within the context of these two novels, Coetzee turns *Foe* into a narrative that stages the absurdity and adaptability of the conflation of marginal positions in counter-discursive texts. The emasculation of Friday stands witness to Coetzee's desire for an ambiguous racial/sexualized space, this space that both enables and disables the parallelism of inequity. Susan Barton discovers Friday's mutilation when he turns quickly in Foe's loose robe; she says that:

> in the dance nothing was still and yet everything was still. The whirling robe was a scarlet bell settled upon Friday's shoulders and enclosing him; Friday was the dark pillar at its centre. What had been hidden from me was revealed. I saw; or, I should say, my eyes were open to what was present to them. (119)

The castration of Friday moves him from the sphere of the black male into that of the black female; he becomes more than Defoe could have written, and emblematic of difference embodied. The black female exists in a meta-marginalized state, definitively *other*, yet existing without a peripheral equivalent seeing as how she marginalized twice over. The castrated male now begins to deconstruct all of the previously assumed gender/race conflations; Friday exists as a man-woman and demonstrates the absurdity of situating inequity systematically.

Women regain relevance in these three texts as we look towards the idea of mothering, and how Coetzee writes-back to Defoe's narrative as a means to examine the potential power of motherhood to displace colonial intent in a novel. Looking at Coetzee's use of mothering, Spivak claims that his intention is to draw attention to the disparity in a narrative that attempts to engage postcolonial ideals with a feminist point-of-view. She says that her "previous remarks on the formal peculiarities of the mother-daughter subplot carried the implication that feminism (within 'the same' cultural inscription) and the anticolonialism (for or against racial 'other') cannot occupy a continuous (narrative) space" (Spivak 168). Rather than assume that *Foe* is incapable of reconciling feminist and anticolonialist ideologies, it may be posited that Coetzee is drawing attention to the inconsistency of equating issues of inequity, which relies on a closer reading of *Roxana* as a means to interpret the relationship between *Foe* and *Robinson Crusoe*.

Where *Robinson Crusoe* is a male-centered narrative, *Roxana* is one that is exclusively female. It is the location between these two novels that allows for a confluence of ideas to emerge from the mother-daughter trope. There are no women in *Robinson Crusoe*, though Coetzee's Susan Barton becomes the central voice in *Foe*. Spivak ponders:

> Who is this female narrator of *Robinson Crusoe*? We know that the original had no room for women. There was the typecast mother; the benevolent widow whose role it was to play the benevolent widow; the nameless wife who was married and died in the conditional mode in one sentence so that Crusoe could leave for the East Indies. (Spivak 161)

Coetzee's insertion of the mother-daughter storyline is in direct contradiction to the male-centered authority that makes up the plot of *Robinson Crusoe*. Male authority becomes conflated with colonial power in this text, with the inevitable result of a trans-gendered slave but no actual women taking a role.

As we follow his progress, we see his whole 'quest' as a journey of self-realization, of coming to terms with a (male) father and a male God: a journey that embodies a transition from the 'feminine' aspect of the male couple, to the 'masculine,' a bildungsroman that is the very essence of that stifling term in the most popular and traditional sense as the hero learns how to achieve mastery over his possessions, his life, 'his' island, and Friday (his 'wife'), and, ultimately, sovereignty over other men (Morgan 84).

Crusoe has no time for mothering on his island, but it finds its way there anyway. Like the mutated marriage of Crusoe and Friday, the mother-daughter relationship in Robinson Crusoe relies on a colonial understanding of gender roles. Friday's interaction with his father, directly after his being saved from the cannibals, reflects a loving and feminized portrayal of a parental relationship. Defoe writes that "when he went in to him, he would sit down by him, open his breast, and hold his father's head close to his bosom, half an hour together, to nourish it" (238). The language and description here denote a mothering between Friday and his father, inverted twice over since they are both men and it is Friday who is cradling the older man. This is a direct juxtaposition to the mother-daughter relationship in *Roxana*, where the younger Susan chases the older in her desire to be recognized. She says "Ay but..., I am sure you are my Mother too; and what have I done that you won't own me, and that you will not be call'd my Mother?" (267). Little Susan is desperate to have that which older Susan would deny her: a mother. This is reflected in *Foe* when Susan Barton tells the young girl "you are father-born. You have no mother. The pain you feel is the pain of lack, not the pain of loss. What you hope to regain in my person you have in truth never had" (91). Susan Barton's refusal to acknowledge her daughter is an act of protest; she demands her own space in this text outside of the domestic space. This feminized interaction between a mother and daughter cannot stand-in for Friday's disempowered colonial subject position so easily as the racialized other is substituted for the sexualized in *Robinson Crusoe*. Instead the two methods of marginalization are clearly demarcated, positioned as irreconcilably different in Coetzee's *Foe*. The import of Coetzee's choice to use *Roxana's* antagonistic filial role in *Foe* gains particular relevance in looking towards the end of Defoe's text. Mother-Susan thinks about her daughter:

> As for the poor Girl herself, she was ever before my Eyes; I saw her by-Night, and by-Day; she haunted my Imagination, if she did not haunt the House; my Fancy show'd her me in a hundred Shapes and Postures; sleeping or waking, she was with me: Sometimes I thought I saw her with her Throat cut; sometimes with her Head cut, and her Brains knock'd-out; other-times hang'd up upon a Beam; another time drown'd in the Great Pond at Camberwell. (325)

This is in the aftermath of Mother-Susan having orchestrated Daughter-Susan's death, as means to safeguard her many sexual affairs and escapades. Susan has killed her daughter to assure her own freedom, a sacrifice to avoid the feminized slavery she sees as submission to male-centered authority. Daughter-Susan's death, as the medium through which to read *Foe* as counter-discourse to *Robinson Crusoe*, becomes the manner in which feminism fails as a partner to anticolonialism. Where the two are insurgents that should fight alongside one another, they are also, irretrievably, separate issues.

Coetzee's *Foe* is a writing-back to Defoe's *Foe*, but only as they are read through Defoe's other novel *Roxana*. It is the examination of Susan Barton, as the main voice of *Foe* and in her capacity in *Roxana*, that the lines of marginality (between feminism and postcolonialism) are delineated. It is Susan's complicity in Friday's subjugation that disallows her assumption of his colonial status, though she suffers from her own social hierarchical disadvantages. Looking at the space that Friday occupies, alongside Susan Barton, Spivak says:

> Yet it is Friday rather than Susan who is the unemphatic agent of withholding in the text. For every territorial space that is value coded by colonialism *and* every command of metropolitan anticolonialism for the native to yield his 'voice,' there is a space of withholding, marked by a secret that may not be a secret but cannot be unlocked. 'The native,' whatever that might mean, is not only a victim, he or she is also an agent. He or she is the curious guardian at the margin. (172)

This space of silent agency is the site of empowerment in *Foe*. It is the moments in which Friday distinguishes himself from Susan Barton that signify him as the subject of the novel. Friday and Susan both suffer under the yoke of a male imperialist structure, but it is Susan, with her access to feminized colonial power, who is locked outside of the marginalized status that Friday holds. Friday becomes the focus of *Foe*, as he demarcates clearly the status of slave and wife, and creates an interpretative space for redefining subjectivity through his representative potential as a counter-discursive character within the larger postcolonial narrative.

WORKS CITED

Coetzee, J.M. *Foe*. New York: Penguin Books Ltd., 1987.

Defoe, Daniel. *Robinson Crusoe*. Ed. Angus Ross. London: Penguin Books Ltd., 1999.

Roxana. Ed. John Mullan. Oxford: Oxford University Press, 1998.

Kossew, Sue. "Women's Words: A Reading of J.M. Coetzee's *Women Narrators*." Wales: University of South Wales, 1990.

Morgan, Peter E. "*Foe*'s Defoe and La Jeune Nee: Establishing a Metaphorical Referent for the Elided Female Voice." *Critique: Studies in Contemporary Fiction* 35.2 (1994): 81-96.

Said, Edward W. *Culture and Imperialism*. New York: Vintage Books, 1994.

Spivak, Gayatri Chakravorty. "Theory in the Margin: Coetzee's *Foe* Reading Defoe's *Crusoe/Roxana*." *Consequences of Theory*. Ed. Jonathan Arac and Barbara Johnson. Baltimore: The Johns Hopkins University Press, 1991.

Tiffin, Helen. "Postcolonial Literatures and Couner-Discourse." *Kunapipi* 9.3 (1987): 17-35.

The Paradigm of Ambivalence in the Women Characters of Rohinton Mistry

8

Anita Myles

Due to a generally accepted notion that her position in society is dualistic, a woman is expected to shuttle between apparent patriarchy and latent matriarchy, gets arbitrarily thrust responsibilities while is sternly denied authority. Tragically, an archetypal nurturer but is, perhaps, never nurtured. Even Rousseau who strongly favoured democracy propagating the principles of liberty, equality and fraternity admits the existence of sexual asymmetry in nature. Observing that passion was natural and necessary in all human beings though in women it was not controlled by reason which was an attribute of men alone. Rousseau stated therefore, that,

> women must be subject all their lives, to the most constant and severe restraint, which is that of decorum; it is therefore necessary to accustom them early to such confinement that it may not afterwards cost them too dear....we should teach them above all things to lay a due restraint on themselves.[1]

Hence freedom to women, according to Rousseau, would terminate into an immense suffering to man. Consequently, a woman must be confined to her subordinate maternal role within the family. History provides myriad proofs of men misusing the authoritative positions entrusted to them establishing certain sexual norms and unlicensed behavioral patterns which forced women to choose a subordinate social and subaltern status in the cultural context. Obviously, such subordination resulted due to the illegitimate use of power. Hence, a truly liberated woman was one who was free from such extreme exploitation which is possible only when the entire social pattern is transformed and metamorphosized. In contrast to this idea of patriarchal authority, the women turned towards their filial and maternal obligations.

Perusal of the works of several contemporary male Indian English novelists exhibits forcefully though unintentionally a regular pattern of themes focusing on feminine ambivalence in the Indian society. Rohinton Mistry is one such novelist with Parsi roots who may not have composed his subject matter with this dual perspective of Indian women in mind yet the female characters in all his works, short stories or novels, portray a definitive duplicated personality. While concentrating on sketching a realistic picture of life, Mistry exposed middle class system as he saw it in Bombay, an in depth analysis of his writings reveals that sufficient space has been allocated to the exploration of gender issues. The status of women in his writings draws the attention of the female readers and critics alike. In fact literary texts reveal more about the intersection of class and gender than one can learn by actually studying the material circumstances and social constraints of characters and authors. Texts by women contain a hidden sympathy for women characters but in the case of Rohinton Mistry it is interesting to observe how during the course of narration he emphasizes, pinpoints and dwells at ease on the contribution of women in sustaining not only family but also society to the best of their abilities.

A woman's being and psychology should be seen within the cultural construct. Since long a belief existed that the man-woman relationship was one of economic and psychological dependencies. Not now as things have changed much resulting in termination of the period of tranquility necessitating the time for action. Apparently women may be epitomes of calm and quiet but they feel just as men do having an urge to exercise their faculties rather than to suffer in restraints resulting in stagnation. This changing scenario finds ample expression in Rohinton Mistry's fiction.

Rohinton Mistry's first collection of short stories entitled *Tales from Firozsha Baag* (1987)[2] depicts women of all age groups, married and unmarried both, in varied roles of a daughter, a wife, a mother, a sister, a daughter-in-law, a girlfriend, a widow and as the mistress of the house supervising servants. Mistry resorts to utmost care while diligently describing housewives and housekeepers especially their concern about managing respective chores without having much desire to go beyond these expectations. As such they lead a life of existence contented. In general, the women in the stories take care to keep the family together more so during festivals when they are particular about observing the various religious rituals meticulously. Interestingly enough, women play a supportive role in the stories, a fine example which may be extricated from the story entitled "Exercises" where Jehangir observes with much satisfaction and pride how his parents had all along been "supporting each other as they slept through heat and dust" (p.206). The mother tries to be supportive when Jehangir falls in love with Behroze urging him to visit Bhagwan Baba for ascertaining whether Behroze was the right girl for him or not. Of course, Jehangir views the whole affair as interference not anything else.

Another realistic picture exhibiting the strength and forbearance in a widow is sketched in "Condolence Visit". As Daulat Mirza sits in the armchair next to what had been her husband Minocher's bed looking at the flickering lamp, she ruminates silently about her life, "Like Minocher, she thought, reliable and always there; how lucky I was to have such a husband. No bad habits, did not drink, did not go to the racecourse, and did not give me any trouble. Ah, but he made up for it when he fell sick. How much worry he caused me then, while he still had the strength to argue and fight back. Would not eat his food, would not take his medicine, and would not let me help with anything" (p. 64). Even memories of a troublesome sick husband were cherished for weighing heavier were memories of supportiveness and happiness which they enjoyed as a couple.

"Swimming Lessons" brings out the unflinching love that a mother has for her son. The son has migrated to Canada while the mother eagerly awaits news from him. Much to her disappointment the letters are extremely brief, inevitably annoying the father, but not discouraging the mother. One fine day she is rewarded with a copy of short stories penned by the son. The parents are delighted, while the mother cannot believe that the reticent son had such deep rooted and vivid memories of his childhood. Mother liked the last story the best as it portrayed Grandpa. She admired the emotional descriptions in some stories while in others she experienced the stirring of emotions within her. A certain mixture of sadness and happiness alike gripped her till she heard her husband say: "You are confusing fiction with facts, fiction does not create facts, fiction can come from facts, it can grow out of facts by compounding, altering, transposing, augmenting, diminishing, or altering them in any way; but you must not confuse cause and effect, you must not confuse what really happened with what the story says happened, you must not loose your grasp on reality, that way madness lies" (p. 250). One wonders if the above statement should be viewed as Mistry's concept of naturalistic fiction. Apparently there exists some substance in the argument which places the novelist amongst great creative experimenters because in such examples we observe a rare combination of autobiography and fiction. Coming back to the story, not discouraged by her husband's verbal irony mother was too overwhelmed by emotions to listen to anything that father said. She was so proud of her son that she sat down to write to him.

Rohinton Mistry does not forget to portray the other side of the picture; the suffering woman. In fact the very first story in the collection "Auspicious Occasion" spells out the travails of sixteen year old Mehroo, married to fifty year old Rustomji, an extremely incompatible alliance leaving Mehroo a completely dissatisfied person. She fails to get either physical or emotional satisfaction in her marriage. She is more like a servant to Rustomji forever at his beck and call fetching his newspaper, cooking for him, preparing his drinks. The monotony of life grips her and throws her in a state of utter despair. However, in both the cases —whether the woman is happy or unhappy. Mistry paints a scenario of compromise where the woman is prepared to accept the situation as it is.

Mistry's first full length novel, *Such a Long Journey* (1991)[3] a family drama of Gustad Noble and his neighbours, Dilnavaz, the wife of Gustad is sketched as a perfectly compatible partner.

They have three children; Roshan, the daughter, Sohrab and Darius, the sons. Roshan is a frail child; throughout the novel she remains sick, convalescing for long periods and then intermittently returning to school. She is loved by the nuns at school as well as the neighbours at home. The two sons do not have a good rapport with their father. Their actions only spell out trouble causing immense tension to Gustad while Dilnavaz endeavours endlessly to strike a balance between the father and the sons. Matters reach to such extremes that Sohrab finally leaves home to live elsewhere. Many a time Dilnavaz would tread upon memory lane recapitulating the childhood of her sons when things were not so bad. One such description is as follows: "Dilnavaz stroked her hair, remembering that when the boys were little, they waited just as anxiously for their Daddy to return from the office. How Sohrab and Darius used to race to the door to open it for him. Now they have grown, and things are so different" (p. 150). Such thoughts usually culminated in deep slumber, for Dilnavaz could not do much about the changes that had taken place in the household. The silent surrender to prevailing circumstances and the ultimate compromise are realistically presented by Rohinton Mistry.

Not only does the novelist portray the psychic life of Dilnavaz but also enumerates her assets as a meticulous housewife. She is basically a down to earth woman who takes care of even the minutest needs of her family catering to the needs to her school going sons, to Gustad as an office worker, simultaneously caring for Roshan, the sick daughter. The patience of both Dilnavaz and Roshan draw admiration. It is rare to find Dilnavaz losing her patience or her temper when things seem to run out of hand.

In Miss Kutpitia, Dilnavaz had a friend to rely upon. She lived in the neighbourhood and had sacrificed her life to take care of her brother's son Farad. She lost her sister-in-law in childbirth. Misfortunes pour down on Miss Kutpitia when she loses both the brother and the nephew in a road accident. The novelist depicts her as a confident woman having the inner strength to set things right when they go wrong. Mistry writes: "Miss Kutpitia had been trying to mend and fix, ever since, in her own peculiar way. Her three and a half decades of reverently observed isolation had allowed the tropical climate to work its rot and ruin" (p.283).

Miss Kutpitia was gifted with the art of taking things within her stride. Once a fire broke out in her house damaging the locked rooms belonging to her brother and nephew. When both Dilnavaz and Miss Kutpitia assessed the damage Dilnavaz was amazed to find her attitude of compromise and complacence. To quote the novelist: "She was surprised that Miss Kutpitia accepted the outcome so matter-of-factly. In fact, Dilnavaz found her positively cheery, looking forward to the chores that lay ahead, enjoying the sympathetic attention of people who had decided to forget her reputation for meanness and crankiness. It was tacitly accepted now that a person so providentially delivered from the jaws of fiery death has the forces of goodness on her side" (pp.290–291). Even the neighbour's marvel at her innate courage to face life as it comes.

Dilnavaz finds a good friend and adviser in Miss Kutpitia. They are more or less like sisters sharing each others joys and sorrows. When Dilnavaz is puzzled by her recurrent family problems she confides in Miss Kutpitia who instantly encourages her to perform certain superstitious rites and rituals to overcome the problems. Very confidently she says, "You see, I don't like to weaken anyone's faith. Miracle, magic, mechanical trick, coincidence—does it matter what it is, as long as it helps? Why analyse the strength of imagination, the power of suggestion, the potency of psychological pressures? Looking too closely is destructive, makes everything disintegrate. As it is life is difficult enough. Why to simply make it tougher? After all, who is to say what makes a miracle and what makes a coincidence?" (p. 289) The words offer the much required solace to Gustad and Dilnavaz, needless to add that the relationship between the two women grows stronger day by day.

Mistry gives vivid descriptions of Gustad's grandmother who was an ardent wrestling fan. Grandma, "in her own way, was a powerful woman" (p. 42). Gustad believes that his sense of endurance has been inherited from her and cherished the memories of his grandmother. Dinshawji's wife Alamai is yet another woman sketched by Mistry. He does not hesitate in calling her "a termagant if ever there was" (p. 239). They had no children. Gustad admired Dinshawji's sense of humour inspite of the fact that most of his life was spent with his "domestic vulture". He would wittingly say—"No need to take me to the Tower of Silence when I die. My domestic vulture will peck my bones clean ahead of time"(p. 239). Rohinton Mistry's depiction of women in their dual response to familial, community and societal expectations as contained in *Such a Long Journey* finds more powerful expression in his next novel *A Fine Balance* (1995)[4].

Dina Dalal (nee Shroff), the protagonist of *A Fine Balance* is known for her "fragile independence". She loses her father at a tender age, marries Rustom against the wishes of Nusswan, her brother and becomes a widow merely three years after marriage. She substantiates her living by sewing clothes (later hiring two tailors to do the job) and renting out one of the rooms in her flat to Maneck Kolah. Dina is intelligent, sharp and shrewd, "a smart little girl (who) knows how to get what she wants." Dina is subjected to much mental and physical torture by Nusswan because as she grew up she became prettier and sexually more attractive. He would often threaten to cut off her tongue and breasts. He invites suitable bachelors to the house for Dina who resembles himself in temperament.

However, Dina gets courage to resist Nusswan's matches and marries Rustom on her own accord. She educates herself by visiting the public libraries of Bombay for Nusswan had discontinued her formal education after the death of their father. Nusswan treated her more like a servant than a sister. Dina also has to avoid the overtures of the priest at the Parsi temple who would habitually fondle the young girls visiting the temple. By dint of her courage and presence of mind Dina manages to survive the onslaughts of fate depicted through her brother and the priest. She ultimately succeeds in having enough money to have a roof over her head.

Dina had the additional responsibility of looking after her widowed mother, Mrs. Shroff who apparently lacked the perseverance, the strength and the mindset to face the unexpected tragedies of life. There is a rich contrast between the mother and the daughter who belonged to different generations. Both Dina's mother and her aunt ("Crazy Bapsy Aunty") lose their mental stability after the demise of their spouses. The two ladies were completely dependent on their husbands and their deaths signified the loss of support necessary for living. They had never known what independence was as long as they were married. Dina had learnt much from the marital lives of her mother and aunt. She was aware of the pitfalls of arranged marriages. She was mindful of the perils involved in later life. According to her, "Families decide everything. Then the woman becomes the property of the husband's family, to be abused and bullied. It is a terrible system, turns the nicest girls into witches"(p. 492). Women in the system have no voice of their own.

Dina's struggle for survival, her courage and perseverance have been skillfully depicted by Rohinton Mistry. She had let out a room in her house to Maneck Kolah, a school friend's son. Maneck admired her efforts to keep squalor at bay. In fact she forgot her miseries in his presence. She would set the dinner table for him, bring out the long preserved cutlery saying, "You've inspired me. It's been twenty-five years since I used these things" (270). Sometimes Dina pondered over her life and how things clouded her future but immediately she would shun her negative thoughts saying, "I never like to look back at my life, my childhood, with regret or bitterness" (p. 418). The attitude of compromise and acceptance is expressively apparent in her words and statements.

Unfortunately, the attempts that Dina makes to survive independently do not bear positive results. She too, becomes a victim of the Emergency which is all of a sudden clamped on the Indian subcontinent. Om and Ishvar, her workers at the sewing shop are disabled after the forced sterilization. The shop goes bankrupt. Dina has to leave her apartment as well as her workplace. She loses her sewing machines but more tragic than that her independence. She has to go back to the fold of her brother, Nussawan, which is as good as a descent into hell. Nussawan is ultimately victorious for he has had his way in shattering the much sought after independence of his sister Dina.

Nussawan's wife Ruby, who once delighted in torturing her sister-in-law, Dina now begins to sympathise with her.

Incidentally the story of *Family Matters* (2002)[5] preoccupied Mistry since 1987 when *Tales From Firozsha Baag* was published. The last story of this collection entitled "Swimming Lessons" deals with an episode that finds a perfect extension in this novel, where a young Indian emigrant to Canada nostalgically describes the care and attention which his sickly mother provided to his grandfather who suffered from Parkinson's disease and osteoporosis and ultimately dies, a family drama meticulously expanded into an impressive novel form in *Family Matters*.

In sustaining various families, the women characters play vital roles as portrayed by Rohinton Mistry. With the exception of Nariman Vakeel, all other male characters are flimsily delineated in comparison to the female characters. The novelist may not have consciously projected the "ladies" of the novel as strong but as a realist he could not ignore the significant role a woman plays in protecting her family and in sustaining the community. Gerda Lerner has rightly pointed out: "While men conquered territory and built institutions which managed and distributed power, women transmitted culture to the young and built the social network and infrastructures that provide continuity in the community."[6] Family strength, religious observances and social succour in *Family Matters* are indubitably provided by various female characters and while the men are engrossed in fruitless dreams or in reminiscences of the past glories, the women successfully conceal their own frustrations in order to succulate the family.

Roxana appears to constitute the most balanced personality of all the significant female characters. In spite of Yezad's pronounced hostility, Roxana continues to take care of her father without complaining and provides his needs to the best of her ability. Once during Roxana's absence Yezad is compelled to help Nariman with the bedpan with his son's assistance, resultantly he wonders how his wife managed alone. Roxana's pleasant and accommodating personality delights Rangarajan, the plasterer who considered her to be an excellent example of womanhood, defending in strong words after realising that she was merely a housewife, "What are you saying, dear lady? Housewifery is the most important calling, requiring umpteen talents. Without housewife there is no home; without home no family. And without family, nothing else matters, everything from top to bottom falls apart or descends into chaos. Which is basically the malady of the West...." (p. 175). Rangarajan's approbatory comments about a housewife are commendable for on a woman's shoulders inevitably rests the responsibility of laying the strong foundation of a family due to her unique puissance of cohesing the household together.

Nariman realizes his mistake in transferring his house in the names of his step children Jal and Coomy equating himself with the foolish King Lear supported by Roxana as the tender loving and caring third child Cordelia. She experiences dire emotional stress in looking after her father in a small apartment. However, at the crucial moment of a possible mental collapse, her training to the children as a responsible mother provides the necessary strength because Murad and Jehangir quickly make the required adjustments facilitating a peaceful co-existence under one roof. The children learn to make minute sacrifices for greater happiness. Ultimately, Yezad is ashamed of his behaviour, succumbs to the overflowing emotions within and offers to help Nariman in the absence of Roxana. Roxana stands against 'the absurd forces of destiny' due to her innate womanly strength capable of supporting her family in the midst of an unabatable tempest.

Yasmin's sacrifices are no less significant who married Nariman three years after the death of her husband Palonji Contractor for the sake of providing security to her children Jal and Coomy, a real sacrifice as she was aware of Nariman's infatuation for Lucy—a non-Parsi whom he was prevented from marrying and hence agreed to marry a Parsi widow. The marital alliance failed to deter Nariman from meeting Lucy every evening who had taken up an ayah's job in the household of Mr. Arjani living in the same building. Yasmin would watch Nariman help Lucy to drop the Arjani children to school, carrying their heavy bags and sometimes take their tiffin as well, though she tolerated all this silently for the sake of her children. Lucy would often climb up the parapet of the topmost floor and sing songs till Nariman brought her down. One day Yasmin decided to go up herself and end this drama. As destiny would have it both the women fell to their respective deaths. Yasmin justifiably died in an attempt to win her husband completely as she could not bear the constant interference of another woman. Yasmin's portrayal presents the dismal state of women in the contemporary Indian society who make sacrifices and yet have the status of second rate citizens. Nevertheless this lady proves her strength of character in surrendering her personal happiness for the sake of her children's welfare tolerating her husband's inordinate flirtations for the sake of family peace.

Coomy, in contrast emerges as a strong headed woman, a typical symbol of feminine sacrifice in upholding the family values. While other young girls of her age enjoyed social life, participated in socio-religious functions, entered courtship with eligible Parsi bachelors and spent time in educational pursuits, Coomy renounces her aspirations for the sake of her psychic mother and later for nursing her ailing step father. She had a chequered childhood witnessing the physical suffering of her father Palonji afflicted with pleurisy and his ultimate death. After the death of her mother she sustains her brother Jal as well. Coomy's death has been described as a sort of sacrificial ritual when while helping the men of the household in repairing the ceiling she is injured by a falling steel girder. The death is not wasted; the repaired house symbolizes the impending unification of the remaining family members.

The three ladies of the Vakeel household constitute metaphorically the feminine power, not physical but mental and spiritual, each fortifying an otherwise broken household. *Family Matters* scrutinizes some other female characters who, though not as convincingly drawn as these three, yet provide a significant insight into the positive role played by women in fashioning a harmonious state in the family, in the community and in the society. Daisy Ichhaporia, the violinist contributes by playing melodious tunes to lull Nariman to sleep or to put aside his depression and unhesitatingly relinquishes an important musical assignment to play Nariman's favorite tune at his death bed marking his end with peace and joy. Similarly, Villie Cardmaster helps Yezad to win in Matka during the moments of financial crises, an apparently insignificant assistance which however sustains the man saving him from possible breakdown and destruction. Another trivially sketched lady Mrs. Kapur exhibits immense strength of character in protecting the family and in spite of her submissive nature firmly advises her husband wherever it is necessary. Mr. Kapur explains his wife's contribution for family welfare when he comments: "But family comes first, Yezad, you understand that. Family service before public service, my wife reminded me"(p. 294).

That women uphold, succour and fortify community is discernible in Rohinton Mistry's *Family Matters*. Nariman Vakeel and his life may appear as a cardinal theme of the narrative but the novel certainly polarizes around women-power. Incidentally, the female characters in the novel are not champions of liberation; they may not claim the right to be Shavian 'New Women' but each one of them is significant for the perpetuation of a healthy social system. Parallel predicaments encounter the society all over the world and inevitably a woman sacrifices her personal essentials, submerging her identity in order to sustain the system. Consequently, through an intensely meaningful portrayal of women characters in this novel, Rohinton Mistry has globalized the theme of contemporary complexity inferring that the modern society beset by the dynamics of culture, confused by cultural cross fertilization, marred by religious fanaticism and converging on inner fracture, the system gets protected from the ultimate fragmentation by one woman or the other.

The portrayal of women characters in male-authored texts have been perceived rather minutely by women critics. The general idea is that male authors cannot speak for women because the delineation of such women characters tends to be filtered through the complex workings of male desires. Obviously the feminist critics would begin with a prejudiced mind and seek records of women's oppression in such a text. From this point of view, one has stark realism in the writings of Rohinton Mistry. He does not hesitate to hide male desires towards women but at the same time, he effortlessly highlights the roles played by women in the social setup about which he writes establishing that women constitute a positive force in society.

All genres of literature and of all ages especially since the European Renaissance have focused around women characters in one form or the other. Infact, Renaissance and Reformation literatures have portrayed some of the most powerful female characters, though during the Puritan age followed by Neo-Classicism in England resorted to satirical delineation of women. However, such literatures did not survive for long resulting in either avoiding discussion about feminism or carefully balancing the male-female roles in the society. French feministic theories and critics ignored many essential issues related to feminine consciousness due to their narrow centric approach to the problem thereby harming the cause of women liberation more than highlighting it.

Strangely enough the efforts of a male writer, that is, George Bernard Shaw, provided the much needed boost to the idea of 'Free Women'. Not only did the dramatist project the concept of the 'New Women' but he also created several powerful women in his plays who could not only protect the family but also sustain the entire social system. Since the time of Shaw English literature has witnessed a great number of established male writers especially in the fields of fiction and drama who have successfully shown the important role played by women in family, community and society. Unfortunately, while the feminist critics concentrated on women writers and how women liberation was projected by them, they failed to interpret the male writers' attitude towards the roles of women.

More or less the same situation exists in the Indian critical scenario. Feminism and related ideas like the subaltern women, ecofeminism, etc. are occupying a prominent place in the contemporary India English Criticism, as a consequence of which women poets like Kamala Das, Margaret Chatterjee, Eunice de Souza and novelists like Anita Desai, Shashi Deshpande, Manju Kapur, Gita Hariharan and Shobha De have invited zealous studies especially how their heroines react and revolt against the male dominated social conventions. This type of limited critical evaluation ignores the image of women as proclaimed in several literary creations especially fiction by men. A fact to be accepted is that a study about women and society as observed through a male eye is usually more rational, realistic and balanced. Whereas women writers may certainly be prejudiced favouring a female character as a champion against injustices and exploitation, a male writer, on the contrary, would observe in an unbiased manner the variety of roles played by a woman in the intricate social setup. In this sense Rohinton Mistry tends to be a significant author of feminine delineation. A deep scrutiny of his novels reveals truthfully the duality faced by women in an attempt to create equipoise in their different roles. Of course, Mistry's universe is limited to the portrayal of Parsi women but the individual and the social issues highlighted by him are by and large universal in nature.

Rohinton Mistry's description of women provides a realistic viewpoint showing women both as symbols of growth and progress as well as being powerful means of withdrawal, regression, decay and destruction. Mistry is aware of the fact that the life of the Indian middle class is marked by struggle: the struggle against poverty, against lack of privacy and personal freedom and against spiritual claustrophobia. To escape this vicious existential circle is almost impossible, one has to submit and compromise, a task avoided by men and left entirely to the women. Some women in his novels portray a negation no doubt, but there are others who emerge as powerful positive forces having the grit to sustain their families. Instantly one realizes the precious nature of family harmony and the significance of the wife or the mother in furthering it. The role of these women becomes well-marked out in the contemporary trend of nuclear families as compared to the traditional joint family system. Thus women in Mistry's writings have an awakened conscience, easily resorting to adjust to the disintegration of old values along with the emergence of a new set of values. He itinerates his women through a critical period of self-analysis and painful introspection while they try to figure out meaning in their lives. True enough Mistry's women characters may not always strike upon radical solutions to existential dilemmas yet she undergoes the process of inner enrichment and even visualizes the ultimate crumbling down of male domination. Perhaps the idea of equality with men is a far cry in the Indian context. Nevertheless, the efforts on the part of the Indian middle class women are highly appreciable.

The portrayal of women characters in the writings of Rohinton Mistry is quite comprehensive. He describes her as a young girl, a daughter, a wife, a mother, a widow, a divorcee and also as a spinster. But above all these he probes her psyche to find that she is a human being at the core with feelings and desires as well. Mistry is honest in his descriptions of social relationships between men and women which are richly coloured by the cultural environment in which they are born and brought up. His women characters are not always victims, they are given ample opportunity to come on the scene with their inevitable grit, courage understanding and forbearance in moments of acute crisis. Their inner strength and respect for self-esteem are undoubtedly appreciable for they unwittingly accept their roles as the preserver of tradition and the guardian of culture even though these are imposed upon her.

Rohinton Mistry's women characters successfully juggle between home life, motherhood, career and spiritual fulfillment. They are reconciled to the fact that further autonomy entails a long process of overhauling the entire cultural system. They are all along aware of the fact that if the position of the middle class women changes it will be only because the men have decided to change and society is in the process of transformation. In India the position of women is seen only in context with the male patriarchal system. The question of competition between men and women does not arise rather it is their moving ahead hand in hand, shoulder to shoulder sharing each others aspirations and experiences.

NOTES

1. *Emile* (1762) London: Dent; 1974 edn. p. 332.
2. Delhi: Penguin Books India; 2002 edn.
3. New Delhi: Rupa and Company; 1991.
4. New York: Vintage Books, 1997 edn.
5. London: Faber and Faber, 2002.
6. *The Majority Finds its Past: Placing Women in History* (London: OUP, 1979), p. 179.

The Rewriting of Personal Narratives in the Exile's Quest for Home: Brian Friel's *Dancing at Lughnasa* and *The Loves of Cass McGuire*

9

Elisa Armellino

The myth of homecoming is one of the main issues at the core of 20th-century Anglo-Irish literature and is still a fertile ground of inspiration for contemporary Irish authors. According to Rosemary Marangoly George: "The search for the location in which the self is 'at home' is one of the primary projects of twentieth-century fiction in English" (Marangoly George 3). The sense of displacement and the need for a sense of belonging is, in fact, a generalized condition of those who, for various reasons, have left their native world behind them and live separated from it. As Edward Said argues in *Culture and Imperialism* (1994), the idea of home is inherent in the experience of exile: "Exile is predicated on the existence of, love for, and a real bond with one's native place" (Said 407).

Thus, the presence of a 'home', whether this is linked with a geographical place or with the dimension of family affections or private memories, appears as something ineluctable with which exiles have inevitably to cope. The image of 'home' is alive even in those cases in which it has been rejected and abandoned willingly, that is, even in the cases in which it is linked with feelings of hatred or resentment. This is also demonstrated by the lives of the Irish writers who choose to abandon Ireland and live abroad, to the point that James Joyce, despite going away from his homeland, depicts the city of Dublin almost obsessively in his works. As Thomas Brook suggests in *James Joyce's Ulysses: A Book of Many Happy Returns* (1982):

> As Joyce must have occasionally done, Bloom also wonders if it is a folly that he is writing. But then Bloom realizes the motivation for writing. He realizes that husbands have no need to write because they are in physical proximity to the object of their love. We write letters only when we are separated from those to whom we write.... Similarly, Joyce writes about Dublin because he is away. Writing, motivated by absence rather than by presence, becomes a way of accomplishing a return. (Brook 96)

This return, which is achieved through writing, reveals that 'home' can be a haunting presence in the mind and that the myth of homecoming is grounded on the impossibility of regaining a world which is absent from present reality. Like Joyce, another famous Irish exile, Samuel Beckett, decided to leave his homeland and, as though he wanted to stress his distancing from it, wrote some of his main works in French, that is, in a language different from his mother tongue. Yet, though the presence of his native country is not so evident as in Joyce's writing, in his texts the image of Ireland often takes shape through the descriptions of Irish landscapes or is recalled through the use of Irish place-names (like those of the imaginary cities of Bally, Ballyba and Ballybaba). Thus, in *Murphy* (1936), one of the characters, Celia, seems to feel a sense of nostalgia towards Ireland: "The sky, cool, bright, full of movement, anointed her eyes, reminded her of Ireland" (*Murphy* 27). In addition, the names of many characters like Molloy, Malone, Moran and Macmann, sound obviously Irish and, according to some critics, even the rain encountered by Beckett's outcasts during their wanderings recalls Ireland's weather conditions. Thus, the decision of the author to distance himself from the homeland does not prevent him from hinting at the dimension of his home country in his works. Interestingly, as Helen Astbury notices:

> Towards the end of *The Unnamable*, the speaker...says in the French version: 'Je me voulais moi, je voulais mon pays, je me voulais dans mon pays, un petit moment, je ne voulais pas morir en étranger'. In the English translation, Beckett did not feel the need to translate 'je voulais mon pays', but

> contented himself with saying: 'I wanted myself, in my own land for a brief space'. (Astbury 4)

Thus, instead of resulting in a break with his roots, the choice of being separated also linguistically from the home country seems, almost paradoxically, to allow the exile to be nearer to it. And, yet, the 'home' which is remembered and approached through a distancing from it is necessarily inscribed in a dimension which is far from present reality. This is why the quest for the native world is reminiscent of the spiritual pilgrimage described by Zygmut Bauman:

> For pilgrims through time, the truth is elsewhere; the true place is always some distance, some time away. Wherever the pilgrim may be now, it is not where he ought to be and not where he dreams of being. (Bauman 29)

Therefore, the 'home' which exists always "some distance, some time away" is both elusive and ineluctable at the same time, like a ghostly presence which haunts the mind but can never be caught.

The elusiveness inherent in the image of home also suggests that the home to which exiles hope or imagine to go back is not merely a geographical place but is a far more complicated and multifaceted dimension. The myth of return described in the works by Irish authors which are included in this research is variously built around different notions of 'home place'. It is quite a task, however, to define the identity of the native world clearly, since, as Declan Kiberd states in *Inventing Ireland* (1995): "[I]dentity is seldom straightforward and given, more often a matter of negotiation and exchange" (Kiberd 1). Ireland, which has an "extraordinary capacity to assimilate new elements" (*ibid*) from other cultures, has been described and defined for long by others: "Through many centuries, Ireland was pressed into service as a foil to set off English virtues, as a laboratory in which to conduct experiments, and as a fantasy-land in which to meet fairies and monsters" (*ibid*). Thus, for those Irish men and women who can look at their homeland only from some distance, Ireland appears as a land wich can be observed from many perspectives without ever being clearly defined. According to

Roberta Gefter Wondrich, who investigates the theme of homecoming in her essay "Exilic Returns: Self and History Outside Ireland in Recent Irish Fiction" (2000):

> What is foregrounded more and more persuasively by [Irish] works of fiction is the idea of a difficult and still conflicting relationship with Ireland as homeland. Or, more radically, what is problematic is the very notion of Ireland as 'home'.... Ireland figures as a country whose identity is shaped by an ongoing process of discontinuity and change, to the extent that even the sense of the nation and the obsession with the national past come to be refigured as a fiction of Ireland, permeated by the elusive sense of that Mother Ireland which Desmond Hogan in *A Curious Street* calls 'the lady of many disguises'. (Gefter Wondrich 2)

The "process of discontinuity and change" which complicates the relationship of Irish people with their native country is also what can leave them with the feeling, once they are 'back' from exile, that their 'home' is a product of their imagination. Indeed, the idea of the home place as a "fiction" is expressed also by one of the best-known exiles of today's literatures in English, Salman Rushdie, who in *Imaginary Homelands* describes an occasion on which he returned to his city, Bombay, and felt that everything, in the place where he had grown up, reclaimed him and his presence, as though he had never departed from it. Yet, when he decided to represent India in his novel *Midnight's Children*, he realized that the home place and the history he was trying to claim back through writing were mere fictions, so that he reflects:

> It may be that writers in my position, exiles or emigrants or expatriates, are haunted by some sense of loss, some urge to reclaim, to look back, even at the risk of being mutated into pillars of salt. But if we do look back, we must also do it in the knowledge—which gives rise to profound uncertainties—that our physical alienation from India almost inevitably means that we will not be capable of reclaiming precisely the thing that was lost; that we will, in short, create fictions, not actual cities or villages, but invisible ones, imaginary homelands, Indias of the mind. (Rushdie 10)

Thus, the impossibility of regaining the lost world of birth and the elusive nature of 'homes' seems inherent in the condition of all exiles, who are for ever dispossessed of their native place and, yet, they can try to rebuild it in new, always different versions. However, the image of the native land as it is re-built and re-shaped by memories, despite being fragmentary and incomplete, can still be precious and meaningful (as Rushdie says: "The broken mirror may actually be as valuable as the one which is supposedly unflawed" (11).

Hence, the journey home is another fiction, that is, it is a narrative built by those who are abroad in order to fulfil their need to preserve their roots, even though they live in a foreign place. This is why, according to the sociologist Rina Cohen and the anthropologist Gerald Gold, the myth of return is a necessary element in the experiences of migration, since: "[It] enables the migrant to postpone his/her total absorption or integration in the host society" (Cohen and Gold 375). Whether the journey back to their native country is achieved or not, the myth of homecoming remains "a wishful fantasy, or belief, of immigrants that, in an unspecified date in the future, they will return permanently to their homeland" (*ibid*). This explains why, as Declan Kiberd notices, the hundreds of thousands of Irish emigrants who had fled to other countries to escape from the famines of the 1840s preserved, from their new dwelling places in the USA, Australia and Britain, the dream of a homeland. As Kiberd says: "[Emigrants] were committed to carry a burden which few enough on native grounds still bothered to shoulder: *an idea of Ireland*" (Kiberd 2).

Some of the most vivid descriptions of the condition of exile are offered by one of the greatest contemporary Irish authors, Brian Friel, in his plays. Many of his characters suffer from a painful sense of displacement. Sometimes, they struggle for being accepted again in the country they have left. Indeed, since the emigrant who is back home is often rejected by his/her people because of his/her different idea of the world, s/he has to struggle to save his/her identity from the assault of the conformist native society. In other words, s/he has to find a way to define himself against the dominant interpretation given about him/her by others. This reaction of self-defence can be considered a form of rebellion against the risk of being totally assimilated by the native community and losing one's distinct identity.

Language is the first means through which the home country tries to control the exile and define him/her as an outsider. Yet, at the same time, it is the means through which those who have returned can establish their difference. By finding a new personal way of expression, the person who is back home again can preserve his/her new identity despite the hostility of the homeland.

In the plays examined, the returned emigrant reacts against the impositions of the place of origin by choosing to express himself/herself differently, using a new and alternative kind of communication. Though in some cases the different language found remains isolated in the mind of the character and becomes a kind of private and concealed world, it stands for a symbol of 'otherness' which challenges the illusion of unity and general consensus of the native society.

This is the case of the realm of dreams into which the returned emigrant falls in Brian Friel's *The Loves of Cass McGuire* (1966). The old people's home Eden House, where Cass is sent by her brother Harry after her return from the USA, becomes the only world in which she can shape her identity freely and imagine a different life. Trilbe and Ingram, the odd couple who live with her in this kind of asylum, succeed in taking her into their mythical dimension. In this way, they offer her an escape from the unhappiness of reality but also a new language (that of rhapsodies) to reinvent herself. This can occur, however, only by distancing herself from the language which her family used in order to define her as an outsider and a failed emigrant.

Before being isolated in Eden House, Cass comes into conflict with the kind of communication employed by her relatives, who speak in the conventional and polite way of middle classes. Indeed, the way in which Cass speaks when she is newly arrived home is deeply aggressive and emphatic. As the stage directions say, she has "a raucous Irish American voice" and "talks loudly and coarsely" (*The Loves of Cass McGuire* 14). In addition, she uses a strongly metaphorical language in contrast with the flat and self-contained one of her family. This is clear even in the way in which she and her brother manifest the joy of reunion. While Harry's expressions are only moderately emphatic and remain inscribed in the formal rules of politeness, Cass uses a nearly aggressive metaphorical image:

> Harry: We were always so close to one another, Cass. Always. I thought the sun rose and set on you. Welcome home a thousand times.
>
> ....
>
> Cass: Home! I can't even begin to tell you what this means to me, Harry. [...] You and Alice and the kids—Jeeze, Harry, I hope it's not too much for me—you know—like a highball on an empty stomach.
>
> (Friel, *The Loves of Cass McGuire* 36)

Yet, for the different voice of Cass no place is left in her brother's house. The way in which she expresses herself is too far away from that of her family to be accepted. Thus, she is slowly subjected to the will of the same world she has willingly returned to. The personal narrative created by Cass during all the years spent as an immigrant in the USA clashes with that of the family. While Cass has believed all her life that she was working hard in a foreign country to help her relatives in Ireland, she is told in the end that all the money she has sent home has never been used. The returned emigrant sees suddenly that all her efforts have been vain and can only regret the richer life she never allowed herself to live:

> CASS: I could ov bought myself a mink coat! So! I could ov put a fan in the bedroom in the summer! Yeah! Another thing—I could ov eaten prime beef every Sunday!
>
> (*The Loves of Cass McGuire* 41)

Even the protests and laments of Cass McGuire are vain. The returned emigrant, who is victim of her own illusions, finds herself powerless in the house of her brother.

The language used by her relatives thus becomes a means to convince her that her life cannot continue in the same house with them (and in their world). Though she is aware that her family has decided "to stick her into [a] workhouse", she has therefore to surrender, in the end, to Harry's version (that is—Eden House is simply "a rest home for elderly people"; 16). Yet, as we have seen, in the new home she can subvert the interpretation shaped by others on her life. In other words, she can reinvent a personal language, which is different, at the same time, from that of her family and from that used by herself when she was still in her brother's house. She discards both the everyday communication of her relatives and the coarse, aggressive expressions she adopted as an Irish-American emigrant.

The rhapsodies she creates are poetic images of imaginary loves. As Richard Pine notices, they are also "predominantly visual in the recollection" (Pine 82) and possess high "sensual intensity" (*ibid*). In these purely invented recollections, facts are important only in reference to the symbolic meaning they are endowed with. Thus, even the smallest events are considered when they can be in some way linked with the idea of affection:

> CASS: One Christmas I saw a man in a green sledge in Central Park, and he was being pulled along by two beautiful chestnuts.... And as he was passing me he happened to look over. And do you know what he done? He lifted his black hat to me....
>
> (Friel, *The Loves of Cass McGuire* 63)

Through the language of rhapsodies, Cass can even rename herself. She shapes new lives to fill her lack of identity in the world outside Eden House:

> CASS: My name is Olsen by the way. My late husband, mebbe you heard of him, General Cornelius Olsen; he made quite a name for himself in the last war, but you just call me Catherine.
>
> (Friel, *The Loves of Cass McGuire* 64)

Yet, these memories, even though in some way consoling, remain mere illusions. As Neil Corcoran argues, referring to the lines quoted from W.B. Yeats and repeated by Cass, Trilbe and Ingram in their rhapsodies:

> The Yeats line which accompanies the restrospect 'But I being poor have only my dreams. I have spread my dreams

> under your feet. Tread softly because you tread on my dreams'—is ominously admonishing: the phantasy knows the precariousness of its own construction. (Corcoran 21)

Despite this "precariousness", however, to construct a world dominated by dreams remains a form of refusal of the 'real' world. Even the identities shaped by Cass McGuire, despite being only imaginary, serve as a means to struggle for life despite all the rejections received from the world outside. The fact that the new autobiographies created by Cass belong to fiction and not to reality does not mean that they are purposeless and void of meaning. As Hugh, one of the characters in Brian Friel's *Translation*, says:

> It is not the literal past, the 'facts' of history, that shape us, but images of the past embodied in language [...]. We must never cease renewing those images; because once we do, we fossilize.
>
> (Friel, *Translation* 445)

Yet, to renew the images of one's life a process of recollection of the past is needed. Memory is therefore a further dimension in which the returned exile can try to rewrite his/her history away from the main interpretation imposed by the native society. As Homi Bhabha suggests in *The Location of Culture*, to regain one's true history one needs to get involved in "a painful remembering, a putting together of the dismembered past to make sense of the trauma of the present" (Bhabha 63). This is done by Michael in Brian Friel's *Dancing at Lughnasa* (1990) to make sense of the events which marked the summer of 1936 in Ballybeg when he was only a child. The return of his uncle, the missionary priest Father Jack, from Uganda, the arrival in the family house of the first radio and the unexpected outburst of emotions of his aunts (the Mundy sisters) challenged, in different ways, the repressive moral code of the small Irish community. The idea of resistance against authority, indeed, permeates the whole play. According to Anna McMullan:

> The main figure of authority in the world of the play, though he never appears on stage, is the village priest. He has the power to punish Kate and the Mundy family by sacking her

> from her school teaching job.... Authority is portrayed within the world of Ballybeg as a primarily repressive and diciplinarian force. (McMullan 92)

The power of Catholic Church, therefore, is the first power to be challenged by the rituals of Father Jack and by the dancing of the Mundy sisters which "provides a release from such relentless self-restraint and subjection to authority" (McMullan 93). In addition, the figure of the returned missionary priest, who instead of preaching in the colonized country has gone native and embraced the culture of the 'savages', disrupts the image of triumphant imperialism. More generally, the Festival of Lughnasa, by recalling the ancient Celtic harvest ritual held in August, reminds about pagan festivities and about the pre-colonial past of Ireland. Both pagan Ireland and the Africa of Father Jack appear, therefore, as distant worlds which challenge the dominant culture of modern times. Yet, all the voices of dissent in the play are silenced by the repressive authority of the society of Ballybeg.

Since the pagan religion embraced by Father Jack in Uganda does not make any distinction, as he explains, "between the religious and the secular" (*Dancing at Lughnasa* 74), his ideas sound particularly dangerous in the native place. Because of the weird behaviour of Father Jack, the Mundy sisters are punished by the strict Catholic community of Ballybeg. Kate loses her job as a teacher, whereas Agnes and Rose, after refusing to begin working in a factory, emigrate to London, where they live in poverty. Thus, even the Mundy sisters, despite going back to a lost freedom and regaining their repressed instincts through dancing, are left without a sense of home in the end. The catharsis they have achieved is regarded by the community as a form of transgression which needs to be punished.

The rebellion against the dominant ideologies of Ballybeg would certainly be forgotten, therefore, if it were not for Michael's remembering. It is only through Michael's recollection of the past that this ephemeral rebellion against the repressive culture of the native society can still preserve a meaning. As Catriona Clutterbuck notices:

> Michael tries to author his own fate and re-author that of his mother and four aunts through an act of memory, [negotiating] the delicate balance between supporting and resisting imperialism in mining out a space for speech—the basic condition of subject-status. (Clutterbuck 104)

Though Father Jack is the returned emigrant who challenges the values of the native place, Michael is the character who, through memories, achieve a final homecoming. The returned missionary priest remains essentially a displaced character who has lost the sense of his roots. He is described as a forlorn figure...shuffling from room to room as if he were searching for something but couldn't remember what (*Dancing at Lughnasa* 8). Michael, indeed, has the power to reconsider the past. He is the narrator of the play and, as such, has the power to build the story according to his personal point of view. His recollection, however, is not a simple return to the past but allows him to go towards the future. As Anna McMullan suggests:

> It is the narrator who moves into the future and leaves Ballybeg behind. At the end of the play, the child Michael finally finds his voice, or rather his vision.... In the narrator's re-membering of his own genesis, the events of 1936 seem to constitute the moment which defines him as a creative individual, differentiating him from the already fractured family around him, who is nevertheless the source of his own history and textual narration. (McMullan 97)

Thus, the act of remembering also becomes an act of self-appropriation in conflict with the general sense of loss which permeates the play. An image, in particular, is brought back by the memories of Michael.

At the end of the play and at the end of his recollection, Michael refers to the image of the summer of 1936 which visits him more often and explains:

> When I remember it, I think of it as dancing. Dancing with eyes half closed because to open them would break the spell. Dancing as if language had surrendered to movement—as if this ritual, this wordless ceremony, was now the way to

> speak, to whisper private and sacred things, to be in touch with some otherness.
>
> (*Dancing at Lughnasa* 107)

The image of the past which Michael preserves in his mind is therefore linked with a further form of language, that is—with the language of dance and movement. Yet, the vision is also suspended, in his memory, above reality. As he states: "What fascinates me more about that memory is that it owes nothing to fact. In that memory atmosphere is more real than incident and everything is simultaneously actual and illusory" (*ibid*). Like Cass McGuire, Michael has to enter a new dimension in order to achieve his only possible return. Unlike the world of dreams of Eden House, however, the kind of language found by Michael is free even from words. The meaning suggested by the silent movements does not need the support of traditional verbal language.

However, the vision of the narrator is not completely optimistic. The characters observed by him in their dances seem "to be floating on [the] sweet sound" (*ibid*) and move "in complete isolation" (*ibid*). This might suggest that the dances of the rebellious characters cannot do anything to affect reality or change it. Yet, in his mental homecoming, Michael saves the meaning concealed in the events of the past and suggests that a form of free expression may still be gained despite all attempts at silencing differences. By entering "in touch with some otherness" (*ibid*), the narrator cannot restore the past, which is for ever lost, but can at least re-establish the importance of the marginal voices which the authority has suppressed. According to Catriona Clutterbuck, the idea of 'otherness' and the right of 'others' to be heard is central in the play:

> The resonance of the play is connected to its articulation of loss in a communal context. It also acknowledges that reaching out to the other as well as seeing ourselves from the perspective of difference is a vital contemporary challenge.... There are many 'other' voices to be heard, if we are going finally to produce a future in which the paralysis of older forms of authority can be transformed into a celebration of the movement of individual and social agency. (Clutterbuck 100)

The homecoming of Michael through the memories of the past is therefore a symbolic act of rebellion against the repression of dissent in the community and a way to exorcise the fear of losing the past and all the meaningful events which are concealed in it.

WORKS CITED

Friel, Brian. *The Enemy Within*. Loughcrew: The Gallery Press, 1979. "Dancing at Lughnasa," in *Brian Friel Plays*.Introduced by Christopher Murray. London: Faber and Faber, 1999. "Faith Healer", *Brian Friel: Plays*, Introduced by Seamus Deane. London: Reinhardt, 1971.

The Loves of Cass McGuire. Dublin: Gallery Books, 1966. *The Home Place*. Loughcrew, Ireland: The Gallery Press, 2005. *Philadelphia, Here I Come!*. London: Faber and Faber, 1965. "Translation", in *Selected Plays of Brian Friel*. Introduced by Seamus Deane. London and Boston: Faber and Faber, 1984.

Bauman, Zygmunt. "From Pilgrim to Tourist—or a Short History of Identity." *Questions of Cultural Identity*. Eds. S. Hall and P. Du Gay. London: Sage Publications, 1996: 18-36.

Bentley, D.M.R. "Remembering and Forgetting". *Mnemographia Canadensis* Vol. 1 (2003). University of Western Ontario. (see: www.uwo.ca/english/canadianpoetry).

Bhabha, Homi. *The Location of Culture*. London: Routledge, 1994.

Clutterbuck, Catriona. "*Lughnasa* After *Easter*: Treatments of Narrative Imperialism in Friel and Devlin". *Irish University Review* (1999): 90-100.

Corcoran, Neil. "The Penalties of Retrospect: Continuities in Brian Friel". *The Achievement of Brian Friel*. Ed. Alan Peacock. Gerrards Cross: Colin Smythe, 1993: 14-28.

Friel, Brian. *Philadelphia, Here I Come!*. London: Faber and Faber, 1965.

"Translation", in *Selected Plays of Brian Friel*. Introduced by Seamus Deane. London and Boston: Faber and Faber, 1984.

Gaillard, Anne Marie. *Migration Return: A Bibliographical Overview*. New York: Center for Migration Studies, 1994.

Gefter Wondrich, Roberta. "Exilic Returns: Self and History Outside Ireland in Recent Irish Fiction". *Irish University Review* 30.1 (2000). 1-16.

Marangoly George, Rosemary. *The Politics of Home*. Berkeley,Los Angeles and London: University of California Press, 1966.

McAuslan, Ian and Walcot, Peter. *Homer*. New York: Oxford University Press, 1998.

McGrath, Francis. *Brian Friel's Post-Colonial Drama*. Syracuse, New York: Syracuse University Press, 1999.

McMullan, Anna. "'In Touch With Some Otherness': Gender, Authority, and the Body in *Dancing at Lughnasa*". *Irish University Review* 29.1 (1999): 90-100.

Peacock, Alan, ed. *The Achievement of Brian Friel*. Gerrards Cross: Colin Smythe, 1993.

Pine, Richard. *Brian Friel and Ireland's Drama*. London: Routledge, 1990.

Pitto, Cesare. "The Return of Immigrants to their Native Communities", in *Writers in Transition*. The Proceedings of the First National Conference of Italian-Canadian Writers. Eds. Dino Minni, Anna Foschi Ciampolini. Montréal: Guernica Editions, 1990.

Reynolds, Mary, ed. *Joyce: A Collection of Critical Essays*. Englewood Cliffs, NJ: Prentice-Hall, 1993.

Riley, Joan, and Briar Wood, eds. *Leave to Stay: Stories of Exile and Belonging*. Virago Press: London, 1996.

Ross, Bruce. *Remembering the Personal Past*. New York: Oxford, Oxford University Press, 1991.

Rogers, Rosemarie. "Return Migration in Comparative Perspective". *The Politics of Return: International Return Migration in Europe*. Ed. D. Kuban. Staten Island: Center for Migration Studies, 1984: 277-298.

Rubin, David. *Autobiographical Memory*. Cambridge: Cambridge University Press, 1986.

Rushdie, Salman. "Imaginary Homelands". *Essays and Criticisms* 1981-1991. London: Penguin Books, 1991.

Sayre, Robert. "Autobiography and Images of Utopia", in *Salmagundi* n. 19. Skidmore College: Saratoga Springs, NY, 1972.

Schlossman, Beryl. "Retrospective Beginnings". *James Joyce Quarterly* 29.1 (1991): 85-99.

Scott, F.R. and A.J.M. Smith, eds. *The Blasted Pine: An Anthology of Satire, Invective and Disrespectful Verse*. Toronto: MacMillan, 1957.

Shaun, Richard. "Brian Friel: Seizing the Moment of Flux". *Irish University Review* 30 (2000): 254-271.

Inner Progression of a Repressed Soul in Anita Desai's *Fasting, Feasting*

10

Meenakshi Raman and *Sushila Rathore*

Indian English Fiction has a long history to cherish in the realm of delineating the aspirations, sufferings and struggles faced by women since Ages. To start with, there has been a long list of writers who have taken up the ordeals faced by women in this patriarchal society as the core of their novels. Among them Kamala Markandaya, Ruth Prawer Jhabvala, Shashi Deshpande, Bharti Mukherji, Anita Nair, and above all Anita Desai are some of the prominent writers writing in English today. Anita Desai has created an unparalleled stature in Indian English fiction by centralizing in her fiction the mental agonies, the internal strife and trauma faced by the women protagonists with a difference. As has been said by K.R.S. Iyengar,

> Her forte is the exploration of sensibility—the particular kind of modern Indian sensibility that is ill at ease among the barbarians and the philistines, the anarchists and the amoralists. Since her preoccupation is with the inner world of sensibility rather than the outer world of action, she has tried to forge a style supple and suggestive enough to convey the fever and fretfulness of the stream of consciousness of her principal characters. The intolerable grapple with thoughts, feelings and emotions is necessarily reflected in the language, syntax and imagery, yet the reader's first impression on reading Anita Desai's novels may very well be that the emotions are too many, and are often the result of excessive cerebration on the author's part and not always determined by the movements in the consciousness of the characters.

> Nevertheless, Anita Desai's is an original talent that has the courage to go its own way....[1]

Anita Desai has given a new direction to Indian English fiction and has created a specific niche for herself by delving deep into the human psyche of her female characters; she brings forth their agonies, mental yearnings and trauma in stark nudity. She presents dexterously the struggles faced by them in this world where women have been accorded a secondary status. She has several works to her credit like *Cry the Peacock*, *Where Shall We go this Summer*, *Clear Light of the Day*, *In Custody*, *Journey to Ithaca*, etc. Her interest in the fragmented internal life of the characters and not in the outer atmosphere is the remarkable quality which allocates her a unique place among the other women novelists. For her it is "depth which is interesting, delving deeper and deeper in a character or a scene rather than going round about it"[2] whereas writers like Kamala Markandaya, Nayantara Sahgal and Ruth Prawer Jhabvala are more inclined towards politics, east-west encounter, and social themes.

Anita Desai does not refrain herself from acknowledging the fact that she is more concerned with the mental rather than physical being of her women protagonists;

> My writing is an effort to discover, underline and convey the significance of things. I must seize upon that incomplete and seemingly meaningless mass of reality around me and try and discover its significance by plunging below the surface and plumbing the depths, then illuminating those depths still they become more lucid, brilliant and explicable reflection of the visible world.[3]

Her novel *Fasting, Feasting* analyses in the same vein the internal anguish faced by Uma, the central character in the novel with great aplomb. Uma, the eldest daughter in her family, after being denied the desired love and affection, always feels isolated and insecure. Uma fulfills all the roles assigned to her—taking care of her brother, attending to each and every need of her parents, but despite that she fails to elicit affection from them. From the very beginning the parents depend on her and ironically she never gets her share of importance. She gets overshadowed by her sister Aruna because she is an average student in her studies whereas her sister Aruna is not only excellent in her studies but also smart in every other sphere.

Uma has been brought up differentially and always been treated as a nuisance. She has been exploited since her childhood and has never been treated with equality. Uma is not as beautiful as her sister Aruna and hence she is made to feel ugly in front of people. This indifference in the hands of her parents makes her feel insignificant and she starts loosing confidence. She longs for the attention of her parents who always gives her a secondary treatment in comparison to her sister Aruna.

Her parents cherished the desire to have a son and when Arun is born they stop caring for the daughters. Overwhelmed by the birth of the son they ask her to leave the school. This show of unrestrained happiness at the birth of a son in front of the daughters is indicative of the inconsequential status of daughters in the family. "Papa, in his elation, leaping over three chairs in the hall, one after the other, like a boy playing leap-frog, his arms flung up in the air and his hair flying.'A boy!' he screamed, 'a bo-oy! Arun, Arun at last!'" (p. 17).

The exclusive concern and care allotted to the son pricks the mind of Uma to a great extent. Starting from the birth of Arun till his school, Uma has been assigned the responsibility of taking care of him. Though she is a weak student she is never given the freedom to have tutors to teach her. On the other hand, her father arranges tuitions for Arun in all the subjects. All the love and care is showered on the son and the daughters are never even paid any consideration and treated merely as an obligation. This discrimination has worked positively for Aruna, as just after this incident she starts asserting herself very strongly in all the matters. She couldn't digest the open prejudice meted out to them only because of their sex. Consequently, she never allows anyone to suppress her in any way. Her father has to do everything related to her marriage as she wants. On the other hand, this injustice after the birth of Arun works rather negatively for Uma. Her innermost self is smothered as a result of the open biasness shown by her parents after the birth of a son. Hence, she never reaches a stage where she can be confident and firm.

She has that sense of fear and segregation that she constantly considers herself a weakling, a discarded one among her own family members. She is forced to leave the school as she has to take care of the most important person in the household, i.e. the son. Due to this, she really feels herself fed-up because she also wants to study like other children.

At the birth of her brother she is not very old despite that she is forced to do all the work starting from changing his nappies to giving him food. Her consciousness is torn between her deepest desire to go out and play and over the captivity imposed on her by her parents. Her childhood just elapses in all these household chores, she is neither allowed to study nor allowed to enjoy with the children of her age. Whenever she expresses her desire to study, her mother silences it, 'I have to go and do my homework,' she told her mother. 'I've got to get my sums done and then write the composition'.—'Leave all that,' Mama snapped at her (p. 18).

Uma endures all the pain and internal helplessness without complaining to anyone, though there are instances where she really blurts out her desire strongly but is always silenced either by her mother or father. There are moments when she wants to communicate her feelings of distress through her silence for instance when she locks herself in the room and didn't come out irrespective of repeated calls of her parents. The parents are not seriously interested in educating her; they always search for opportunities where she can be kept at home to take care of their son. After Uma failed in her exams her mother got the chance to keep her in the home for always:

> You know you failed your exams again. You're not being moved up. What's the use of going back to school? Stay at home and look after your baby brother. What's the use of going back to school if you keep failing, Uma? You will be happier at home. You won't need to do any lessons now. You are a big girl now. We are trying to arrange a marriage for you. (p. 22)

In all these situations Uma really finds herself incarcerated without any freedom to choose and decide on her own, for instance she just hates taking care of the child because she really finds herself inept in managing these things. All her quests and her frustrations are restricted to her thoughts without any outlet. But still she has that sense of understanding where she never really questions the favours given to her brother and sister, who gets everything according to her wishes merely due to her quality of being a very influential child. Uma fails to get the things just because she lacks the power to assert herself strongly. But there are instances where even she becomes impatient sometimes for small things and doesn't want to compromise. She asserts her desire to go out and enjoy by going with her cousin Ramu against her parents wishes.

The desire to go out and study is so strong in her that one day she runs away secretly to meet Mother Agnes, her teacher to request her to persuade her father to send her to school, as she says—'But I will work very hard mother!' She yelled, 'I will pass next time. Please tell him, Mother—I will pass next time!' (p. 28).

Uma tries a lot to convince her parents to send her to school but they do not agree at any cost and as a result she really starts having a sense of seclusion where she feels that her wishes and desires carry no meaning for anybody in the house. Uma has got the heart of a child, even after being a grown up woman as she is not very skillful in managing the sensitive issues. For instance, she is happy at the thought of Anamika being sent to her parents' house forcefully by her parents-in-law. She doesn't know the way to participate in such discussions. For example when she comes to know that her cousin Anamika has been sent to her house by her in-laws she expresses her happiness by saying that now they will be able to meet Anamika. Hence her parents never consider her fit to take part in such sensitive social issues and try to keep her away.

The disparate and irrelevant treatment she suffers in the hands of her family is responsible for the ruining of her future also. Uma's parents search for a match for her but they do not take much interest in finding out the exact information about the groom and his family and consequently it leads to a failure. They just wanted to get rid of her and hence they were in hurry to marry her. The fake engagement costs them a huge sum for which Uma is blamed ultimately. As she is not very beautiful and intelligent the grooms are more interested in her sister Aruna than in her. After repeated failures in getting a suitable match for her everybody in the home starts blaming her. All these instances of allegations cast a great impact on Uma and she starts feeling herself a burden on the family. Even her sister starts speaking in a sarcastic way and everybody starts feeling sympathetic towards her. When Aruna said to her, laughing 'Uma, why don't you cut your hair short? Like Lila Aunty? It will suit you, you know,' she retorted. 'Tchh! What silly ideas you have,'and was not only annoyed but hurt as well: she had caught the mockery in Aruna's tone (p. 85).

She is not very pretty but does not want to put on make-up to look attractive. She is a very simple girl and moreover she has little sense of grooming in comparison to her sister Aruna who is very skillful at dressing up and in talking to people. Uma also does not know how to lie, she is innocent as a child and when her mother tells her to lie to the grooms' parents about the preparation of dishes she doesn't agree to that. But even in this case the family considers her a total fool as she doesn't know the ways of the world.The sarcasm that she suffers perforates her always but she has no separate existence of her own and not even the strength to face people and do something in order to prove herself.

Since her childhood she has not been a confident child and despite all her efforts she couldn't acquire it only because of the indifference and lack of importance meted out to her by her own family members. Even she has to take permission of her father to make a telephone call and they don't even allow her to talk to anybody. Their apathetic and rude behavior has never allowed her to become a mature person. They are responsible in making her a diffident child having no inclination towards creating a separate existence of her own and whenever she has tried to do it they have tried their best to evade it.

The stage of repeated failures to marry her off proves to be very crucial and Uma's childlike persona is being taken over by maturity. "Uma's ears were already filled to saturation with mama's laments, and Aruna's barbs. Had anyone looked they might have noticed that Uma's face was losing its childish openness of expression and taking on a look of continual care" (p. 86).

After a long search, Uma was married to a man who later turned out to be an already married man with children and a wife to support. She came to know a little about it when she was taken back to her house by her father. She was never informed about the legal proceedings being involved in terminating her marriage, which ultimately ended in a divorce. A victim of hatred in the hands of everybody without committing a single mistake, she has no space to call her own in that house. The parents decided the marriage and it was cancelled also without even informing her. However, the parents were responsible for this whole episode but they never considered it to be their fault and blamed Uma's fate only. This incident brings a lot of change in Uma and she becomes quite introvert after this unpleasant incident. As a result of this failure, all the attempts to marry her off were put to an end and she acquired the place of a permanent problem in the family.Uma feels pangs of rejection after witnessing the behaviour of her parents which has even worsened after this event. She just lies down in her bed hearing the barking of dogs in the complete darkness of the night, "That was what Uma felt her own life to have been—full of barks, howls, messages and now silence" (p. 61).

She tries a lot to control her shattered life. There are moments in her life which gives her some consolation for instance whenever her Mira-masi, an old widow relative visits their house, she accompanies her on her religious pilgrimages. The company of Mira-masi helps her in her moments of distress and she acquires courage to compromise with her present situation. Mira-masi utters words of consolation for Uma: "She is blessed by the Lord. The Lord has rejected the man you chose for her because He had chosen her for Himself" (p. 97).

Her attempts to go out and work with people like Mrs. O'Henry never become successful. Depressed, broken, irritated, secluded, estranged and lonely; Uma finds herself nowhere neither in the category of married nor unmarried. The novelist writes:

> That she had not had their experiences, that hers was other: that of an outcaste from the world of marriage, the world which all the murmuring, and whispering and muttering implied, was all that mattered. Retreating to her own room, she sank down on the floor, against the wall, put her arms around her knees and what it would have been like to have the Lord Shiva for a husband, have Him put his arms around her. (pp. 96-97)

Uma really feels pangs of isolation even in the so called close knit family, as there was no one with whom she could share her agonies and her torn self between her duties as a daughter and as an individual. As Anita Desai writes, "The tightly knit fabric of family that had seemed so stifling and confining now revealed holes and gaps that were frightening—perhaps the fabric would not hold, perhaps it would not protect after all" (p. 86).

She finds herself completely alone and feels suffocated in the confines of that household where everyone is just concerned about the son and his affairs. She also feels herself unwanted and segregated when her father spends a lot of money in the marriage of Aruna. Nevertheless he does everything as dictated by her. Here also she feels herself incomplete as a human being where no one values her more than merely as a custodian of the house. She feels tormented at the open partiality her father displays at the time of Aruna's marriage. Despite doing everything for the family she is not treated as an integral part of it rather an outsider who is just living there for survival. She feels that she has no identity in that home except as a caretaker of the house whom everyone can ask to work for them. She understands everything but the life long suppression suffered in the hands of her parents never lets her open her mouth.

There is an utmost longing in Uma to cast out the forced life she has been leading and in order to assert herself she speaks through her silence. Her parents have never allowed her to go out not even allowed her to spend sometime in her own room, all these things really prove to be suffocating for her and in order to show her anger over this unending captivity not only on actions but also on her thoughts she shuts the door in front of her mother. These types of incidents are not for once but many times. She is full of fury as she is not even allowed to even spare some time for herself. For instance she reacts very strongly when her mother forces her to leave everything else and bring the tea for her father. At this she puts tea with a clatter on the table—"Here, her eyes flash through her spectacles, this, this is what I know. And you, you don't. He takes the cup from her, too startled to protest" (p. 137).

Uma has no freedom to even go out and meet someone without the permission of her parents. Initially, she has done according to their wishes but there were occasions where she has also expressed and advocated her need to enjoy very intensely. When her invitation to a coffee party by Mrs. O'Henry is quickly brushed aside by her parents, she openly expresses her anger on this constant oppression.

> 'Mrs. O'Henry—she has invited me to a coffee party.' Uma can hardly speak; she would like to keep this treasured invitation to herself alone, after all—and would have preferred not to divulge it. Of course that is out of the question.
>
> 'Why?' Asks Papa.
>
> 'Coffee? Why coffee?' asks Mama.
>
> Uma jerks her head back. 'Why'? She snaps back at them. 'She is giving a party—a coffee party, not a tea party—and she has invited some ladies, and me.' (p. 112)

Uma's slightest wishes are not granted and she is always repressed by her parents. Her neighbours' daughter Moyna has started working as she wants to be different, on hearing this there is an inmost urge in Uma and she also wants to work and have a career of her own. One day, she talks to Dr. Dutt secretly and requests her for a job. At this, she agrees and comes to her house to seek the permission of her parents. Dr. Dutt is not been considered a lady of repute as she is single and working, though she belongs to a well reputed family. When she informs Uma's parents about the requirement they have in the dispensary for nurses and suggests Uma's name they are awestruck. They do not like the idea at all and start making excuses:

> Papa looked incredulous and Mama outraged. Dr. Dutt clasped Uma's arm. 'Don't look so frightened,' she urged. 'I know how well you look after your parents. I know how much you helped Mrs. O'Henry with her work, I am confident you can do it' But Uma was not confident. 'I have no degree,' she faltered, 'or training.' 'This kind of work does not require training, Uma' Dr. Dutt assured her, 'or degrees. Just leave that to me. I will deal with it if the authorities ask. You will agree, sir?' She turned to Papa, smiling, as if she knew how much he adored being called sir. (p. 142-43) But Papa did not appear to have noticed the honour this time. He was locking his face up into a frown of great degree. (pp. 142-43)

Both the parents do not like the idea and Uma's Mama pretends in front of Dr. Dutt that as she is ill she needs Uma at home to take care of her. On knowing this Uma is full of anger and she feels like shouting and telling Dr. Dutt that her mother is hale and hearty and she is lying as she doesn't want her to be independent. Uma has undergone this discrimination in the hands of her parents since her childhood, where girls have been considered as burdens on the family. But after her sisters marriage and also as her brother is also a grown up man and has become successful, she also wants to have a career of her own. But selfishness and discrimination is so much rooted in her parents that they don't even allow her to do a job. After this incident, Uma stops all her attempts to even try for anything that can make her self-sufficient and she shuns all her anger and frustrations and compromises with the current situation.

To sum up, dejected, torn, and alienated self of Uma never achieves a stature where she can become an independent woman. A struggler throughout her life, Uma toils with her own wishes, her own desires that have never been provided, an outlet neither by her nor by her own family members. Although there are times in her life wherein she wants to assert her own likings but on being rejected by her family members, she learns to maintain silence. She surrenders to her present state and undergoes insults, tumults, rejection, hatred and lack of freedom with tolerance.

Her psyche has become accustomed to the discrimination meted out to her as a part of the female race and consequently, she tries to adjust and seeks fulfillment in the household chores. However, she senses the suffering and the injustices meted out to her and acquires the courage to express but she never crosses the boundaries of family and tradition. After undergoing all the segregations and indifferences she achieves a stature of tolerance and maturity where she finds herself an inseparable part of the family in which she is living and rather than discarding them for her own aspirations she compromises with the situation and gets ready to lead it the way her parents wanted. As said by Anita Myles, 'Anita Desai portrays Indian woman as fighter, a victim and as a heroine and ultimately a winner because of her indomitable spirit and attitude of compromise'.[5]

NOTES

1. K.R. Srinivasa Iyengar. "A note on Anita Desai's Novels", *The Banasthali Patrika*, (January, 1969), p. 64.
2. Jasbir Jain. "Anita Desai: Interviewed." *Rajasthan University Studies in English*, 12 (1979), pp. 61-69.
3. Anita Desai. "Replies to the Questionaire," *Kakatiya Journal of English Studies*, 3, No. 1, 1978, pp. 1-6.
4. Anita, Desai. *Fasting, Feasting*, London: Chatto & Windus, 1999, All the Quotes hereby cited are from the same edition quoted along with page numbers.
5. Anita, Myles. *Feminism and Post Modern Indian Women Novelists in English*, New Delhi: Sarup and Sons, Ist Edition, 2006.

Bridges in the Gap between British and American Women Poets: A Feminist Reading of Selected Poems of Sylvia Plath and Hilda Doolittle's *Helen in Egypt*

11

Rosalyn M. Mutia

Summary

Feminism is one of the terminologies of the phenomenon of women's oppression on the basis of their gender. This phenomenon can be traced to an age-long tendency for women to be classified as the "other" of the male who is considered as the norm. Twentieth century theoretical debates on feminism show a marked lack of consensus between women scholars whose varied political and socio-cultural environments necessitate different worldviews and perspectives of appreciating reality. However, a study of the poetry of women poets who take up the pen in their various societies points to vast similarities in themes and gender role attributions among the women writers. This paper examines and analyzes the feminist issues in selected poems of a twentieth century British woman poet Sylvia Plath and in the epic poem of an American woman poet Hilda Doolittle, in order to bring out the vast similarities in their treatment of the issue of otherness.

Introduction

Criticism of British and American women's literary creativity begins as far back as with the work of such renowned literary giants of the Romantic period like Madame de Stael, Elizabeth Barrett Browning and Virginia Woolf. This is followed during the Victorian era by works of equal importance by women poets like Emily Dickinson. The critical treatment of women's poetic creativity at this time was highly misogynistic as it emphasized both female incapacity for poetic invention and women's inferiority in matters of experience, knowledge, and education. Women's image as poetess was satirized in male texts, and this seems to have had an effect on continuous female creativity, resulting in a silence of women on the art of poetry. Margaret Homans (1980) has argued that women experienced an incompatibility between femininity and poetic subjectivity in the Romantic period that hindered their success.

In Acheson and Huk's *Contemporary British Poetry: Essays in Criticism*, Claire Buck's essay, "Contemporary Women's Poetry in the British Women's Movement" locates a difference between women's poetry in Britain and that in the United States:

> The cultural location of feminist poetry in Britain emerges as most clearly different from that of poetry in the U.S. even despite the influence of the United States Women's Movement on British Feminism. (99)

Buck notes the confidence that American women have had in the important part that poetry plays in the Women's movement and attributes this confidence to "the professionalization of the poet's role within the academy in the United States" (100). This professionalization, Buck remarks, is a much more recent and limited development in England. According to Claire Buck, the odd split in British politics between a more progressive social policy and a model of good culture has been very limiting to women. Her allusion to this split is reminiscent of the Victorian insistence on decorum and high culture and as she insinuates, this tradition is perpetuated in modern British society by an aristocratically inflected nostalgia for recognized forms of high culture, designed for the edification of the middle class. Because of this tendency for critics to always point at the differences between British and American women's creativity, this paper intends to show that the similarities between the two traditions outweigh any form of difference. This will be done using feminist criticism.

Analysis

Though feminist poetry often refers to the poetry written by women within the realms of the women's liberation movement, feminism or at least the feminist spirit is an age-long phenomenon which predates the women's movement, finding its predecessors in women poets like Sylvia and Hilda Doolittle, among others, who wrote as far back as the 20th century. Even today, women are still writing feminist poetry. This paper analyzes and compares the written poetry of two women poets from Britain and America respectively, who wrote in the mid 20th century—Sylvia Plath and Hilda Doolittle. It brings out the gender roles that are attributed to British and American women in the poetry to show that the roles attributed to women in patriarchy make them victims of their socially constructed gender. The paper also shows that in spite of their varied historical and socio-cultural backgrounds, these women poets deal with the same issues in their works.

Sylvia Plath was born the oldest child in Boston Massachusetts on 27th October, 1932 to Otto Plath a biology professor at Boston University and Aurelia Plath who was a high school teacher, but who, at her husband's suggestion, had to give up her job because of their marriage, to become a home-maker. By the time Plath wrote her poetry she had lived in Britain for quite some time and had become British by marrying the British writer, Ted Hughes. So her poetry can be classified as British.

At the time she wrote, single-parenthood was not a common phenomenon. Motherhood, therefore, implied the notions of marriage and wifehood. Talking about life in their home, Aurelia Plath, Sylvia's mother, says:

> Social life was almost nil for us as a couple.... He (Otto) had never known the free flow of communication that characterised my relationship with my family and talking things out and reasoning just didn't operate. (Basnett 7)

Subordination of her mother in this stringent family life was later to have a bearing on Sylvia Plath as she writes about the roles attributed to women and the effect on their lives. In her collection *Ariel*, the poem "Daddy," presents a family situation in which the woman is totally subordinated to her husband. In fact, she is just a very insignificant part of human existence and her role is subsumed in a patriarchal halo. "Daddy" is therefore an unnerving assault at the male parent for this subordination of the woman in the poem. In this poem the speaker considers that the life of a woman is similar to that of a foot locked up in the father/husband's black shoe, never even daring to breathe or express the feeling of pain or any other emotion:

> You do not do, you do not do
> anymore, black shoe
> in which I have lived like a foot
> for thirty years, poor and white
> Barely daring to breathe or ach'oo.
>
> ("Daddy")

In this "shoe" known as the life of a woman in a patriarchal society, the speaker has lived for thirty years. The word "Ach'oo" has an onomatopoeic effect echoing the sound of sneezing. Sneezing is an involuntary, (sometimes), unconscious act which is difficult to control. Yet in this "shoe" the speaker barely dares to express even such a reflex emotion. Everything must be put in total control. This image points to complete subordination because in it the speaker, who is a mother, is not even a complete human organism. She is only a foot. As a foot, the woman has no opinions or even if she has, she has no way of expressing them. The speaker once more complains of this:

> So I never could tell where you
> put your foot, your root.
> I never could talk to you.
> The tongue stuck in my jaw.
>
> ("Daddy")

And then: "I have always been scared of you/ With your Luftwaffe your gobbledyggo." But this fear was not the fear of reverence. It was the fear that results from the gaze of subordination.

Hilda Doolittle deals with this same issue of women's subordination in "Helen in Egypt". The poem is a series of lyrics of irregular free verse with varying length and interspersed with prose commentaries sometimes longer than the lyrics. In it Doolittle reconsiders the social stereotypes attributed to women by which society regards a woman as nothing but the representation of physical beauty and therefore a sex object and shows how that function subordinates her. It is divided into three parts. In Part I entitled Pallinode, the setting is an Egyptian temple near the coast and the time is after the Trojan War. The speakers are Helen of Troy and Achilles (the Trojan prince now apparently dead and ship-wrecked in Egypt). It is in this setting that Doolittle allows her heroine to transcend the courtly love traditions of her class (being the wife of King Menelaus) and play the roles of mother and wife; roles which continue to expose the woman as a subordinated victim.

Subordination of the woman as a mother is seen in the first part of the poem which begins with a dramatic encounter between Helen and Achilles in Egypt. Almost dead, Achilles is ferried away from the heat of battle to Egypt. It is in Egypt that Helen takes care of him, though he cannot recognise her. In doing this, Helen assumes the role of a mother. In fact, when Achilles grieves with outrage at suffering the mortal fate of a mere man, Helen comforts him by praying for him like a mother would:

Let me love him, as Thetis, his mother,
For I knew him, I saw in his eyes
The sea-enchantment, but he
Knew not yet, Helen of sparta,
Knew not Helen, Hated of Greece.

("Pallinode")

But even as helpless as Achilles is at this point in time, his subconscious mind is still totally under the grips of the gender biases of his society. So when he finally recognizes Helen, he identifies her as the "Other"—the negative object to the man who is the defining and dominating subject. This identification makes him even the more remorseful for he cannot imagine himself the all-powerful Achilles totally dependent on a woman. So he clutches her and tries to strangle her: "[he] clutched my throat/with his fingers remorseless steel." This attempt at strangulation stems from Achilles refusal to accept the woman as no more than a subordinated human "other" and not someone needed by men.

Another feminist issue discernible in the poems of these two poets is women's reaction to this subordination in their rejection of motherhood as an institution and their acceptance of it as an experience. For Plath, when motherhood became an institution of patriarchy, then the life of a married mother was like being locked up in unbeatable doldrums. Her poetry shows women and mothers as being confined in plaster, in a bell jar, a cellar or a wax house, and being liberated from such by a maddened or an ugly avatar of self. Though she recognized that her writing could offer her an escape from the traditional female role, it could not release her from the system of values that drove her to excel at conventional motherhood as well as at writing and thus to strain too hard at both.

Plath's poem, "Three Women", presents three women with differing views on the theme of motherhood depending on their careers and their stations in life. The poem shows that while women will like to experience motherhood, they will vehemently reject it as a patriarchal institution, since as an institution, it is meant to stifle their ability to exercise their other capabilities. Plath's presentation in this poem is recast in the total configuration of class demarcations into which women have been socialized. In the poem, there is first of all the happily pregnant woman who "cannot help smiling" because of the joy she feels that a baby is growing in her.

When I walk out, I am a great event
I do not have to think or even rehearse.
What happens in me will happen without attention
The pheasant stands on a hill;
He is arranging his brown feathers
I cannot help smiling at what it is I know
Leaves and petals attend me. I am ready.

("Three Women")

There is secondly a secretary who yearns to experience motherhood through childbirth but whose office job makes it impossible for her to carry a child to term. There is thirdly the college student who considers motherhood as an imposition of patriarchy and therefore as a means of stifling her academic career. She therefore rejects the child she conceives.

The working woman (secretary) manifests a dire yearning to have children. But as a working class woman, she keeps having miscarriages because her public life conflicts with the private.

When I first saw it, the small red seep, I did not believe it ...
And the man I work for laughed; Have you seen something awful?
"You are so white, suddenly." And I said nothing.
I saw death in the bare trees, a deprivation.
I could not believe it, it is so difficult
For the spirit to conceive a face, a mouth?...
There is this cessation, this terrible cessation of everything.
("Three Women")

The third woman in "Three Women" is most probably a college student, representing another class of women, and considers pregnancy in particular and motherhood in general as a patriarchal institutionalized duty. For this reason, she feels repulsion towards the progress of her pregnancy.

I saw the world in it—small mean and black
Every little word hooked to every little word, and act to act.
A hot blue day had budded into something.

So, because of her class as a budding intellectual, she rejects the functions of mothering, though biologically she has the capability to mother. Mothering, it would appear, is considered as an impediment to her career prospects. It is something that can "murder her:"

I am not ready for anything to happen.
I should have murdered this that murders me.
Her cries are hooks that catch and grate like a cat
It is by these hooks she climbs to my notice.
("Three Women")

The baby's cries, the chores associated with taking care of her and the entire institution of motherhood are presented as a threat to the intellectual woman's identity, and in the poem, the persona therefore decides to give the baby up in order to return to the university. The poet's attitude is complete identification with the need to reject the antipathy that exists between maternity and social and mental independence for women.

Plath, however, presents children in themselves as very enriching and satisfying, and even at times as the only salvation for the tortured soul. In his innocence, the child offers solace to his mother. In "Nick and the candlestick" for example, Plath writes about her child:

You are the one
Solid the spaces lean on, envious.
You are the baby in the barn.

Similarly, Hilda Doolittle's poem "Helen in Egypt" tackles women's rejection of the subordination inherent in motherhood as an institution, while they accept it as an experience to be enjoyed. Resisting this mythical stereotyping and subjugation of women, Doolittle makes Helen to appeal to another woman in order to be free from Achilles' grip. When Helen resists instead of succumbing to Achilles' power to subdue and subordinate her in her role of mother, she does so by resorting to another female, to a mother image, to Thetis, who is actually Achilles mother. At this point she becomes transformed. She is now the phoenix rising from the ashes of the heat of war and battle. She gains a better status as Thetis indoctrinates her about the enormous power that lies dormant in women who must not therefore succumb to patriarchy. She also acquires the ancient wisdom of Egypt. She has become "the Phoenix/ [that] has vanquished/ that ancient enemy, sphinx" ("Pallinode" *Helen in Egypt*). Just as Plath had "to kill" Daddy in "Daddy," so also Helen resists male power and by so doing gains control over her mind. Like the intellectual college student in Plath's "Three Women," Helen in Doolittle's "Helen in Egypt" can now pursue a better course of life for herself. In the poem, this is the point at which she begins to understand the hieroglyphs on the temple walls of the god, Amen-Thoth:

the lords have passed a decree,
the lords of the hierarchy,
that Helen be worshipped.

be offered incenses
upon the altars of Greece
with her brothers the Dioscuri. ("Pallinode")

In the second part of "Helen in Egypt" known as "Leuke," the prose commentary reveals that "Achilles is said to have married Helen who bore him a son, Euphorion." But it is clear that Helen's desire to experience motherhood is as a matter of choice and not of imposition. This is because before this point in the poem, Helen rejects Paris' marriage offer to her. Just like in Plath's poetry, Helen sardonically rejects Paris and the notion of motherhood as an institution.

Plath and Doolittle, equally show concern in their poetry with the feminist issue of childbirth and/or women's sterility. In this way, they treat the theme of motherhood as an embodiment of the double mystery of life: just as life is a juxtaposition of the good and the ugly, of fecundity and decay, and of death and rebirth. Childbirth exposes the woman to the joys of motherhood, while sterility shows the dilemmas and frustrations that any shortcomings of this role can throw the mother in.

In "Two sisters of Persephone" Plath demonstrates the sorrows that crowd and sadden the motherhood of a barren woman and hereby shows that sterility is a problem to mothers of all races. In it, the imagery vividly captures and contrasts barrenness with fecundity and praises fecundity:

Two girls there are, within the house
One sits, the other, without
Day long, a duet of shade and light
Plays between these.

The girl within the house is in "a dark wainscotted" room and

works problems on
a mathematical machine, at this barren enterprise,
rat shrewed go her squint eyes.

But the other girl outside has more space and possibility and is not therefore restricted to the barren banal activity of mathematical calculations. The sky is her limit and there is no horizon to her possibilities. So she

burns open to the sun's blade
...freely becomes sun's bride...
grows quick with seed. ("Two Sisters of Persephone")

and "grass-couched in her labour's pride/ she bears a king". The barren unfertile girl is described in such imagery that the reader's compassion and pity are evoked. First, her room is draped in dark wainscoted shades. Her actions are mechanical and lack interest because the opportunities are limited. Her eyes are described as "rat-shrewd" and "squint" indicating some kind of unease, insecurity and boredom. It is a gloomy picture. The other girl, however, is as free as a bird. In a kind of imagistic dislocation, the sun becomes a bridegroom and the girl the bride and then in their union, she "grows quick with seed" and delivers not only a child but also a king, or better still, a queen. In this, this second girl experiences the joys of motherhood, the joy of being no more only an object subjected to a man but also a subject on whom the growing baby in the womb depends. In fact, as Simon/e de Beauvoir remarks: "Life is but condition of existence; in gestation, it appears as creative..." A pregnant woman is therefokre "no longer an object subservient to a subject [a man for example]," neither is she a "subject afflicted with the anxiety that accompanies liberty; she is someone with that equivocal reality: life. Her body is at last her own, since it exists for the child who belongs to her" (467).

On the other hand, Plath dreads sterility. In the "Munich Mannequins", the speaker regards perfection as a kind of sterility:

> Perfection is terrible, it cannot have children
> Cold as snow breath, it tamps the womb
> Where the yew trees blow like hydras
> Unloosing their moons month after month to no purpose.

The womb of a sterile woman is portrayed here as a place "where yew trees blow". Yew trees are usually planted in churches and graveyards and this, therefore, is a perfect image of death. Barrenness, therefore, renders the mother a victim of the scorn of society.

Hilda Doolittle on her part shows in "Helen in Egypt" that even when women reject patriarchal stereotyping of themselves as sex objects of male pleasure, they still feel a compulsive pressure to mother. So in this poem, Helen, who has repudiated all strictures of courtly love as the wife of king Menelaus, decides to marry Achilles and to bear a child, Euphorion. Similarly, she considers Paris as her adolescent child, engendered by the new transformations in her personality, which have led her to marry Achilles because the latter limps to her as a sign of masculine weakness. It is only when these two "children" have become hers that the binary distinctions of male/female, weak/strong, and powerless/powerful, get fused together, engendering new definitions for Helen's selfhood and powerful possibilities for womanhood as a whole. Her desire to have children overshadows even her relationship with Achilles as she tells Theseus that "Beyond all other the child,/the child in the father/the child in the mother,/the child-mother yourself...." As the child-mother, Helen has thus borne out a new personality and a new sense of selfhood for herself. This new female self becomes the "melting point" of all patriarchal binaries and masculine dualities:

> Thus, thus, thus,
> as day, night
> as wrong, right,
> as dark, light,
> as water, fire,
> as earth, air
>
> as storm, calm,
> as fruit, flower,
> as life, death,
>
> as death, life;
> the rose deflowered,
> the rose reborn
>
> Helen in Egypt,
> Helen at home
> Helen in Hellas forever.
>
> ("Leuke")

An analysis of these two poets from varying cultures and historical epochs has thus shown that contrary to the differences inherent in theoretical feminism, feminist issues in the poetry of women from varying socio-cultural and historical milieus reveal a heightened degree of unanimity with feminist concerns and themes. Perhaps it is because women's literature in general and poetry in particular, has to do with such intimate universal experiences of women's lives that every woman can identify with. Through this poetry, we can discern hidden pointers to the need for sisterhood and coalition building among women and possibilities for women in different cultures to unite and this lays the groundwork for contemporary feminist theories and creative works which intend to explore and connect with the implications of diverse experiences, ethnic definitions and convergent goals.

REFERENCES

Basnett, Susan. *Sylvia Plath*. Towata, New Jersey: Barnes and Noble, 1987.

Buck, Claire. "Contemporary Women's Poetry in the British Women's Movement." *Contemporary British Poetry: Essays in Criticism* (ed). James Acheson and Romana Huk. Albany: State University of New York Press, 1996.

De Beauvoir, Simone. *The Second Sex*. Trans. H.M. Parshley. New York: Bantam, 1961.

Doolittle, Hilda. *Helen in Egypt*. New York: Grove Press, 1961.

Homans, Margaret. *Women Writers and Poetic Identity: Dorothy Wordsworth, Emily Bronte and Emily Dickinson*. Princeton: Princeton University Press, 1980.

Homer. *The Iliad* (Oxford World Classics Trans. Robert Fitzgerald). London: Oxford University Press, 2004.

Hooks, Bell. *Feminism is for Everybody*. Cambridge: South End Press, 2000.

Mies, Maria. *Intergrative Feminisms: Building Global Visions, 1960s to 1990s*. New York: Routlege, 1996.

Plath, Sylvia. *Ariel*. New York: Harper and Row, 1966.

Immigrant Experience and Pain of Exile in Jhumpa Lahiri's *The Namesake*

12

Srutimala Duara

There is a great tradition of writing in American literature about the immigrant experience. Recalling guidos, gavones and gedrools, Maria Laurino presents in *Were You Always an Italian?* a concise but stimulating look at Italian-American culture as a model for the immigrant experience as a whole. The author, a third-generation Italian-American, grew up in 1950s New Jersey as a minority whose ethnicity was long stifled. In Bharati Mukherjee's *Jasmine*, Jasmine's metamorphosis, with its sudden upheavals and its slow evolutionary steps, illuminates the making of an American mind; but even more powerfully, her story depicts the shifting contours of an America being transformed by her and others like her. In his debut novel, *American Son*, Brian Ascalon Roley details the Filipino immigrant experience through the troubled relationship between two brothers and their struggle to assimilate into the culture of Southern California. In *Grass Roof, Tin Roof,* about a Vietnamese family resettling in the isolation of California gold country, Dao Strom investigates the myth of westward progress and the consequences of cultural displacement. *The Namesake* continues to develop further the themes of cultural alienation and loss of identity that the immigrant faces in making a new home in a foreign country. Jhumpa Lahiri introduced us to people who left behind family and friends and the familiar heat and bustle of India to build a new life in America—a cold, bleak land of strangers and new customs. Addressing the themes of immigration, collision of cultures and the importance of names in *The Namesake*, Lahiri demonstrates how much of a struggle immigration can be. According to Dubey, "The immigrant experience is complicated as a sensitive immigrant finds himself or herself perpetually at a transit station fraught with memories of the original home which are struggling with the realities of the new world". This constant struggle is portrayed in *The Namesake*, as first generation immigrants and their children struggle to find their places in society.

A major international best-seller, *The Namesake* is the debut novel from Jhumpa Lahiri, the author of *Interpreter of Maladies* that bagged the 2000 Pulitzer Prize for Fiction, and won critical acclaim for its "grace, acuity, and compassion in detailing lives transported from India to America." *The Namesake* is a cross-cultural, multigenerational story of a Hindu Bengali family's journey to self-acceptance in Boston. Jhumpa Lahiri masterfully explores the themes of the complexities of the immigrant experience and foreignness, the clash of lifestyles, cultural disorientation, the conflicts of assimilation, the tangled ties between generations and paints a portrait of an Indian family torn between the pull of respecting family traditions, and the American way of life. It's a tale of love, solitude and emotional upheavals with an amazing eye for detail and ironic observation. In it she revisits issues that she knows well—those of cultural displacement, sense of identity, and belonging with one foot in two worlds.

The Namesake takes the Ganguli family from their tradition-bound life in Calcutta through their fraught transformation into Americans. On the heels of their arranged marriage, Ashoke and Ashima Ganguli settle together in Cambridge, Massachusetts. An engineer by training, Ashoke adapts far less warily than his wife, who resists all things American and pines for her family.

There's a passage early on where the young woman who's just recently come to the United States is pregnant, describing how she feels. "But nothing feels normal to Ashima. For the past 18 months, ever since she's arrived in Cambridge, nothing has felt normal at all. It's not so much the pain, which she knows somehow she will survive; it's the consequence, motherhood in a foreign land. For it was one thing to be pregnant, to suffer the queasy mornings in bed, the sleepless nights, the dull throbbing in her back, the countless visits to the bathroom.

Throughout the experience, in spite of her growing discomfort, she had been astonished by her body's ability to make life exactly as her mother and her grandmother and all her great-grandmothers had done. That it was happening so far from home, unmonitored and unobserved by those she loved, had made it more miraculous still. But she is terrified to raise a child in a country where she is related to no one, where she knows so little, where life seems so tentative and spare."

The Namesake opens with Ashima Ganguli trying to make a spicy Indian snack from American ingredients—Rice Krispies and Planters peanuts—but "as usual, there's something missing." Ashima tries and makes over her home in Cambridge to remind her of what she's left behind in Calcutta. Throughout *The Namesake*, Jhumpa Lahiri uses food and clothing to explore cultural transitions—especially through rituals, like the annaprasan, the rice ceremony. When Gogol is born, the Gangulis meet other Bengali families with small children, and Ashima finds that with a new baby "perfect strangers, all Americans, suddenly take notice of her, smiling, congratulating her for what she's done."

In his youth, Ashoke Ganguli is saved from a massive train wreck in India. When his son, Gogol, is born, Ashoke thinks, "Being rescued from that shattered train had been the first miracle of his life. But here, now, reposing in his arms, weighing next to nothing but changing everything, is the second." The title *The Namesake* reflects the struggles Gogol Ganguli goes through to identify with his unusual names. Gogol loses first his public name, his *bhalonam*, and then his private pet name, his *daknam*. He tries to remake his identity, after choosing to rename himself, and what is the result? Lahiri shows how our names precede us in society, and how they define us.

Turning her sights on the next generation, on Gogol's life after he begins to make his way in the world as a first-generation American, Lahiri proves herself nearly as adept as when she focuses on the particular struggles of the parents. When their son is born, the task of naming him betrays the vexed results of bringing old ways to the new world. Ashoke and Ashima's son "Gogol" is born in America and named after his father's favorite author by the name of Nikolai Gogol, author of *The Overcoat* in memory of a disaster years before. This is the namesake of the title. *The Namesake* chronicles the life of Gogol (Nikhil) Ganguli from his birth in the '60's to the present. He is given the name by his father who, before he came to America to study at MIT, was almost killed in a train wreck in India. Rescuers caught sight of the volume of Nikolai Gogol's short stories that he held, and hauled him from the train. Ashoke gives his American-born son the name as a kind of placeholder, and the awkward thing sticks. Young Gogol of course, knows nothing of this and resents his name extremely: "He hates that his name is both absurd and obscure, that it has nothing to do with who he is, that it is neither Indian nor American but of all things Russian after the Russian author, Nikolai Gogol. Gogol goes to Yale, changes his name to Nikhil. "I hate the name Gogol. I've always hated it," he tells the judge in charge of his name-change application. He re-creates himself as the person he'd like to be—hanging with friends, going to parties, meeting girls—but never fully shakes his old identity. "At times his name, an entity shapeless and weightless, manages nevertheless to distress him physically, like the scratchy tag of a shirt he has been forced permanently to wear." In a scene central to the novel's theme, Ashoke gives his son a volume of Nikolai Gogol's short stories for his fourteenth birthday, hoping to explain the book's significance in his own life. Gogol, a thoroughly Americanized teenager, is indifferent, preoccupied with his favorite Beatles recording. Such quietly revealing moments give the narrative its emotional power. The loneliness of lives lived in exile is most poignantly revealed in the late night family telephone calls from India, always an announcement of illness or death.

Gogol grows up a bright American boy, goes to Yale, has pretty girlfriends, becomes a successful architect, but like many second-generation immigrants, he can never quite find his place in the world. Like every American kid, Gogol eventually moves away from home. He does not hate his parents. Far from it he is very devoted to them. But sadly, there is hardly any genuine emotion depicted in the parent-child relationship. There are a few poignant moments that involve Ashoke and Gogol, but beyond that the feelings seem to be lost in the humdrum of daily lives. None of the characters have much to grieve about in their comfortable lives, but it seems as if the environment is one of drabness and permanent mourning. Ashima, for one is a perpetually depressed character who goes through the motions of life without any enthusiasm. Is she sad because she misses her country? Is she sad because her relationship with her husband is not what she hoped it would be? Does the family never do fun things together? Lahiri never tells us.

The things Gogol's parents say do not interest him and their Indian way of life means nothing to him. He detests the way they hold on to Indian traditions and functions that are of no importance to his American mind. He hates it when his parents whisk them off to Calcutta, a place the couple still considers home, for months together, disrupting his entire schedule. In spite of his yearly sojourns to Calcutta, he does not feel bound to India as they are. Unfortunately, his parents fail to understand him too, though they do try to give him the best of both worlds by religiously celebrating every American and Indian holiday. But the host of Bengali acquaintances he meets at these gatherings tends to put him off and distances him further. Like his American friends, Gogol drinks, smokes pot and has more than one romantic relationship and is able to dissociate himself from the memories of his girl friends, although with great difficulty. What strikes the reader is the monotony of his life even when it is full of ups and downs. Later one realizes that the monotony is not in his life, but in his mind. It is the way Gogol perceives things that make him what he is and shapes the story of his life. An atypical hero, he goes about his life without a sense of purpose, going where fate leads him. Gogol never thinks to do otherwise. He does take a few drastic steps in his life, but they are motivated more by his rebellious streak against his upbringing rather than a genuine desire to swim against the current. His unfortunate choice in marriage stems from an instinctive desire to cling to his Indian roots.

During the first semester of his freshman year, he goes home "unwillingly but obediently" every other weekend. His father meets him at the station; his mother does his laundry. Then one day he sits next to an attractive woman he recognizes from campus, the daughter of now-divorced hippies, raised on a commune and home-schooled until 7th grade. "He cannot imagine coming from such parents, such a background, and when he describes his own upbringing it feels bland by comparison," Lahiri writes. But the woman is fascinated as Gogol tells her about his childhood visits to Calcutta with his family, the layout of his maternal grandparents' apartment, its view of corrugated tin roofs: "He tells her the way tea was served, how it was brought through the window from men on the platform who served it from giant aluminum kettles, the milk and sugar already mixed in, and how it was poured into crude clay cups that were smashed afterward on the tracks. Her appreciation for these details flatters him; it occurs to him that he has never spoken of his experiences in India, to any American friend."

The Namesake provides important insights into the challenges often faced by people who live bicultural lives. There's a section where he dates a wealthy, cultured young Manhattan woman who lives with her charming parents. One telling scene has Gogol at a party with his American girlfriend's parents and their friends. One woman comments that Gogol and his family must be immune to illness when they travel to India and Gogol tries to explain that they often do get sick while in Calcutta. "But you're Indian," the woman answers. "I'd think the climate wouldn't affect you, given your heritage." When Gogol's girlfriend's mother tries to intercede on Gogol's behalf, she does more harm than good. She insists that he's American, that "he was born here," but then turns to him, bewildered for a moment. Gogol sees immediately that after months of knowing him, she still isn't sure. "Weren't you?" she asks.

After graduating and going through a number of relationships with American girls, his father's sudden death, forces Gogol to look back at his own culture that he has dismissed. His mother sets him up on a blind date with the daughter of a Bengali friend, and Gogol thinks he has found his match. In order to please his mother and friends, he attempts an ill-fated marriage to a Bengali childhood friend. It ends in disaster as he struggles to try and balance the American and Bengali parts of his life. Moushumi, like Gogol, is at odds with the Indian-American world she inhabits. She has found, however, a circuitous escape: "At Brown, her rebellion had been academic...she'd pursued a double major in French. Immersing herself in a third language, a third culture, had been her refuge—she approached French, unlike things American or Indian, without guilt, or misgiving, or expectation of any kind." Lahiri documents these quiet rebellions and random longings with great sensitivity.

Eventually Gogol reaches some sort of compromise, but it is never entirely satisfactory—there is always a sense of sadness that he is neither fully of one world or the other. Lahiri brings great empathy to Gogol as he stumbles along a first-generation path strewn with conflicting loyalties, comic detours, and wrenching love affairs. We see Gogol grow and as a first generation American struggle with a name he is embarrassed by, and deal with a heritage he is not sure of either. We see him fighting with himself over family loyalties, we see him funny escapades and crazy love affairs. While the Gangulis are trying hard to assimilate into American culture, Gogol rejects all of the old ways and ancient traditions of the family and becomes thoroughly Americanized. Torn between his parents' ways and customs and those of the modern culture in which he lives, Gogol finds himself on a path of divided traditions and heartbreaking love affairs that eventually lead him back to the old ways of his parents. Gogol grows up, moves out, and goes through life suffering personal tragedies that also shape his identity. Ashoke passes away and after his father's death Gogol makes a kind of peace with him. In addition, Gogol suffers through two jinxed romances before finally marrying a fellow Bengali American, Moushumi Mazoomdar. Despite a few tragedies, the end of the book is strangely liberating as we see young Nikhil finally coming into his own.

Lahiri's book is less of an insightful study and more of an autobiographical description of the Indian immigrant experience and how it can sometimes go awry. Lahiri's essays and interviews suggest that she herself is a victim of the "humiliating", her own adjective, process of immigration. But like Gogol, Lahiri says she herself has now reached the stage in her life where she thinks that bicultural upbringing is a rich, albeit imperfect thing. Yet, by her own admission a part of her yearns to be completely American. We may call it a contradiction of sorts, just like every other contradiction in Gogol's life.

Jhumpa Lahiri was born in London, England in 1967. She is the daughter of parents who emigrated from India. She moved to Rhode Island as a young child with her Bengali parents. Lahiri knows the terrain like the back of her hand: the community of expatriate Bengalis in the Boston area; their peculiarly lonely lives with ersatz extended families made up of fellow expatriates; the customs and world view through which they see their own everyday experience; and the struggle of their American children with their own questions of identity and belonging.

Although they have lived in the United States for more than thirty years, Lahiri observes that her parents retain "a sense of emotional exile" and Lahiri herself grew up with "conflicting expectations...to be Indian by Indians and American by Americans." Lahiri's abilities to convey the oldest cultural conflicts in the most immediate fashion and to achieve the voices of many different characters are among the unique qualities that have captured the attention of a wide audience. Although Lahiri grew up in the United States and considers herself an American writer, she has found that it is sometimes difficult to see herself as an American. Her parents always considered India their home, even after living abroad for thirty years. "It was important to my mother to raise her children as Indian, thinking and doing things in an Indian way, whatever that means," Lahiri recalled to Mervyn Rothstein in the *New York Times*. While growing up, Lahiri visited India often, usually every few years, and her visits there lasted from three weeks to as long as six months at a time. Still, Lahiri did not feel at home in that country either. "I've often felt," she told Barbara Kantrowitz in *Newsweek*, "that I am somehow illegitimate in both cultures. A true Indian doesn't accept me as an Indian and a true American doesn't accept me as an American."

Lahiri's own experience as a writer echoes Gogol's. In her Charlie Rose interview, Lahiri revealed, that "Jhumpa" is her pet name rather than her good name. Growing up in America, however, she has chosen it as her official, public name. The gesture annoys some members of Lahiri's family, who must find the public use of a private, family name to be inappropriate. But it is a gesture that allows Lahiri to continue to claim the version of herself she knows best, and that she wants others to know.

In an interview with Jeremy Brown, Jhumpa Lahiri admits, "It's what my world is, and what I've always been aware of. My parents came from Calcutta. They arrived in Cambridge, much like the parents in my novel. And I found myself sort of caught between the world of my parents and the world they had left behind and still clung to, and also the world that surrounded me at school and everywhere else, as soon as I set foot out the door. So I've never not been aware of that division in my life, and I wanted to write about that in the book."

Lahiri has said, "The question of identity is always a difficult one, but especially for those who are culturally displaced, as immigrants are...who grow up in two worlds simultaneously." What Gogol wants most from his life is different from what his family wants for him, and what they wanted when they first came to America to start a family. Jhumpa Lahiri has said of *The Namesake*, "America is a real presence in the book; the characters must struggle and come to terms with what it means to live here, to be brought up here, to belong and not belong here." The marriage of Ashima and Ashoke is arranged by their families. The closest intimacy they share before their wedding is when Ashima steps briefly, secretly, into Ashoke's shoes. Gogol's romantic encounters are very different from what his parents experienced or expected for their son.

Lahiri explores in several ways the difficulty of reconciling cross-cultural rituals around death and dying. For instance, Ashima refuses to display the rubbings of gravestones young Gogol makes with his classmates. And when Gogol's father suddenly dies, Gogol's relationship with Maxine is strained and quickly ends. Their love affair can't survive Gogol's grief. The loss of Gogol's father turns him back toward his family. It also changes Sonia and Ashima's relationship. In the last few pages of *The Namesake*, Gogol begins to read *The Overcoat* for the first time—the book his father gave him, by his "namesake."

Regarding the Indian immigrant experience that differentiates it from the experience of other immigrants to America Lahiri says, "For me, it was always a question of allegiance, of choice. I wanted to please my parents and meet their expectations. I also wanted to meet the expectations of my American peers, and the expectations I placed on myself to fit into American society. It's a classic case of divided identity, but depending on the degree to which the immigrants in question are willing to assimilate, the conflict is more or less pronounced. My parents were fearful and suspicious of America and American culture when I was growing up. Maintaining ties to India, and preserving Indian traditions in America, meant a lot to them. They're more at home now, but it's always an issue, and they will always feel like, and be treated as, foreigners here. Now that I'm an adult I understand and sympathize more with my parents' predicament. But when I was a child it was harder for me to understand their views. At times I felt that their expectations for me were in direct opposition to the reality of the world we lived in. Things like dating, living on one's own, having close friendships with Americans, listening to American music and eating American food—all of it was a mystery to them. On the other hand, when I was growing up, India was largely a mystery to Americans as well, not nearly as present in the fabric of American culture as it is today. It wasn't until I was in college that my American friends expressed curiosity about and interest in my Indian background. As a young child, I felt that the Indian part of me was unacknowledged, and therefore somehow negated, by my American environment, and vice versa. I felt that I led two very separate lives."

The Namesake is about this perpetual dilemma faced by immigrants as they struggle to maintain their identities while trying to shake them off at the same time. It is about the series of distressing choices they are forced to make every day as they try hard to avoid being misfits in a foreign land.

The Namesake encompasses 30 years in the life of a family. The action takes place in and around Boston and New York between 1968 and 2000. For Ashoke Ganguli and his wife Ashima, getting to understand American culture is never easy. But even as the immigrant couple tries to make sense of the world around them, they have to watch their two children, especially son Gogol, wrestle with the question of who they are. The experience of immigrant children differs little from that of their parents. The question of identity is always a difficult one, but especially for those who are culturally displaced as immigrants are, or those who grow up in two worlds simultaneously, like the children of immigrants. In a way, it is easier on the older generation to live in the new world. They bond with fellow immigrants; they have ties to cultural organizations and to temples. But the children have to fend for themselves, in a sense. They too carry considerable amount of tension about their own identities. Jhumpa Lahiri's observations about immigrant life (Bengali or otherwise) are astute: "Every weekend, it seems, there is a new home to go to, a new couple or young family to meet," she says of the young Gangulis settling into Cambridge, "They all come from Calcutta, and for this reason alone they are friends." Gogol's moving away from his parents, in seeking a life separate from theirs might be interpreted as an exercise in cultural displacement: "he didn't want to go home on the weekends, to go with them to *pujos* and Bengali parties, to remain unquestionably in their world." Yet as Lahiri herself pointed out, there is a definite universality to the process of finding one's place in the world. Of course as most children of immigrants do, Gogol inhabits two worlds, often comparing or pitting one against the other. In one such telling passage in *The Namesake*, Gogol contrasts the vacation experiences of his girlfriend Maxine's against his own as a child. A secluded vacation destination like the one Maxine's parents return to year after year would have been out of the question for his own parents, Gogol observes correctly, "They would have felt lonely in this setting, remarking that they were the only Indians."

Instead Gogol remembers summer vacations in rented vans visiting Toronto or Atlanta or Chicago places where his parents had "other Bengali friends."

The novel is an evocative and deeply felt portrayal of family life and the complexity of relationships, the difficult process of trying to assimilate into a new culture and maintain their own cultural connections and identity. This poignant treatment of the immigrant experience is a rich, stimulating fusion of authentic emotion, ironic observation, and revealing details. The novel is about misplaced homelands, about misunderstandings between generations, about the pain and pining of an immigrant, about family values and about an individual who learns from a series of engaging events and conversations the significance of everything he considered meaningless and perhaps, foreign. *Namesake* is a novel that is brilliant in the description of typical immigrant Bengali families, and does a laudable job in capturing the essential conflicts within and among the family members of immigrant families.

REFERENCES

Jhumpa Lahiri—Wikipedia, the free encyclopedia.

Jhumpa Lahiri Summary—References, Selvaduarai, Shyam (ed.) "Jhumpa Lahiri: This Blessed House".

VG: Artist Biography: Jhumpa Lahiri.

SAWNET: Bookshelf: Jhumpa Lahiri.

Jhumpa Lahiri: *The Namesake*: Book Review.

2007 Seattle Reads *The Namesake* by Jhumpa Lahiri—A conversation with Jhumpa Lahiri.

A Busse Reading Guide for *The Namesake* by Jhumpa Lahiri—NPR's Melissa Block interview on "All Things Considered".

Bookreporter.com—Author Profile: Jhumpa Lahiri.

Re-writing the Myth: Romantic Love in Margaret Drabble's *The Waterfall*

13

Ranu Uniyal

Simone de Beauvoir reflects that woman's "otherly" position, that is, her status as the other in society is primarily a constructed notion and has been correlated to the myth of romantic love. It is in romantic love that a woman seeks to build a landscape of desire. She is ready to enter this landscape with little hesitation and having entered she desires neither freedom nor separation: "Only in love can woman harmoniously reconcile her eroticism and her narcissism" (de Beauvoir, 1975: 657).

For a "woman in love" the sole objective is to merge her identity with that of her beloved and she does this by complete submission. Her love is tinged with mysticism. She derives pleasure in the thought of submersion:

> ...with closed eyes anonymous, lost, she feels as if borne by waves, swept away in a storm, shrouded in darkness: darkness of the flesh, of the womb, of the grave.
>
> (de Beauvoir, 1975: 658)

In *The Waterfall*, Jane Gray writes her story of passion and survival. She looks at love, a "natural disaster", in a serio-comic manner. Love is marked with upheavals and remarkable changes in Jane. At the beginning of the novel we see her alone in childbirth, in a "cold empty house" (W 8) unwilling to set herself "against fate" (W 7). It appears from her account that marriage to Malcolm failed to fill the internal void and she, like a "lonely virgin in her personage" (W 84), welcomes James, "the Holy Ghost". And it is "through him...being is transmuted into worth (de Beauvoir, 1975: 659). At the end of her story Jane

Gray asserts that love has changed her. She acknowledges: "James changed me beyond recognition" (W 228). She is delighted that she, who had been "a disaster area", has now blossomed into a "new landscape" created by love and desire (W 228, 229).

The novel is set against the background of formulaic conventions of romantic love. Nineteenth-century novels by women provide a constant parallel to the modern romance and Margaret Drabble gives an ironic twist to the classic plot in her story. Unlike the medieval concept of courtly love, the romance plot was treated with a genteel ambiguity in the nineteenth-century romances. It worked towards respectability, aimed for marriage. Where it did not succeed it ended in death. And Drabble subverts the aim and the conclusion of the romance plot. *The Waterfall* does not aim for marriage nor does it end in death. It ends in self-awakening of the female protagonist. As a strategic discourse it becomes a restructuring of male sexuality and sexual relations in female terms. Woman does not remain an attendant, or a passive recipient in the story. She manoeuvres the course of the romance plot with self-awareness and playful open-endedness.

Published in 1969, *The Waterfall* echoes some of the values of its time. The common catch-phrase of the sixties "You've never had it so good" signified a dramatic change in the perceptions of the people. After the post-war austerity, Britain entered a period of golden optimism; marked with an increasing prosperity, the rapidly growing middle class foretold a change in attitude. Larkin concedes the sixties as a period of drastic change:

> ...And every life became
> A brilliant breaking of the bank,
> A quite unlosable game.
>
> So life was never better than
> In nineteen sixty-three. (Larkin, 1974:34)

Drabble is aware that in an atmosphere of sexual and social liberation romantic love too would have to be treated differently. Unlike nineteenth-century romances like *Jane Eyre* or *Villette* or even perhaps *The Mill on the Floss*, Drabble's *The Waterfall* begins with childbirth and her heroine is neither unmarried nor a virgin. For a late twentieth-century woman, childbirth is not a restriction, it does not call for a closure but opens "new course" and furnishes the traditional romance plot with an unconventional perspective.

In the opening chapter an underwater world is reconstructed and here Jane Gray waits like a "victim". What we see emerging, then, is not merely a movement from darkness into light, not just a birth of a child but a landscape of desire, of birth and of love. The warmth ensuing from childbirth is in sharp contrast to the snow outside. Inside she could "feel the blood flowing from her into the white moist sheets" (W 9). From a state of absolute nothingness which is probably marked with a desire for salvation, the birth of her baby brings with it a prospect of equanimity:

> The colours of the scene affected Jane profoundly: they were the violent colours of birth, but they were resolved into silence, into a kind of harmony. (W 10)

Outside is the external landscape, from which Jane is excluded by her confinement. She can only see it through "the uncurtained window" (W 9). The falling of the snow is not just an externally visible phenomenon but is symptomatic of the change in Jane Gray's life. It is the blank surface on which her new future will be written. It corresponds with the landscape of birth. The woman's body in "suspension" (W 9) is surprisingly calm after delivery. The "cold and empty house" (W 8) wherein she lies "empty, solitary, neglected, cold" (W 8) is in effect, an explicit mirror of her inward self. The bloodied sheets and the "warm and sodden" newspaper create another visible landscape within the confines of the room. The blue walls, the red glowing fire, the white towels, a yellow pudding bowl, and the sight of the dozing black mid-wife, seemingly create an interior landscape of colour, life and maternity, which subsequently brings the "victim" out of her self-imposed exile. And in it the figure of Jane Gray becomes both a participant and an observer. We shall see that the red and white and blue colours of birth are adequately colours of passion and reprieve in *The Waterfall* and it is in this atmosphere that Jane Gray commits herself to "waiting" (W 37). And it is these female colours of birth that seduce James, invoke in him a desire for Jane. From a loveless state of being she is transposed into a world of harmony and happiness. In other words, the drowning protagonist however "unwilling" to save herself realizes after delivery that she is intact and whole and desired. What had earlier been a state of indifference is now marked with a state of expectation. The changes in her physical circumstances signify a change in her mental attitude. There follows a close connection between the release of the baby and that of the emotions.

The opening of *Jane Eyre* reveals some striking similarities to *The Waterfall*. The "cold winter wind" and the "penetrating" rain outside is in sharp correlation to the world inside where "the chidings of Bessie" and the sharp "penetrating" glances of her three cousins make Jane as much a loner as Jane Gray in labour. In one of her stormy encounters with Aunt Reed she is accused of being "passionate". Unloved and isolated, the orphan Jane Eyre receives warmth as an adult in Rochester's house. She waits for affection, for love and is rewarded with it only at the end of the novel.

In the nineteenth-century portrayal of romantic love in George Eliot and Charlotte Bronte, one reads landscape as a major connecting device between the heroine's outer and inner worlds. It is for them an expression of moods and anxieties, of pleasures lost and repressed. Drabble asserts how after having been "exiled from the landscapes of her youth" (LL 83), Eliot attempted to enact and exorcize her relationship with her estranged brother Isaac: "...the tragic drama of *The Mill on the Floss*, gathers around remembered place" (LL 83). The Red Deeps and Maggie's "kinship with the grand scotch firs" represents the woman's desire to connect herself with what is prohibited. Ellen Moers points out that:

> Guilty pleasure and renunciation are two of the themes with which female writers set off the landscape of female self-indulgence; others are ecstasy, even of a mystical nature; and freedom, and independent assertion, and fear. (Moers, 1986: 254)

Maggie's fascination for the Red Deeps and her self-consuming guilt over pleasure forms the very texture of the novel. She is so filled with ideas of renunciation that she fails to respond to her own desires and needs. Instead of saying "yes" to temptations, she prefers to die. Maggie has wanted to retain her fascination for the world of innocent childhood and thus she aspires towards the company and love of her family. In order to be accepted by them she forces herself into self-denial. Maggie's story highlights a woman's failure to adjust in a world of mature passions. *The Mill on the Floss* uses landscape as a trope for feminine desire. Neither love nor friendship can save Maggie Tulliver. What saves her from becoming an anti-heroine is her death. She is redeemed by her death. It is this situation that is viewed rather mockingly by Jane Gray in *The Waterfall*:

> She drifted off down the river with him, abandoning herself to the water, but in the end she lost him.... Maggie Tulliver never slept with her man: she did all the damage there was to be done, to Lucy, to herself, to the two men who loved her, and then like a woman of another age, she refrained. (W 153)

To Jane Gray, Maggie's "no" is least satisfying. Jane Gray, the twentieth-century woman, believes there is less gained and much lost if one refrains from one's most urgent passions and desires. In writing her own story she is conscious that:

> We drown in the first chapter. I worry about the sexual doom of womanhood, its sad inheritance. (W 153-154)

Drabble parallels the Victorian situation with that of the twentieth century. Maggie suffers actual death by drowning. In an age of moral prudery Eliot's heroine has no choice but to die. Death alone can save her from further humiliation. Drabble's Jane Gray suggests that the twentieth-century woman has no such compunctions; although she does not suffer physical death, being a woman she is unable to avoid "the sexual doom" which is perhaps manifested in her desire for sexual salvation. The modern woman gives way to Eros and drowns in the first chapter. Desire carries a legacy of "sad inheritance" (W 154). It is exacting. Being a woman one ends up inheriting "thrombosis or neurosis" (W 239). But she is able to comfort herself with the little she has gained by loving, by experiencing sexual gratification (which was unacknowledged by the Victorian heroine). And then she acknowledges her concern:

> How can love preserve itself in death?...What do the dead care for fidelity? It is the living who need to keep it, for their own sake, for the dignity of their passion, for the lost value of what they risked for it. (W 201)

Conscious of the temporality of romantic passion Drabble's Jane feels that she is no longer compelled to follow the fate of her literary sisters. Guilt does not force her to renounce her passion like Maggie Tulliver. Unlike Charlotte Bronte, who uses the external landscape imagery to accommodate her violent and intrusive emotions, we see the body itself becoming a landscape of desire for selfhood in this case. It is passion that changes her "beyond recognition" (W 228). Sexual fulfilment requires an object to be desired and it is James' love that can fill this void in Jane. He is an object with multiple functions. In him, Jane sees not only her protector but also her lover, mother, child and her saviour.

The depiction of the body as landscape corroborates the cycle of change, and cannot be comprehended in isolation. As a landscape of desire, the body is subject to upheavals, convulsions, guilt and passions. In Jane Gray, it wrenches and tears, splits and wears and at the close of the novel subsides into a desire to set "her own house in order" (W 225). Once the body, as a parched landscape, desiring love and fulfilment, ceases to preoccupy the central protagonist, she directs her focus outwards. She takes charge of the social world.

Like Jane Eyre, the protagonist Jane Gray uses her creative energy. One expresses herself in painting, the other in poetry and fiction. The drawings of Jane Eyre are the most intense expression of her repressed self. The "spiritual eye" (JE 126) is aware of the split between her inner and outer world. Faced with rejection at the hands of the outside world, she can derive an inner strength and "one of the keenest pleasures" (JE 127) in drawing. The natural imagery of "the swollen sea", the "strange sea birds" and hair like "a beamless cloud torn by storm or by electric travail" (JE 126) are all significant signs of her longing for autonomy. Her inner restlessness and agony, her desire for love and friendship can find no outlet but in her "elfish", "peculiar" and "solemn" (JE 127) drawings. Tormented by fear of loneliness and unrequited love she restructures "the spiritual eye" (JE 126) and is able to maintain her outward calm and sanity. Charlotte Bronte's Jane Eyre refuses to enter into bigamy and accepts Rochester only after he is widowed. Before making her fall into a confirmed social order Charlotte Bronte reverses the balance of that order. Power, both physical and economic, is transferred into the hands of its female protagonist. Rochester both blind and maimed, however, is the one who pays the price for love while Jane without losing her femininity becomes his caretaker. If romantic love is about transcendence, then *Jane Eyre* is certainly about transcendence both at a spiritual and socio-economic level.

The Jane Eyre story does not, however, end with Charlotte Bronte. Its versions are being repeated and restructured in twentieth-century fiction. Daphne du Maurier's *Rebecca* is one such writing. Unlike the hero Maxim, its heroine is inconspicuous and single. She is without a name. And the rival woman is portrayed as vicious and mad like Rochester's Bertha. The twentieth-century romance story retains the "classic" romance structure by repeatedly readjusting power relations.

The Waterfall does not have a "neat" or "a feminine ending" like *Jane Eyre*. It does not end in the marriage of the two lovers. Conscious of the fate of Jane Eyre, Jane Gray deliberately chooses a different ending. She sees a possibility of death, or that of a permanent handicap, but is neither attracted nor compelled to live it. She chooses transcendence not at the cost of physical well-being but on her own terms. She dwells on the possibility:

> Or I could have maimed James so badly, in this narrative that I would have been allowed to have him, as Jane Eyre had her blinded Rochester. But I hadn't the heart to do it, I loved him too much. (W 231)

Her fate was different and "Nothing like what Jane Eyre had to put up with" (W 231). James recovers from his accident and in the ambiguous interplay of narrative Jane Gray admits that her love would not let him be "maimed" or "blinded". She would have him whole. Unlike the classic romance story *Jane Eyre*, the lover is saved from being handicapped in *The Waterfall*. But a price is to be paid and in the words of Jane Gray: "The price of his restoration was his loss" (W 223). As we read the story of Jane's love, we are led to believe that love despite its not so "neat" ending does follow a "text book pattern of relationship" (W 232), that is, it derives strength from its predecessor romance plots.

As suggested earlier, the female body, as in a text, maps out a landscape of desire and establishes on its own terms a unique "pattern of relationship" (W 232) in *The Waterfall*. Conscious that it is impossible to write a conventional romance in the present times where love itself has become a commodity, Drabble chooses to defy it with comic deception. Conscious of living in an age where romantic love has disseminated into popular fiction Drabble has no intention of treating it as tragic. She is playing with the idea of *liebestod*. Unlike the classic romance Jane Gray's story does not end in tragic dispute. Perhaps she is aware that the dull, monotonous reality of her everyday existence can be made bearable in writing. Writing the romance gives life a flavour and a meaning, and it not only saves her from receding into unimaginable despair, but the imagination of her mind, nourishes and nurtures her back to normal life.

By being able to write her fantasy, Jane Gray is able to absolve herself from silence and suffering, from isolation and emptiness. It is the fantastic that enables her to restore her physical and mental health. It provides her with a new lease of life and through it she is able to recognize herself. It is the fantastic that appeals to Jane the story-teller. Further, Jane Gray not only justifies her plunge into adultery but sees it as a "necessity".

E.C. Rose reads it not as a passionate love story but as "a novel about how to 'tell' that affair". She sees Jane Gray as "a woman struggling...to find a voice with which to speak her own experience" (Rose, 1988: 88). From being the figure in a landscape she writes and creates a landscape of her dreams, she becomes a writer of landscape. And in doing so Drabble has managed to subvert the dominant "classic" discourse:

> She assaults patriarchal thinking on the most fundamental terms, in the domain of discourse, by suggesting that word does not have power-over[sic], that language is powerless to control or meaningfully to structure reality. (Rose, 1988: 88)

The Waterfall is not only about love but also about being in love. It is not only about having an affair but is also a "writing" of that passion. Using Angela Leighton's expression, Jane Gray, the novelist and the poet, prefers "not waiting but writing" (Leighton: 1989: 1). She not only imagines but creates. She lives her affair in writing. "But instead, I wrote about love" (W 227). And in doing so she becomes a woman who "write(s) herself" (Cixous, 1976: 875). It could be argued that romantic love is not without its object in *The Waterfall* But it is increasingly difficult to assess the desired goal, for it is certainly not marriage, it could however be "writing". It further explores the dilemma of a modern writer. Drabble's *Jane Gray* joins the debate on romantic love. Does one give in completely to the obsessive passion or stay away from it and live with it as a construct of the mind? As in *Villette* where the ambiguous ending of the text is inexplicit about Lucy's position, Jane Gray too fluctuates between the various possible endings. She finally decides to let things move in a positive direction. For her love is not an end in itself, she makes it permanent by shifting it to the world of poems in print. Written word takes precedence over felt emotion. Drabble's pragmatic approach to life leaves *The Waterfall* with its unorthodox ending, that is without a closing. She, in the words of Lorna Irvine, is "for affirmation rather than denial, for continuance rather than ending" (Irvine, in E.C. Rose, 1985: 74).

The Waterfall is suggestive of a change in feminine subject position. As a child Jane had succumbed to silence while her heart craved to speak. Unable to release her aggressive eroticism in early years, Jane continues to hold on to her repressed desires. Marriage to Malcolm forces her into deep closure and pushes her to the world of "waiting". What is ironical is that Jane reviews her own situation and concludes that her need for James was borne out of "necessity". She was offered a loan which she accepted without shame or regret:

> I accepted it, being more interested in possession than in the terms of possession. (W 219)

She simply accepted the loan without counting, weighing, judging or questioning the terms involved in such a transition. Seemingly the tenancy of love is without a bargain. It is by mutual consent.

The feminization of its male protagonist is perceived as one of the chief features of the novel. The male lover becomes feminized and seeks to fulfil the infantile longing for nurturance in *Jane Gray*. The birth of the baby and falling of the snow prepare the ground for the woman's deliverance. While James' entry into the maternal realm ensures that no such censorship is required for romance to flourish in modern times, in fact it flourishes in the most unlikely landscape. It chooses to be different. In this case it is promoted in the "most dangerous of places" (W 44), it is the bed where the woman is lying all covered in blood, in sweat and milk after the birth of the baby. Cut off from the outside world by snow and her situation, Jane Gray experiences multiple orgasm through the sexual juices (blood and milk), the amniotic fluid flowing through her body. One of the most striking aspect of their relationship is that James not only becomes her saviour but claims to be saved by her:

> "I'd have died," he said, "I'd have died if you'd told me I had to go and sleep in that child's bed, by myself. I wanted to be here so much". (W 35)

He has entered the predominantly female enclave and under his care she becomes more herself. The self becomes a landscape prone to changes both personal and historical. By looking after her, the mother in childbirth, James not only becomes her protector but also defies the male order by mothering her. He becomes her mother. As a critique of motherhood *The Waterfall* explores a different terrain. In her account of Object Relations theory Chodorow claims that much of one's sexuality is structured in the formative years of childhood. In a child "Internalization is mediated by fantasy and by conflict" (Chodorow, 1978: 50). In *Jane Gray*, the process of growth is surprisingly delayed. Possibly, she had failed to experience a lasting symbiosis in infancy and this desire remained latent in her even though she had become a mother. Without surprise, she continues to be a child of the imaginary. Romantic love alone can save her from lasting infancy. Being in love is a return to the womb. Before she can become a fully mature and integrated mother she needs to be reborn herself. Jane needs to go back into the maternal element and paradoxically James provides her with such a recovery. Romantic love moves her to the world of personal and social obligations, where as an adult she learns to accept division, fragmentation, responsibility and is reconciled to childhood. The sinking, drowning, dying drive gives way to the living instinct in her. Peculiarly so, romantic love in Jane Gray's case does not precede death. Like a newborn infant who is "totally dependent on parental care until it can develop adaptive capacities" (Chodorow, 1978: 58), Jane Gray too becomes James' child. In childbirth "she committed herself to waiting" (W 37).

> "You're my prisoner, here, in this bed," he said, "but if you're good and wait quietly, I'll look after you, I'll bring you meals, and books to read, and cups of tea". (W 37)
> (emphasis mine)

"This bed" alone can fulfil James' desire for sexual love. It is "this bed" where he hopes to imprison her and then have her. The bed becomes an interesting mediator between the two characters. It serves to bring them together. And one recognizes in James' assertion not only a desire to serve but be rewarded in love. He is struck by the beauty of the maternal body:

> It's so lovely here, it's like heaven in this room...I couldn't stay away, all the time I wasn't here I was thinking of you and of how warm it must be in that bed, and of how near I could be if you would let me, of how you might even let me touch you...when I sat there in that chair, the first time, and watched you fall asleep, I felt—I don't know, I felt as though you were mine. (W 36)

In James is a note of urgency. He provides her with maternal care and in the process wishes to bridge all distances between him and her. He too, is the infant who wishes to be reborn. There is, however, a reversal of roles here. It is James and not Jane, who decides to be at the beck and call of the other. He is her caretaker. Once in bed with him Jane is astonished to see a thawing of her emotions. James has succeeded in relieving her from a state of indifference, salvaged her destiny. He has inspired in her a desire for sexual gratification. "That a desire so primitive could flow through her, unobstructed, like milk, astonished her" (W 45).

Using the female body as a metaphor of fruition and fulfilment Drabble charts out a landscape which is essentially feminine:

> Who would have thought he would ever take such pains to make good in me the new courses, the new ways, the new landscapes? I spoke of violence and convulsions, but he made the new earth grow, he made it blossom. (W 229)

These are the words of a woman whose discovery of love leaves her spell-bound. Romantic love not only enlivens the cold arid zones of her virgin mind but also opens up "new courses" and makes "the new earth" blossom. It is the nature of desire itself that undergoes a rapid change and like a mother's milk flows "unobstructed". Struck with the forces of her tumultuous desire the female body itself becomes a retinue of changes both physical and emotional.

Love becomes what de Rougement calls an experience of a lifetime that not only alters but also enriches "it with the unexpected...with enjoyment ever more violent and gratifying" (de Rougement, 1983: 282). For we also see Jane developing certain "adaptive capacities" (Chodorow, 1978: 58). At the end of the narrative one does not read her situation as that of a helpless infant. Having tasted love she is more relaxed, self-assured, and decides to settle herself amidst "shining paint work and well swept floors" (W 232). The desire for the romantic sublime and the return to the imaginary has been fulfilled, giving way to "new-found desires to see my poems in print" (W 232).

Romantic love—pre-social, pre-interpersonal, bisexual, narcissistic, a struggle between Eros and death—is, for a man, a return to his earliest self, a search for the self-completion that, on entering the world of being only a man, was taken from him. Male romantic love looks backwards, or if it looks forward, it looks only to death—which is itself a return to the inert from which we came.... The romantic love of women looks forward, forward to marriage (Mitchell, 1984: 113-114).

James and Jane's story explodes this myth of romantic love. Like Jane Eyre, the female protagonist does not look forward to marriage nor does exist merely as an idea. Physical and emotional boundaries have been traversed in modern love and it elicits a desire to look forward to life. She does look backward and writes about this romantic fallacy allowing her the comfort that by doing so she can purge herself from guilt and self-pity.

The visit to Goredale Scar and the sight of the waterfall establishes the terms of the narrative. The sexual imagery of the waterfall is highly suggestive "a lovely organic balance of shapes and curves, a wildness contained within a bodily limit" (W 236), and is juxtaposed with Jane's bodily experiences. *The Waterfall* becomes a metaphor for continuity. It leads from somewhere to somewhere and is not an end in itself. And like it, romantic love pursues a similar course, refusing to remain still. Her desire is a wildness "within bodily limit" and the waterfall in flow is both Jane and her congress with James and her need to write. The natural waterfall with its "wildness" refuses to accept closure. Just as the waterfall leaping down from the rocks flows unrestricted and formulates its own "curves and shapes", romantic love desires to be free and looks forward to self-abandonment. Jane Gray having once traversed the enforced enclosure seeks "deliverance" like the waterfall. It could however, be argued that she can do so only within bounds. She chooses to become "the object of the tale" (Mitchell, 1984: 114) and writes her own romance. The fact that she can write her affair intensifies the case that writing is a choice that enables her to understand the erotic nature of her subjectivity. She seems to understand that there is no point wallowing in self-pity or self-justification. It is interesting to hear her say "He changed me forever and I am now what he made" (W 229). We see next, that there is price to be paid for Eros. However, the modern woman does not pay it in physical death as did Maggie of *The Mill on the Floss*. Jane develops thrombosis and has to stop taking contraceptive pills.

Accident is the necessary impediment in the text. It strikes us as inevitable denouement and reveals "the futility of human effort against the power that holds us" (W 185). It is James' accident that saves Jane. Drabble finds fate and character irreconcilable and her novels attempt to draw "a balance between the two":

> I believe in the possibility of accident because anyone with any common sense must believe in accident. I suppose I'm trying to do what one has to do in life, to reconcile the importance of fate, the destiny, the character, and the accidents that hit you on the way (Preussner, 1980: 567).

The sense of "possibility" is a significant feature in Drabble's fiction. Though confined within her women explore the nature of possibilities. Jane Gray has often been accused of being a failure, of not being able to save herself:

> Drabble fails, however to make Jane's salvation through sexual passion compelling or convincing, let alone attractive. Jane remains almost pathologically helpless and cloyingly dependent on James. (Korenman,. 1980: 63)

This recalls Hardin's interview and Drabble's account of Jane as "feeble"—"the dottiest, the nearest to madness, of all the characters" (Hardin, 1973: 294,290). Joan Korenman sees Drabble as reaching an "impasse". What is intriguing to the reader is the fact that Jane understands the split in her personality. The imagery of the plant on her window-sill echoes the state of Jane's being, "leafless, withered, unwatered twig" with "faint green horseshoe scars on its brown stem that proved some hidden life" (W 41). The plant on the window-sill survives despite neglect. She resembles the neglected twig, and is disposed to live, to fight. Inertia is a temporary phase, for we are led to believe that Jane has not only overcome her impasse but having discovered "some hidden life" she strives to maintain it. It could also be argued that inertia is a necessary phase for her to be reborn.

As a poet, a novelist, a wife, a mother and also a lover she carries within her the divided core of feminine subjectivity. She lives in more than one world. She receives nurturance from more than one source. That is what makes her story so complex and poly-vocal. Her fate is as undecided as some of her Victorian sisters. Yet, she is unquestionably different from them. *The Waterfall* as a modern love story can also be read as an exercise in literary self-consciousness. It displays an overwhelming force of literary history. There is a constant underplaying of the plot, situation and names. Drabble is paying tribute to the mother of the story, Charlotte Bronte. But love does not remain a wicked, inaccessible passion. Like Lucy Snowe, she has lived for long with the idea of romantic love in her mind; unlike Jane Eyre who seeks consummation in marriage Jane Gray cared not what she "lost in the future, so long as the present could be mine" (W 154). If death by drowning was Maggie Tulliver's fate then love in drowning (perhaps living in drowning) is Jane Gray's.

In *The Waterfall*, Drabble explores the landscape of desire through the recurring image of the water. Throughout the narrative, the protagonist and the writer Jane Gray seems to be confounded with the thought of death by drowning. As she listens to James she is:

> Hopelessly moved by his willing blind suicidal dive into such deep waters: the waters closed over their heads, and they lay there, submerged, the cold dry land of non-loving abandoned, out of sight, so suddenly and so completely out of sight. (W 36-37)

James' proposal takes her by surprise. She knows that she would respond to his appeal for love, for she herself is much in need of it. The process of healing has started:

> Ah, perfect love. For these reasons, was it, that I lay there drowned was it, drowned or stranded, waiting for him, waiting to die and drown there, in the oceans of our flowing bodies, in the white sea of that strange familiar bed. (W 67)

Once again, the natural imagery of the "sea" structures the nature of sexual passion. It emphasises the link between life and death. We notice further, that the protagonist and writer is equally conscious of the symbol of body as landscape prone to disaster and how it differs from a natural disaster. Passion is equated with violence, with destruction. But unlike the destruction of the world which can be ascribed to outside forces and influences, to a universe which is "hostile, ill-ordered", human bodies cannot choose forces outside themselves: "The violence is us: is me" (W 152).

> The meaningless violence of the world—the Lisbon earthquake, the Titanic, Aberfan-...but at least these disasters are external, and can be ascribed to a hostile, ill-ordered universe: not so the violence of our own bodies, as unwilled, as fore-ordained, as the sliding of mountains, the uprooting of trees, the tidal waves of the sea. (W 152)

She takes the blame on herself. It is she and James who have willed such a disaster. They had waited. They had desired and longed for it. And yet, as we see her assessing her situation, her story, our own understanding of it gets more and more complex. For is it not Jane who claims that her entry into the landscape of desire alone could have saved her? She deemed it a necessity. Desperate as she was, she "had not cared who should drown, so long as I [she] should reach the land (W 152). The fluidity and the incommensurability of the sea is in contrast with the solid assurance and the safety of the land. One enriches the body, the other protects the mind. One provides sustenance, the other imagination. If one is foreign, the other is familiar. In addition, the return to the land is seen by the protagonist as a sign of resurrection. Only drowning woman can hope for resurrection. She has to undergo the overwhelming experience of death by drowning to be able to appreciate the moment of salvation:

> ...James and I, parched and starving: and we saw love as the miraged oasis, shivering on the dusty horizon in all the glamour of hallucination: blue water, green fronds and foliage breaking from the dry earth. Like deluded travellers we had carefully approached, hardly able to trust the image's persistence, afraid that it would fade into yet more dry acres as we drew nearer: believing ourselves blinded by our own desires.... (W 208-209)

This is a language steeped in desire. This is, after all, a landscape dealing with desire. The metaphor of the land becomes central to the metaphor of desire. It speaks of the figure in search of a landscape which would satisfy their "parched and starving" bodies. They have been offered a landscape of love and the interaction between love and desire is holistic and real. It is not a mirage. It exists. The water is, Jane Gray asserts, sweet and the sea inexhaustible. Beyond it lie patches of green, of life and living. In short, love that was seen as a "miraged oasis" is real as an experience. Love alone can save body from further disintegration.

Unlike the actual "sea" the literary-ness of passion can be explored. Its unboundedness and sublimity is both a face-saving device and an act of deliverance. "...I wrote about love" (W 227), says Jane Gray further complicating the task of the reader. Is it the love that she had experienced as a woman or endeavoured to create as a writer? Is she attempting to live her desire for love in writing? Is it simply "some Brussels of the mind"? The "dusty Victorian house, the fast car, the race tracks, the garages, the wide bed" suggest simultaneously the desired life, that is James, and the life which she can never have, for "it was some foreign country to me" (W 84), it was a life beyond her reach, since he is already married to her cousin and has children, and it can only be reached through writing. The "creation of the woman in love" is viewed as "an enterprise of heroinism" by Moers (Moers, 1986: 165). She argues that the "modern adultery novel has simply been a compelling vehicle for heroinism" (Moers, 1986: 155). Whatever Drabble's objective might be writing of love is certainly more convincing than waiting. "Merely waiting" would not have been a suitable recourse to salvation in Jane Gray's case. She looks at Charlotte Bronte:

> Which was Charlotte Bronte's man, the one she created and wept for and longed for, or the poor curate that had her and killed her, her sexual measure, her sexual match? (W 84)

Drawing the personal from the fictional or vice-versa Jane Gray seeks to question and create "some Brussels of the mind" (W 84). Supposedly, in recreating the love of her life in *Villette*,

Charlotte Bronte had managed to voice the experience of her mind. Brussels continues to reflect a yearning for love and fulfilment. Although Jane Gray tries to make her position clear (she asserts the success of her passion and possession of James) one is as unsure of modern love, one is unable to pin-point which is Jane's man, the James she wept and longed to have an affair with, a perfect romance, or the ordinary James she met in the vicinity of her room? Is it the real James, her cousin Lucy's husband that she desired and had for herself, or is it the hero of her mind that she wished to fall for and created in fiction to salvage her mind, fulfil her desire of him? Is he as foreign and distant and unavailable to her as was Charlotte Bronte's hero of the mind, or the man she fell in love with in the city of Brussels? Or is he a mediation between the two, that is a literary go-between? It could be argued that *The Waterfall* is a mediation between real love and the consciousness of writing about love. Drabble problematizes the situation of being romantically caught up in love. The near death of James is suggestive of the image that is killed in the car crash. It brings with it a destruction of the fantasy.

In this landscape of desire, which is of her making, Jane Gray functions as a body and a mind, a woman and a writer? She is both the receiver and the received. And this is achieved through romantic love outside marriage, outside convention. A dangerous yet a tempting proposition is available to the modern woman in love. Like the game of cards whence:

> the cards fell, in an amazing careful rhythm, interleaving, dovetailing, one by one, joining and melting as they fell into one pack. (W 149)

The game of the cards is also known as the game of the waterfall. Its unpredictability is its charm and the success its reward. Modern romantic love is equated with the game and carries a similar sense of risk and challenge. It can either be a coup de grace or a coup d'e'tat. Explaining the intricate nature of this delicate game, James says to Jane "One can't take these risks too early in a relationship, you know" (W 149). But Jane and James take the plunge and surprisingly "It worked". The game of cards playfully suggests the erotic undertones of love. And with Jane one is left wondering whether love is love or simply a game? Using de Rougement's words does it consist of silence or speech? Is it that having once become a desire it becomes "the dialogue of bodies":

> There are only two philosophies: that of the desire and that of the act...Desire makes us divine; the act makes us human. (de Rougement, 1976: 41-42)

Desire and act are simultaneously represented as human and preserved as divine in "writing" in *The Waterfall.* If one is to look at it as a "Brussels of the mind where I trembled and sighed for my desires" (W 84), the story reveals an attempt by Jane Gray to recapitulate the experience of gratification in love through the narrative.

Repudiating de Rougement's concept of romantic love as purely mystical, Mitchell sees "narcissism and bisexuality" as erotic states. Drawing on Freud's ideas who later saw Eros and the death drive as contradictory to each other she sees Eros and death drive "intertwined" in romantic love:

> Romantic love is about the self, it is erotic, but does not have a sexual object that it is ultimately different from itself. (Mitchell, 1982: 111)

Romantic love accordingly is a desire for wholeness, completion. In the character of Jane Gray, Drabble perceives and articulates such a desire. Both Jane and James suffer from "internal incompleteness" (Mitchell, 1984: 112) and seek their lost halves in each other. "She was his offspring, as he, lying there between her legs, had been hers" (W 151). Equally significant is the recovery once the "search for self" (Michell, 1984: 114) is over; Jane's discovery of love ends neither in bondage nor in conflict. Its apotheosis is neither death nor marriage. The state of sexual bliss has, in consequence, given way to "new-found desires to my poem in print" (W 232). Apparently such a love has encouraged woman to recognize and accept her writerly position without creating a loss of individuality. It has enriched and inspired her.

If "to love is to live" then Jane Gray's passionate affair has certainly pulled her out of enforced confinement and enabled her to welcome both poetry and children, cleanliness and a circle of literary friends in her orbit.

The shifting of the I / She voice creates a diffusion of tone in the course of the narrative. The "broken and fragmented piece" (W 46) is how Jane sees the entire event. "Lies, lies, it's all lies. A pack of lies" (W 84) says the first person. Jane Gray sees the telling of the story as an act of misrepresentation where the truth fails to appear on paper, it is beyond it. There are constant fluctuating tones: "And yet I haven't lied. I've merely omitted: merely, professionally, edited" (W 46).

We all know that we cannot take Jane at her word. The unreliable narrative voice has been deliberately used in the text to highlight the chasm between fiction and reality. Being a writer puts Jane at liberty to add to or subtract from her own story. She edits, cuts down unnecessary details, and in the process subsumes the tragic bit of her story into the comic. Like "Scotch and Dust" (W 238) that get mixed up in the dark of the hotel leaving an unpleasant taste in the mouth, Drabble's Jane (despite her denial of it) is aware that once initial sexual euphoria is gone she will be haunted "by the grotesquely false position" (W 220), she is in:

> Perhaps love can't survive a context: perhaps it dies if it admits the outside world, or crumbles to dust at the breath of coarser air. But that air is the real air... And yet love has a reality, a quotidian reality. (W 84-85)

In her appraisal of love, Jane Gray reaches an understanding of the emotion. The struggle between her desire for love and her acceptance of it has left her with an awareness that it is fragile. Love cannot last. And yet, she admits the experience of it is infused with something real. It might suffer at the hands of the outside world, but the creative imagination keeps it alive. The "Scotch and dust" (W 238) affair stresses the protagonist's "adaptive capacity" to laugh at her stupidities however painful and damaging they might be. Clever though she may be in masking her true feelings, Jane Gray reveals herself in slips and digressions. While the third-person narrative explains the course of romantic love that was hampered by rejection in childhood and physical violence in adulthood, the first-person narrative appraises the entire situation with a detached propensity: "the feeling that nothing at all is expected of me: I am merely a woman, merely an attendant woman" (W 75).

Prominent among it is her frustration in marriage. In choosing to love and write about love Jane Gray makes it clear that she desires not to be an attendant. In love she is attended and does not attend. A contrast is visible in *Jane Eyre*. The use of multiple narratives shows a constant shift from "lyrical romanticism to caustic cynicism" (Creighton, 1985: 56).

Drabble's use of multiple voice triggers off a series of responses. On one hand Jane's affair can be read as a satiric comment on the whole of the sixties where sexual promiscuity stands for liberation. And on the other, it can be read as a "textbook pattern" (W 232) where love itself is a

> Revealing perspective on Drabble's technique. (Fox-Genovese, 1979: 244)

As an "artist in concealment and evasion [Jane Gray] had always believed that her passions, if revealed, would in some way scorch and blister and damage their object" (*W* 39). In this case James. She decides to protect her artistic image by talking about love in writing. As for the female image, Jane Gray struggles with it and reconciles to child-care. If one enables her to exploit her creative imagination at its best, the other leads her into the social world.

What seems striking is the way the landscape of the body which constitutes the female self-consciousness gets intertwined with "some Brussels of the mind" (*W* 84), where artistic self-consciousness prevails. The woman and the artist in her is aware of the complexity of the task and seeks to establish a relative code of action. The body becomes the reservoir of intense experiences, as in a natural disaster, it feeds on its own "accoutrements". The mind of the artist with its penetrating gaze sees beyond the eye and strives to create romantic sublime. While the woman experiences, the writer feels, the female waits and the writer writes—a duality is established through the multiple narrative. It not only exposes the split consciousness but also confronts it with an irony based on the knowledge of literary history.

Comparing literature to other discourses Spivak argues:

> In the general discourse of the humanities, there is a sort of search for solutions, whereas in literary discourse there is a playing out of the problem as the solution, if you like. (Spivak, 1988: 77)

It is in this context that one reads *The Waterfall* as "the playing out of the problem". Following Spivak, one agrees that Drabble writes within a "class bound" situation but does manage to fill "the void of the female consciousness with meticulous and helpful articulation" (Spivak, 1988:89). She makes up for this absence by taking into account other aspects of the problem:

> She engages in the microstructural dystopia, the sexual situation in extremis, that begins to seem more and more a part of women's fiction. (Spivak, 1988: 89)

The "micro-macro opposition" is understood with its varied limitation and Drabble's narrative is plotted within this category.

The Following abbreviations have been used for the major texts

W: *The Waterfall*

LL: *A Writer's Britain: Landscape in Literature*

WORKS CITED

The date of first publication, where different, is given in square brackets.

—— (1972). *The Waterfall.* Harmondsworth: Penguin Books, [1969].

—— (1979). *A Writer's Britain: Landscape in Literature.* London: Thames & Hudson.

Abel, Elizabeth (ed) (!979). *Writing and Sexual Difference.* Hemel Hempstead: Harvester Wheatsheaf.

Beards, Virginia K. (1973). "Margaret Drabble: Novels of a Cautious Feminist." *Critique.* 15, 1: 35-47.

Beauvoir, Simone de (1975). *Th~S g4Sex* translated by H.M. Parshley, Harmondsworth: Penguin Books. [1949].

Brontë, Charlotte. (1952). *Villette,* Introduction by May Sinclair, London: J.M. Dent & Sons, [1853].

——(1981). *Jane Eyre.* Oxford: Oxford University Press, [1847]

Brontë, Emily. (1965). *Wuthering Heights.*Harmondsworth: Penguin, [1847].

Chodorow, Nancy J. (1978). *The Reproduction of Mothering.* Berkeley: University of California Press.

——(1989). *Feminism and Psychoanalytic Theory.* New Haven & London: Yale University Press.

Cixous, Hélène. (1976). "The Laugh of the Medusa", translated by Keith Cohen and Paula Cohen, *Signs.* 1,4: 875-93.

——(1981). "Castration or Decapitation?" translated by Annette Kuhn, *Signs* 7, 1:41-55.

Creighton, Joanne V. (1982). "An Interview with Margaret Drabble", in *Dorey Schmidt* (ed.), pp.l8-31.

——(1982a). "The Reader and Modern and Post-modern Fiction." *College Literature.* 9: 216-30.

——(1985) *Margaret Drabble.* London: Methuen.

——(1987) "Sisterly Symbiosis: Margaret Drabble's *The Waterfall* and A.S. Byatt's *The Game", Interdisciplinary Study of Literature.* 20, 1:15-29.

Du Maurier, Daphne. (1975). *Rebecca* London: Pan, [1938].

Eliot, George. (1974). *The Mill on the floss.* Harmondsworth: Penguin, [1860].

Fox-Genovese, Elizabeth. (1979). "The Ambiguities of Female Identity: A Reading of the Novels of Margaret Drabble". *Partisan Review.* 46: 234-48.

Hardin, Nancy S. (1973). "An interview with Margaret Drahble", *Contemporary Literature.* 14, 3: 273-95.

Irvine, Lorna. (1985). "No Sense of an Ending: Drabble's Continuous Fictions", in E.C. Rose (ed.), pp.73-86.

Korenman, Joan (1980). 'The liberation of Margaret Drabble", *Critique.* 21: 61-72.

Larkin, Philip. (1974). "Annus Mirabilis" in *High Windows.* London: Faber & Faber, p.34.

Leighton, Angela. (1989). "Not Waiting but Writing: The Woman Poet and Love", Erasmus *Occasional Paper 5.* Hull: English Department, University of Hull.

Mitchell, Juliet. (1984). "Women: The Longest Revolution" *Essays in Feminism, Literature and Psychoanalysis.* London: Virago.

Moers E. (1986). *Literary Women.* London: The Women's Press, [1976].

Preussner, Dee. (1980). "Talking with Margaret Drabble", *Modern Fiction Studies*. 25:563-77.

Rose, E.C. (1985). *Critical Essays on Margaret Drabble*. Boston, MS: G.K. Hall.

——(1988). "The sexual Politics of Narration, Margaret Drabble's Feminist Fiction (The Ice age, The Middle Ground, The Needle's eye)", *Studies in the Novel*. 20, 1:86-99.

Rougement, Denis De. (1976). *The Growl of Deeper Waters* translated by S. Hazo and B. Lucy, Pittsburgh: University of Pittsburgh Press.

——(1983). *Love in the Western World*. Princeton, NJ: Princeton University Press.

Silver, Brenda R. (1983). "The Reflecting Reader in Villette", in Abel, Hirsch, *Langland* (eds), pp. 90-111.

Spivak, Gayatri Chakravorty. (1988). *In Other Worlds: Essays in Cultural Politics*. New York, London: Routledge.

Third World Women and the Politics of Feminism

14

Anita Singh

Problematics of Nomenclature

The terms 'Third World' and 'Third World Women' are by no means stable categories. Rather, these terms are a locus of contention not only between first world feminism and third world women, but also between third world women themselves within the complex field of postcolonial studies.

Spivak explains the term 'Third World' as initially coined in 1955 by those emerging from the old world order: "the initial attempt in the Bandung conference (1955) to establish a third way—neither with the Eastern nor within the Western bloc—in the world system, in response to the seemingly new world order established after the Second World War, was not accompanied by a commensurate intellectual effort. The only idiom deployed for the nurturing of this nascent Third World in the cultural field belonged then to positions emerging from resistance within the supposedly 'old' world order—anti-imperialism and/or nationalism" (270).

Kum Kum Sangari argues that the term 'Third World' not only designates specific geographical areas, but also imaginary spaces. According to Sangari, "Third World is a term that both signifies and blurs the functioning of an economic, political and imaginary geography able to unite vast differentiated areas of the world into a single underdeveloped terrain" (217). Sangari is critical of the way Third World is used by the West to indiscriminately lump together vastly different places.

Chandra Talpade Mohanty defines the third world geographically: "the nation states of America, the Caribbean, Sub-Sahara Africa, South and South-East Asia, China, South Africa, and Oceania constitute the parameters of the non-European third world. In addition Blacks, Latino, Asian and indigenous peoples in the US, Europe, Australia, some of them have historic links with the geographically defined third worlds, also define themselves as the third world peoples" (5). Cherly Johnson Odim explains that,"the term third world is frequently applied in two ways: to refer to underdeveloped/overexploited geopolitical entities i.e. countries, regions even continents; and to refer to oppressed nationalities from these world areas who are now resident in developed first world countries" (315).

The same instability characterizes the nomenclature of 'Third World Women'. The use of the term third world women by western feminist has been widely critiqued. Mohanty uses the term interchangeably with 'women of color' (7). She argues that "what seems to constitute 'women of color' or 'third world women' as a viable oppositional alliance is a common context of struggle rather than color or racial identification. Similarly, it is third world women's oppositional political relation to sexist, racist and imperialistic structures that constitute our political commonality" (7).

Within this discourse is also African feminism. Its development is associated with concepts such as "Womanism" (Walker 1983, Ogunyemi 1985, Kolawale 1997), "Africana Womanism" (Hudson-Weems 1993), "Motherism" (Acholonu 1995), "Stiwanism" (Ogundipe-Leslie 1994), "Negofeminism" (Nnaemeka 1995), "Femalism", "Black Feminism" (Kohrs-Amissah 2002) and "Gender Activism and Femalism".

The term postcolonial feminism is often used interchangeably with the term third world feminism. The field of postcolonial feminism arose from the gendered history of colonialism. Colonial powers often imposed westernized norms on colonized regions. This is a field inhabited by theorists and critics like Gayatri Spivak, Sara Suleri, Trinh T. Min-ha, Lata Mani, Kum Kum Sangari, Rajeshwari Sunder Rajan, Chandra Talpade Mohanty among many others. Such questioning of dominant western theoretical models from a postcolonial feminist perspective is not new in itself. Works like *This Bridge Called my Back* (ed. by Cherrie Moraga and Gloria Anzaldua, 1981), *Third World Women and the Politics of Feminism* (ed. By Chandra Talpade Mohanty, Ann Russo and Lourdes Torres, 1991), Scholars like Swasti Mitter (*Common Fate, Common Bond: Women in the Global Economy*, 1986) have shown how color and sex are the main principle behind the most recent international divisions of labour. Hazel Carby ("White Women Listen! Black Feminism and the Boundaries of Sisterhood", in *The Empire Strikes Back*, 1982) marked the boundaries of sisterhood as demarcated by differential understanding of the role played by race in defining women's experience and as an analytical category in feminist thought. Ann Jones (*Writing the Body: Towards an Understanding of l'ecriture feminine*, 1981) showed that the notion of female identity and pleasure in French feminist theory are deeply ethnocentric. Pratibha Parmar and Valerie Amos (*Challenging Imperial Feminism*, 1984) have described Euro American feminism as imperial because it erases the experience of non-white and third world women. Angela Davies (1982) pointed that although black as well as white women are oppressed within the family, the family as an institution carries different connotations for them. The African American critic Bell Hooks has argued that feminism has its roots in a world outlook colored by racial imperialism. While Chris Weedon has reminded us that the crucial question is 'who speaks for whom', underlying the relevance of voice and representation. In this sense, in her well-known essay of 1988, "Can the Subaltern Speak?", Gayatri Spivak postulates that the subaltern female subject is not allowed to voice herself. Also, critics like Trin T. Min-ha, Naila Kabeer, Ketu Katrk, Chandra Mohanty, Padmini Mongia, Benita Parry, Sara Suleri, Lata Mani, Rajeshwari Sunder Rajan among many others represent a significant tradition of oppositional critique and alternate theoretical formulations which have shaped the contours of postcolonial feminism.

Postcolonial feminism offers a wide range of theoretical and historical approaches, dwelling upon various complex constellations of concerns. Yet, perhaps, some of its general contours are well exemplified in:

(1) Its persistent critiques of western imperialism and its problematic representations of the other.

(2) Also postcolonial feminism radically and strategically situates the third world female subaltern in an attempt to complicate and contest the dominant feminist (in Spivak's term 'hegemonic feminism') narratives produced, packaged and circulated from the metropolis.

(3) Postcolonial feminism confronts and contests unequal power relations and production on both local and global scales.

(4) In the 1940's and 1950's, after the formation of the UN, former colonies were monitored for what was deemed 'social progress' by western standards. The advancement of women, among other variables, has been monitored by arguably western organizations such as the United Nations. As a result, traditional practices and roles taken up by women—seen as distasteful by western standards can be considered a form of rebellion against colonial aggression.

(5) An underlying theoretical premise of postcolonial feminism is that concepts of freedom, equality and rights stem from the enlightenment and privileged western and European norms, rather than representing a universal value system.

(6) Postcolonial feminism often criticizes western forms of feminism, notably radical feminism and its universalization of female experiences.

(7) Much postcolonial feminism argues that oppressions relating to the colonial experience, particularly racial, class and ethnic oppression have marginalized women in postcolonial societies.

(8) They interrogate the spatio-temporal specificities of (western) theory that is based on facile universalism.

(9) They challenge the assumption that gender oppression is the primary force of patriarchy. Also, they argue that

oppression cannot be ranked at all, as to do so would be to misrepresent their lived experiences.

(10) While challenging oppression within their own cultures, postcolonial feminists also fight charges of being western as some within their own cultures would contend.

The history of colonial-imperial power/knowledge networks variously subalternizing third world identities and culture has not reached its end.

The Third World Feminist Project

Third World Feminist writing challenges the Eurocentric gaze and urges the value of third world feminist to a global feminism. Third World Feminist criticism focuses on three major issues:

(1) On the politics of universalism.

(2) On cultural controls and misrepresentation.

(3) On the homogeneity of the canon. (Humm: 252)

Any discussion of the intellectual and political construction of third world feminism must address itself to two simultaneous projects:

(1) The internal critique of hegemonic western feminism and

(2) The formation of autonomous geographically, historically and culturally grounded concerns and strategies.

The first project is one of deconstruction and dismantling and the second one is of building and constructing (Mongia: 2006:172). The revolt of the particular against that masquerading as the general of what Donna Haraway has called 'situated' as against 'disembodied knowledge' has brought to the fore theoretical and political questions regarding positionality and identity of the third world women vis-a-vis the Euro American women. One locus of such discussion in the Euro American context has been the related struggle over racism and white centredness of dominant feminism (Moraga, Anzaldua, Hooks, Amos among many others) and its replication of elements of colonial discourse (Spivak, Mohanty, Trin T. Minha). Feminists have called for a revised politics of location—revised because unlike its initial articulation the relation between experience and knowledge is now seen to be one not of correspondence, but fraught with history, contingency and struggle.

Johnson Odim identifies problems some third world women have with first world feminist: "while it may be legitimately argued that there is no one school of thought on feminism among first world feminist who are after all not all monolithic—there is still among third world women a widely accepted perception that feminism emerging from white, middle class western women narrowly confine itself to a struggle against gender discrimination" (314-15).

From its inception in early 1700's, feminism in the west had consistently held universalistic aspirations and feminists have argued for women's rights as human beings. It can be argued that the first wave and second wave feminists theories were Eurocentric, basing their ideas and actions on the lives of white women in Europe and North America and ignoring and undervaluing the lives and experiences of women in the third world and the ways in which these lives have been affected by conditions of colonialism. Thus, white middle class, western women were claiming to speak not only for all women in these societies but for women everywhere, universalizing from their own experiences and life situations and ignoring the effects of capitalism, racism and colonialism which proved decisive force.

The African American critic Bell Hooks has argued that feminism had its roots in a world outlook coloured by racial imperialism referring exclusively to the experience of white women, so different for instance from that of black woman. In her novel *The Bluest Eye* (1981), Toni Morrison graphically depicts the effects of the legacy of nineteenth century racism for poor black people in the United States. The novel tells of how the daughter of a poor black family, Pecola Breedlove, internalizes white standards of beauty to the point where she goes mad. Her fervent wish for blue eyes comes to stand for her wish to escape the poor, unloving, racist environment in which she lives.

For a long time, mainstream white western feminism paid scant attention to the question of racism. Racism was seen secondary to patriarchy and at best the problem of non-white women. One of the key challenges to the supposedly Eurocentric and essentialist nature of feminism has come from black feminist, who have challenged white women's ability and indeed their right to speak for black women. A key black feminist theorist whose work has underlined this problem of feminism and racial difference is bell hooks, who, in her book *Ain't I a Women* (1981), writes about the history of black women in the US. The brutal assaults on black women during the periods of slavery in the US led to a devaluation of black womanhood that permeated the psyche of all Americans and shaped the social status of all black women once slavery ended (1981: 52). Thus even now, a century after the abolition of slavery, US society still perceives and represents black women as fallen women, whores and prostitutes.

In 1980, one of the most poignant and powerful critiques of white western feminism came from the radical black lesbian feminist Audre Lorde who wrote: "by and large within the women's movement today white women focus upon their oppression as women and ignore difference of race, sexual preference, class and age, there is a pretence to a homogeneity of experience covered by the word sisterhood that does not in fact exist" (Lorde 1984a: 116). Some differences can be located in the feminist analyses of family. Many feminists have argued that the family is one of the major structures of patriarchal society and thus a prime site of women's oppression. Although family may be a site of sexist oppression for black women, it can also be a site of strength and resistance to racist oppression (Carby: 1957). Further, the feminist model of family as a site of economic dependency for black women very often who were the chief income earner and head of the family with men economically dependent, so any feminist theory that seeks to provide a universalized account of the family as an oppressive force does not necessarily apply to all women's situation. Black women's specific experiences were ignored for example the pro-abortion campaigns of the 1970's did not take into account black women's struggles, which was around the right to keep and realize their fertility. For these women, abortions, sterilizations and depo provera were all too easily available, and were often administered without adequate consultation and/or under the shadow of poverty (Aziz: 1997:70). So we see that as the white women were fighting for rights to their bodies—right for abortion for the black women it had a different meaning—they were fighting for the right to retain their fertility. To quote another instance: Mainstream feminist were clamoring for right to work for women, ironically black women have always been workers not so much by choice as by necessity. The blanket cover of sisterhood conceals a veneer of separatism. The white were also charged with the failure to acknowledge their part in the racist structure of society. As Hazel Carby writes: "Black feminists have been, and are still demanding that the existence of racism must be acknowledged as a structuring feature of our relationships with white women" (1997:46).

In 1984 black American feminist Barbara Smith spoke warmly of being part of a third world feminist movement: "and not only am I talking about my sister here in the United States—America, Indian, Latina, Asian-American, Arab American—I am also talking about women all over the globe...third world feminism has enriched not just the women it applies to, but also political practices in general" (Smith 1984: 27).

Ideology of Separatism/the Gendered Subaltern

Eurocentric tendencies of women in the West lead them to see their societies and cultures as models for the rest of the world. Third world feminist are still in the process of contesting the Eurocentric gaze that privileges western notions of liberation and progress and portray third world women primarily as victims of ignorance and restrictive culture and religions.

Third world women are arguably housed in an 'identifiable margin'. Once again as Gayatri Spivak suggests the margin is at the service of the centre. When an identity is thrust upon one which Deleuze and Guattari refer to as third world zones/ minor/deterritorialised minor zones of nonculture and underdevelopment. Metropolitan demands for marginality, consolidates and moves the non-west as interminably marginal. Spivak insists that the prescription of non-western alterity as a tonic for the ill-health of western culture heralds the perpetration of a new orientatation. Trin T. Min-ha in *Women, Native, Other* firmly attributes the rise of 'the Third World Women' to the ideological tourism of the western/liberal feminism. Trinh's book elaborates through a fictionalized yet all too familiar account of the paternalistic and self-congratulatory tokenism which sustains 'special third world women' readings, workshops, meetings and seminars. At every such event Trinh argues the veneer of cross-cultural sisterly colloquium disguises an unpleasant ideology of separatism, where she goes, the native women is required to exhibit her ineluctable difference from the primary referent to western feminism: "it is as if everywhere we go, we become someone's private zoo"(Trinh 1989). "The voyeuristic craving for the colorful alterity of native women seriously compromises the seemingly egalitarian politics of liberal feminism. by claiming the dubious privilege of preparing the way for one's unfortunate sisters", the western feminism creates an insuperable division between "I –who-made-it" and "you-who-cannot make it" (*ibid.*).

Spivak also deserves mention for her relentless challenges to all those specious knowledge systems which seek to regulate the articulation of what she calls the 'gendered subaltern'. Almost all her works touch upon the touchy politics of knowing the other; her early essay *French Feminism in an International Frame* (1987) is exemplary in its attention to the narcissism of the liberal feminist investigator. Spivak's incisive reading catches the authoritative knower in the act of epistemic violence or authoritative knowing. In this essay, Spivak details the problematic elisions which run through Kristeva's *About Chinese Women*, a text which emerged out of the sporadic French academic interest in China. *About Chinese Women* is really a book about Kristeva; a text which develops once again the difference of the Third world women as grist to the mill of western theory. Spivak expresses deep suspicion of any positivist and determinist notions of identity; that is to say, for Spivak, identity cannot be neatly inscribed in a language, location or biology. In relation to women, it is contended that the subject/object position cannot be easily applied to all women in all contexts. The applicability depends on the specific women's political, social situation, consequently, first world feminist academy need to unlearn their own sense of privilege and re-learn it as loss in order to be taken seriously by the other "female constituency" (Spivak: 1970: 35-49).

In *Under Western Eyes: Feminist Scholarship and Colonial Discourses* Chandra Talpade discusses against a simplistic binary formula that ignores racial, ethnic, national and class differences: "men exploit, women are exploited" (31). Talpade laments the residual traces of colonialist epistemology which are all too visible in the "appropriation and codification of scholarship and knowledge" about women in the third world by particular analytic categories" (1994: 196). She argues that much western feminist writing about third world women "discursively colonize the material and historical heterogeneities of the lives of women in the third world, thereby producing/representing a composite, singular third world women, an image which appears arbitrarily constructed, but nevertheless carries with it the authorizing signature of western humanist discourse" (Mohanty: 1991: 53). She also claimed that western feminism too often portrayed non-western women as different from themselves—Victims of male control, restrictive cultures, more oppressed, tradition, religion and family oriented, legally unsophisticated, illiterate and embattled in nationalistic revolutions. This facilitates and privileges the self-representation of western women as "educated, modern, as having control over their own bodies and sexualities, and the freedom to make their own decisions" (1994:200). Western women come to function as a norm against which the third world women are measured.

White women need to avoid alienating and marginalizing other women by objectifying them or speaking for them. Moraga argues, for example that: "some white people who take up multicultural and cultural plurality issues mean well but often they push to the fringes once more the very cultural and ethnic groups about whom they want to disseminate knowledge (Moraga: 1981a:xxi).

To a large extent Trinh and Talpade's critiques of liberal feminist imperialism draw upon Said's understanding of colonized discourse as the cultural privilege of representing the subjugated other. Both Said's Orientalist offenders and Talpade's feminist opportunists seem to speak the third world through a shared vocabulary which insists, they cannot represent themselves they must be represented.

Imperial gaze and the colonized women/Representations/who speaks for whom

In the Nietzsche inspired post-representational domain of post-structuralist and postmodernist theories, the question of 'representation' is not merely caricatured but is decisively dispensed with—or even declared dead—on the very assumption that representations are no longer possible in the way that the signified is now impossible. Spivak as well as Marxist critics like Aijaz Ahmed—already advanced critiques of such poststructuralist post representationalism, dominated as it by despotism of the signifier.

With reference to the issue of third world feminism we cannot dispense with the question of representation, as such, but rather confront it through zeroing in on the problematic of representations of the third world women that seem to replicate what we can call 'colonialist stance' towards third world women and cultures to explain why these representations are both problematic and colonialist. With the above end in view third world feminists attempt to read, deconstruct and understand the 'worlding' of the third world (to use Spivak's phrase), and analyze the production of third world women as a singular monolithic subject in western feminist texts. For Mohanty, Spivak and Sara Suleri—the central problem occurs when western feminist employ 'women' as a category of analysis based on the notion of a shared oppression. This is problematic because it assumes that women are a coherent group prior to their entry into the social, cultural and family structures. Any analysis of women needs to be based on particular local contexts. Any feminist analysis needs to take account of local cultural practices, class and kinship patterns and socio-historical circumstances. Consequently, they highlight the ethnocentricism that occurs in the western texts, especially when assumptions are made about women from other cultures without taking account of local, often complex, social structure.

One of the classic instances of colonial discourse concerns the program of social reform that the British rulers of India devised in the first half of the nineteenth century, especially over the issue of sati, the interpretation and assignment meaning to the custom reveals many of the attitudes of colonial rule and its construction of an 'other' in India. Third world feminist attempt to deconstruct the representation of the Indian tradition of Sati or widow immolation in mainstream feminist discourse and particularly in Mary Daly's classic radical feminist text *Gyn/Ecology: the Metaethics of Radical Feminism* (1979). The ahistorical colonialist power/knowledge networks of western feminism tends to epistemologize and ontologoize and fix and freeze the entire Indian culture as being patriarchal vis-a-vis the practice of sati.

Uma Narayan (1997) analyses colonial modes of representation in her critiques of Mary Daly's treatment of sati. Narayan argues that while Daly's work addresses third world women's issues, "it does so in a manner that misrepresents what is at stake 'reproducing some common and problematic western understanding of third world contexts and communities" (Narayan: 1997: 45). In Narayan's view Daly fails to give due attention to history in her work on third world practices and, as a result of this, the third world emerges as timeless and unchanging. Comparing Daly's accounts of sati and her accounts of European witch burning, Narayan points to the absence of historical information provided on sati. Moreover, Narayan argues, Daly pays no attention to questions of class, caste, religion or geographical location. The picture produced is too simple and monolithic, lacking internal differences and complexity.

Western imperialism and its impact on women in colonized countries is an area that is often neglected in Eurocentric western feminist analyses, although some feminists such as Cynthia Enloe (1990), have paid close attention to the impact of colonialism on women worldwide. Enloe argues that the relation between colonizers and colonized involved a particular form of gender relations and gendered dominations. Colonized women were represented in ways that both eroticized and exoticized them, making them sex objects for men: "women as symbols, women as workers and women as nurtures have been crucial to the entire colonial undertaking" (Enloe: 1990: 44). Moreover representations of colonized women often serve to justify imperial domination as western men pointed to women's supposedly subservient and unemancipated positions in their own countries and argued that they required the projection and civilizing influence of western men. One example of this type of justification for colonialism was the issue of the veil or headscarf worn by Muslim women, with many colonizing powers attempting to 'liberate' Muslim women by persuading or forcing them to remove their veils. The French colonial power in Algiers undertook a campaign to try to persuade or force Algerian women to remove their veils. This issue of the Muslim veil or headscarf is one that concerned not only colonial powers but also nationalist movements. Enloe (*ibid*: 52) remarks that no practice has been more heatedly debated by nationalists cause by covering themselves with a veil or taking it off. One of the aims of the colonial governments in Muslim countries was almost always to persuade or force women of those countries to remove their veils. They saw this as part of a civilizing mission, and the more the women of a colonized country adopted western dress, the more the colonizing power believed it had succeeded in its mission to assimilate the country to its western, Judaeo-Christian values. In France, for example, the exclusion of Muslim girls from school on the grounds that their wearing head scarf's or veils contravenes the laws on secularism in education. This issue has spilt feminists with some groups supporting the girls' right to wear headscarf to school and the other arguing in favor of the ban on the headscarf on the grounds that they are symbols of the patriarchal oppression of women and of the French society as superior. They ignored ways in which gender is constructed within a set of global power relations and in asserting the superiority of French culture over patriarchal Muslim culture, many French feminists fell into the trap of ignoring their positioning as white women within a set of postcolonial power relations.

This pressure from colonizers put Muslim women in a difficult position, making the veil a highly political issue and meaning that taking off the veil was seen as a statement of compliance or agreement with the colonizing power. This debate continues today, both with the rise of Islam in Iran, Afghanistan, Algeria and elsewhere and in connection with the immigrant Muslim population in western countries.

Analyzing the issue of genital mutilation, Evelyn Accad explains how women in Sudan are voicing opinions against it, through radio programs, stage plays, teaching people about the disastrous consequences, educating midwives "a very different picture of third world women's relation to genital mutilation found in the work of western feminist, for example in Daly's *Gyn/Ecology: the Metaethics of Radical Feminism*. Discussing the issue of gender mutilation in Africa, Sudan and the Middle East (the goal of such gender mutilation was to mitigate sexual pleasure and satisfaction of women) Fran Hosken claims that all women in these countries are victims of male control and male violence. Fran Hosken indicates that sexual control of women is a universal fact in these countries. Hosken writes: "purdah, rape, polygamy and genital mutilations are all violations of basic human rights" (1981: 11). Hosken equates purdah with rape. So institutions of purdah are, thus, denied any cultural and historical specificity. Wearing veils in each of these countries has a specific meaning attached to the practices. Well-known Iranian middle class women veiled themselves during 1979 revolution to indicate their solidarity with their working class sister. Veils have been sometimes used as a revolutionary gesture and sometimes imposed by the state. Such cultural practices must be theorized and interpreted within specific societies in order to both understand and effectively organize to change it.

Britain for instance, manipulated the women's oppression in India and Pakistani culture to legitimate virginity tests, immigration controls and policing of Asian marriages and family life. This civilizing racist British state has placed feminists in Britain in a position analogous to that of 19th century Indian male social reformers, who defend culture and women in a similarly over-determined context.

Western feminist have used third world women as a category of analysis. In their texts third world women are constructed as homogenous powerless group who are victims of male violence (Fran Hosken); victims of colonial process (Maria Cutrufelli); victims of the economic development process (Beverley Lindsay); and finally as victims of Islamic code (Patricia Jeffrey). These types of issue highlights the ways in which western feminists have been guilty of a Eurocentric approach that ignores the experiences and views of women from other countries and other cultures and imposes western norms of patriarchal oppression, and their agency is ignored. They are represented primarily as beings that are passive and acted upon. In other words we are left with the common figure of Eurocentric feminist discourse: the third world women as "always, already Victim" (Mohanty: 1991) what is forsaken here is the notion that women's oppression is a multifaceted and contradictory social process. When Indian feminist speaks of women as victim it is in a complex material sense. Chandra Mohanty, for example points out the ways in which western feminists discussions of issues such as gender mutilation, the Islamic family code, and so on, result in third world women being constructed as powerless victims (Mohanty et al. 1991: 57). This is a complex issue, as Avtar Brah points out: "our insertions into these global relations of power are realized through a myriad of economic, political and ideological processes" (1993: 207). If feminists are wary of this eurocentricism they must be aware of the global postcolonial power relations within which they are operating.

Colonial or Eurocentric discourses on India and on the third world women more generally have an abiding presence in the USA and Britain, TV, documentaries, scholarly works and popular wisdom circulate such notions as centrality of religion, pervasive oppression, poverty, and backwardness. Dowry murders in India are framed, focused and even formulated in US academic feminist discourse, while pointing up the dangerous problems kept alive by western culturalist epistemological approaches to third world subjects, identities, traditions and cultures.

One contemporary example of scripting of the third world authors is the case of Taslima Nasreen, a Bangladeshi author whose escape to the West became an international incident in Europe in 1994, and a national embarrassment for Bangladesh. Early in those events, she was nicknamed: "the female Rushdie" on a NPR show, 'All things Considered'. Very few commentaries on her work in the west (she has been available in translation) focus on *Lajja* for which she had a fatwa issued against her. Her status as a victim of Islamic religious intolerance has dominated all conversations on Nasreen. Descriptions of her escape present the west as coolly rational—the free democratic spheres of speech and action—and the third world as a chaotic tropical realm; for instance, an article in the Financial Times, titled "safe from screams of tolerance" tells of Nasreen's escape from "steamy streets of Dhaka" to her new hideout in "cool Swedish forests". The third world authors are often consumed as subalterns in a historical script shared by the reading public in the first and third world's, authors have become free floating signifiers who are placed within pre-existent western scripts of freedom, progress and expression of individuality. Another author scripted and canonized in the west is Bharati Mukherjee. Her fictions reiterate the discourse of freedom from (Eastern) oppressions so essential for the consolidation of Euro-American feminist libratory agendas. Mukherjee's work is typically taught as immigrant literature and women's literature. Her narrative of escape from India, a place of tradition and backwardness, find reverberations in the American rhetoric of citizenship and the new world. The back cover of *Jasmine* includes a blurb from the Baltimore Sun bears witness to the texts popularity: "poignant...heartrending...this is the story of the transformation of an Indian village girl, whose grandmother wants to marry her off at 11, into an American woman who finally thinks for herself". The spurious connections between euro-American feminism and colonial modernity makes it possible for such a text, argues Grewal, to gain "literary value" over texts such as Meena Alexander's *Nampally Road*, a work trenchant in its criticism of the nightmare of immigrant existence (1994: 45–74).

South Asian communities often collude with the western representations, uncritically orientalising themselves in the media

When Arundhati Roy won the booker award for her novel *The God of Small Things* a blurb in 'India Today', Oct. 27th, 1997, summed up things well: "Arundhati Roy opens up global market for Indian writing in English" . This was followed by a description: "slim hipped Roy, her carelessly curled hair cascading over her face, her nose ring twinkling with naughtiness, and her language flapping with originality, excited the stodgy English establishment". This loaded sentence echoes gestures of exoticization extended to south Asian women in the West.

Western writing on third world women is not a mere production of knowledge about a certain subject. It is directly political and discursive practice in that it is purposeful and ideological. Western scholars on the third world women must be seen and examined precisely in terms of its inscription in these particular relations of power and struggle. Similarly, Western feminist writing on third world women must be considered in the context of the global hegemony of western scholarship i.e. production, distribution, and consumption of information and ideas.

Critique of the Third World Feminism

(1) These third world critics raise significant and trenchant objections to the western feminist investment in postcolonial matters, and yet their own critique suffers from serious limitations. Trinh, Talpade, and Spivak each idealize and essentialise the epistemological opacity of the real third world women.

(2) They paradoxically re-invest the third world women with very iconicity they set out to contest. This newly re-claimed figure is now postulated as the triumphant site of anticolonial resistance. Trinh valorizes the racial gendered body itself as revolutionary archive. While spivak, somewhat feebly urges the academic feminist to speak to the subaltern women to learn from her repository of lived experience.

(3) Each of these critics under consideration is guilty of the sort of reversed ethnocentricism which hunts Said's totalizing critique of Orientalism.

(4) There is a necessity of recognizing the partial and composite structure of all (western as well as Third world feminist) theoretical formulations.

(5) Sara Suleri in *Women Skin Deep: Feminism and the Postcolonial Condition* (1992) calls for a reassessment of the term under which we study gender and race particularly as it is manifested in the discourse of postcolonial feminism. She is critical of the view that the academy ceding itself to the issues of marginalized group in the name of political correctness. She takes up the collapse of multiple cultural and historical matrices under the term postcolonial women. She argues that the move away from historical specificity towards an identity structured around gender and race ultimately fails by collapsing important differences and incongruities. She notes the important distinction between the academic study of race and gender which requires a sort of coalitional identity politics around which scholars can organize, and the specific historical situations of any given racialised women, which must necessarily exceed any given category (such as postcolonial women) to which it is assigned.

Goals of the Third World Feminism

The academy must see then its goal not as creating and shoring up coalitional identities, but rather building coalitions around identities in order ultimately to expose and explore what Hazel Carby calls "a Locus of contradictions". Suleri calls for a shift away from the study of lived experiences and personal narrative which tends to totalize the subject of women and towards a study of specific cultural institution of racism and sexism via analysis of laws and how they formulate and oppress specific groups of racialised women.

In her latest book, *Feminism without Borders* (1992), Mohanty argues that "rather than focusing on differences feminism should mount an anti-globalization struggle against global economic and political processes [that] have become more brutal, exacerbating economic, racial and gender inequalities" (230). Feminist's goal should be a solidarity that recognizes local differences, but is without borders, since globalization effects all.

Complex discussions of ethnocentricism and oppositional criticism are contained in the writings of Rosaria Castellanos and the more recent writings of Chandra Mohanty, Gloria Anzaldua, Rey Chow, Trin T. Min-ha, Gayatri Spivak and Chela Sandoval in particular. These writers are setting an agenda for feminist literary criticism for the 1980's and beyond.

Third world feminist critics are:

(1) Identifying key writers
(2) Creating new representations and Non-ethnocentric critical languages
(3) And analyzing the politics of feminist criticism (Humm: 252).

If third world feminism is to be "worldly" (Said: 1983: 1-30) or "situated" (Haraway: 1988), or engaged, it must take account of the worlds in which it speaks. Perhaps, to Bruce Robbins's suggestion, that theory is a 'when' and 'what', (1988: 18) we should also add the notion of a 'where'.

Third world countries have their own indigenous women's movements concerned with the specificities of their countries, far from being an imitation of western feminism. Narayan argues third world feminism is very much a response to local issues In third world countries: "issues that feminists groups in India have politically engaged includes problems of dowry-murder and dowry-related harassment of women; police rape of women in custody; issues relating to women's poverty, health and reproduction; and issue of ecology and communalism that affect women's lives. Indian feminist political activities clearly make feminists and feminism part of the national political landscape of many third world countries". I am arguing that third world feminism is not a mindless mimicking of western agendas' in one clear and simple sense-that, for instance, Indian feminism is clearly a response to issues specifically confronting many Indian women (Narayan: 1997: 13). Narayan argues that third world feminists need to challenge "the larger pictures of nation, national history, and cultural traditions...that conceal their own historicity and their own status as representations—suggesting that the nation and its culture are 'natural givens' rather than historical inventions and constructions that they are" (20–1).

Third world feminism can be linked to the political project of creating a global climate in which differences can be lived as enriching and valuable rather than as the oppressive effect of hierarchical binary oppositions. This is a perspective developed by Gloria Anzaldua in her writing: "Theorists of color are in the process of trying to formulate 'marginal' theories that are partially outside and partially inside the western frame of reference (if that is possible), theories that overlap many 'worlds'. We are articulating new positions in these 'in-between', Borderland worlds of ethnic communities and academies, feminist and job worlds. In our literature, social issues such as race, class and sexual difference are intertwined with the narrative and poetic elements of a text, elements in which theory is embedded. In our *mestizaje* theories we create new categories for those of us left out or pushed out of the existing ones. We recover and examine non-western aesthetics; recover and examine non-rational modes and 'blanked-out' realities while critiquing rational, consensual reality; recover and examine indigenous languages while critiquing the languages of the dominant culture. And we simultaneously combat the tokenization and appropriation of our literature and our writers/artists" (Anzaldua: 1990a: xxvi).

In the rapidly globalizing economies and the accompanying environmental havoc being wrecked on the lands of the third world people, women have acted to mitigate in particular, the cultural effects of both colonialism and neocolonialism which have caused untold environmental damages to their natural resources. These third world practitioners are often adept at taking action to mitigate the environmental devastation neocolonialism/globalization causes. Hence, it is not surprising that many of the concerns of the third world feminism are closely interwoven with those of ecofeminism. Many projects conducted by third world women to resist the ill-effects of development have also been viewed by ecofeminists. From the vantage point of their particular locations third world women who are resisting adverse neocolonial impacts understand the costs of development and how these costs are occurring. They can and do provide us with valuable empirical knowledge concerning the ill-effects of development projects, in the developing world, where adverse neocolonial impacts spawn protests on the part of third world women. Some of the more familiar example is in environment and ecological movements. Two well-known actions are in Chipko movement in India and the Green belt movement in Kenya.

Third world feminism can contribute to this positive recognition of difference in the struggle to redefine its meaning, as Audre Lorde writes, "The future of our earth may depend on the ability of all women to identity and develop new definitions of power and new patterns of relating across difference. The old definitions have not served us, nor the earth that supports us. The old patterns, no matter how cleverly rearranged to imitate progress, still condemn us to cosmetically altered repetitions of the same old exchanges, the same old guilt, hatred, recrimination, lamentation and suspicion" (Lorde: 1984: 123).

Third World Feminism must be attentive to the micro politics of context, subjectivity and struggle as well as to the macro politics of global economic and political systems and processes. Mohanty (1991) discusses Maria Mies study of the lace makers of Narsapur as a demonstration of how to do this kind of multilayered, contextual analysis to reveal how the particular is often universally significant—without using the universal to erase the particular or positing an unbridgeable gulf between the two terms.

Third World Feminist tackle a whole constellation of intertwined issues thrown up by contemporary globalization and migrations to see how the racist and patriarchal logic of global/corporate/late capitalist continues to homogenize, dehistoricise and de-nationalize third world cultures in the interest of value and profit on both local and global scales and thus perpetrating violence on the land, labour, language and the body of the third world female subaltern.

REFERENCES

Anzaldua, Gloria, Ed. "Making Face, Making Soul". Haciendo Caras. *Creative and Critical Perspectives by Feminist of Color*. San Fransisco: Aunt Lute Books,1990.

Accad, Evelyne. "Truth versus Loyalty". In Bell & Klein, *Radically Speaking: Feminism Reclaimed*. London: Zed Books, 1996.

Aziz, R. "Feminism and the Challenge of Racism: Deviance or Difference?" in H.S. Mirza Ed., 1997.

"All Things Considered". *NPR Show*, 14th Jan. 1994.

"Arundhati Roy Gets Booker for First Novel". *The Statesman*, 6th Oct. 1997.

Brah, A. "Difference, Diversity, Differentiation: Processes of Racialisation and Gender" in J. Wrench and J. Solomos. (Eds), *Racism and Migration in Western Europe*. Oxford: Berg, 1993.

Carby, Hazel. "White Women Listen! Black Feminism and the Boundaries of Sisterhood", in H.S. Mirza (Ed.), *Black British Feminism*. London: Routeledge, 1997.

Daly, Mary. *Gyn/Ecology: The Metaethics of Radical Feminism*. London: The Women's Press, 1979.

Enloe, Cynthia. *Bananas, Beaches and Bases: Making Feminist Sense of International Politics*. Berkeley, CA: University of California Press, 1990.

Grewal, Inderpal. "The Postcolonial, Ethnic Studies and the Diaspora". *Socialist Review*, 24.4, 1994.

Hosken, Fran. "Female Genital Mutilation and Human Rights", *Feminist Issues*, 1.3. 1981

Humm, Maggie. *A Readers Guide to Contemporary Feminist Literary Criticism*. Harvester Wheatsheaf, London, 1994.

Hooks, bell. *Ain't I a Woman*. Boston, MA: South End Press, 1981.

Haraway, Donna. "Situated Knowledge's: The Science Question and the Privilege of Partial Perspective". *Feminist Studies*, 14.3.1988.

Weedon, Chris. 'Genderealisations', Cardiff University, 1(2002) http://www.genderforum.uni–koeln.de/genderealisations/weedon.html.

Johnson-Odim, Cheryl. "Common Themes, Different Contexts: Third World Women and Feminism". *Third World Women and the Politics of Feminism*. Eds., Mohanty, Russo, Torres. Bloomington and Indianapolis: Indiana UP, 1991.

Lorde, Audre. *Sister Outside*. Trumansberg, New York: Crossing Press, 1984.

Mongia, Padmini, Ed. *Contemporary Postcolonial Theory: A Reader*. New Delhi, OUP, 2006.

Mohanty, Chandra. "Under Western Eyes: Feminist Scholarship and Colonial Discourse" in Mohanty, Russo, Torres, 1991.

Mohanty, Chandra. *Feminism without Borders: Decolonizing Theory, Practicing Solidarity*. Durham and London: Duke University Press, 2003.

Mirza, H.S, ed. *Black British Feminism*. London: Routeledge, 1997.

Morrison, Toni. *The Bluest Eye*. London: TriadGrafton, 1981.

Narayan, Uma. *Dislocating Cultures, Identities, Traditions and Third World Feminism*. New York & London: Routeledge, 1997.

Min-ha, Trinh T. *Women, Native, Other*. Bloomington: Indiana University Press, 1989.

Robbins, Bruce. "The Politics of Theory", *Social Text* 18, 1988.

Smith, Barbara. "Black Feminism: A Movement of Our Own". In: Karen Kahn (ed.) *Front Line Feminism: 1975–1995, Essays from Sojourner's First 20 Years*. San Francisco: Aunt Lute Books, 1995.

Spivak, Gayatri Chakravarty. *The Spivak Reader*. (eds.) Donna Landry & Gerald MacLean. Great Britain; Routledge, 1996.

Sangari, Kumkum. "The Politics of the Possible". *The Nature and Context of Minority Discourse*. (Eds.)Abdul Jan Mohamed and David Lloyd. New York: Oxford UP, 1990.

Spivak, Gayatri Chakravarty. "Strategy, Identity, Writing", *The Post-Colonial Critic*. (Ed.) Sarah Harasym, New York: Routledge, 1990.

Said, Edward. *The World, the Text and the Critic*. Cambridge: Harvard University Press, 1983.

Suleri, Sara. "Women Skin Deep: Feminism and the Postcolonial Condition". *Critical Inquiry*. Summer, 1992.

"Women in the News! Safe from the Screams of Intolerance". *The Financial Times*, 14th Aug.1994.

The Idea of Selling the Idea of India in Recent Indian English Fiction

15

Shubha Tiwari

We all know and accept that Prem Chand is a great story teller or Jai Shankar Prasad is a great poet. But the game of language is such that these literary stalwarts are not in limelight. Salman Rushdie, Kiran Desai and others are at the centre of attention. The obvious conclusion is that English as a language is dominating the scene. The question arises that if one language is leading, are there certain ideas also that are catchier than others? When an Indian writes a novel, s/he is expected to write about India. Now, what kind of ideas about India sell and what kind of ideas don't. That is the question. Many sectors are selling the idea of India—tourism industry, education industry and so on. In literature also, particular brand of India sells. What is that brand? In the present paper, we will take up certain recent and successful Indian English novels and will try to study the idea of India therein.

The sheer multitude that is India is both a boon and a bane. It is good that majority of Indians do not know as to what is happening in the elite, English dominated literary scene they are busy chanting Shri Ram Charit Manas and singing bhajans. They do not know that they have become a commodity, a hot selling product in the literary market. A particular idea of India sells.

Freedom of expression is of course fundamental to human nature. To point out India's follies is no crime. It is necessary. But if we project a negative image of our motherland in order to make big bucks or fetch international prizes, it becomes

Nature as Metaphor: A Study of Anita Desai's *In Custody*

16

Reena Mitra

A dynamic use of the scenic backdrop to determine the lives of the characters in a novel as in Thomas Hardy's *The Return of the Native* is technically the most piquant and absorbing feature of a work of fiction. The natural milieu, when endowed with such a potent role in the narrative, becomes the overwhelming determinant over which the individual character has little control. Nature as an all-pervasive element in deciding the course of individual life often assumes a dramatic significance that accords it an irreducible solidity in the larger perspective. The growth of a novelist is believed to be commensurate with his increasing ability to cultivate immediacy and tactility in his descriptions. It is when we confront the eternal framework of Nature in a literary construct that we become conscious of the overpowering and undilutable reality of the landscape, which either influences, even if it be in some remote way, the destinies of people or reflects the moods or the states of mind of the protagonist, and by doing so, reinforces the effect of those mental states and moods upon the reader.

Anita Desai, in her article, "Flight of Forms" elucidates the process of creative writing and explains how it is applicable to her own novels. The creative writer, she believes:

> ...writes without knowing why he writes. He writes the way a spider spins; it is all he knows how to do and he does it without thought, almost without consciousness. To him, it is a compulsive and instinctive act. I can think of a number of metaphors to illustrate this act; and it may be of significance that all that occur to me are drawn from nature.[1]

Desai uses evocative language in her descriptions of Nature. She endows words with an irresistible sensuous appeal and exults in the power of her eloquence. She depicts moods, conflicting choices and inner experiences and explores the inharmonious relationships of man springing from the incompatibility of partners in marriage—all with the help of richly suggestive nature imagery.

In Anita Desai's nature descriptions accurate observation and delicate poetic feelings are remarkably blended and stark facts are clad in striking imagery which harmonizes with the mood of the central character. For minute observation and vivid painting of details of natural scenery, Desai is almost unrivalled and often impresses us with microscopic effects. Few novelists have ever dealt with the minutiae of Nature as adeptly as she has. Her nature descriptions are characterized by an accuracy and delicacy of perception, beauty of delineation and felicity of translation into language of that which she perceives.

In Anita Desai's novels, right from her earliest one, *Cry, The Peacock* written in 1963, Nature is a powerful presence that dominates the scene of action and in its fabric are interwoven hope, despair, defeat and illusion. As she herself admits in an interview, the natural landscapes depicted in her novels are important to her—"The visual images and sounds, smells and textures of the places, I know are my material."[2] In *Cry, The Peacock*, the dance of peacocks itself is a blend of bliss and agony and reflects the mental state of Maya, the protagonist. In *Voices in the City*, Monisha's diary throws light on her love of nature. In *Bye-Bye, Blackbird*, too, Sarah's inner landscape is linked to the natural world around her. In *Where Shall We Go This Summer?* Sita finds security in the lap of nature. In *Fire on the Mountain*, the picturesque backdrop of Kasauli and its pine-scented hills provide a lavish fare of flora and fauna in a variety of forms. In *Clear Light of Day* the koel's call sets the tone of the novel.

In Custody is a novel that is distinctively different from all other novels of Anita Desai in that it is for the first time that a male character holds centre-stage in a work of hers and her treatment of Nature, too, is characterized here by a primarily ironic tone, a tone which intensifies as well as mocks at the misery born of the futility of human effort. This ambivalence in tone lends the narrative a compelling vigour and an added dimension.

In Custody, nominated for the 1984 Booker McConnell Prize, presents the antithesis between exaltation and mortification, between misperception and reality in the context of the plight of degenerate Urdu poetry in the contemporary era. Deven, with his inherent poetic sensibility exhibits a total lack of interest and concern in his profession as a lecturer of Hindi. His performance as a teacher reflects this indifference and ennui and he remains unappreciated and unrecognized by all who matter. His vain enthusiasm for Urdu poetry makes him fall prey to Murad's suggestion of his interviewing Nur Shajehanabadi, the famous Urdu poet, for an article in the Urdu magazine, *Awaz*. Lured by visions of name and fame Deven accepts the offer but soon his world of romantic illusions falls miserably apart for he finds Nur hardly measuring up to the poet he had visualized as his idol. Total disillusionment sets in when he actually meets "the man so clearly a hero,"[3] the great poet, the "superior being",[4] who is now no more than an old man engulfed by the intractable whirlpool of worldly reality, a total picture of debility and infirmity. This engulfment of Nur by the blasé world around is symbolically and effectively suggested by reference to the canal water turning "concentrically in a whirlpool."[5] The maelstrom, however, does not spare Deven either and he is encompassed by a sense of defeatism which with great determination he shakes off at the end to emerge as "the custodian of Nur's very soul and spirit."[6] Anita Desai very adeptly uses here nature as metaphor for calamities in life and nature, again, as metaphor for emergence from these calamities.

Deven, like Monisha in *Voices in the City* and Maya in *Cry, the Peacock*, lives in a world of make-belief in which he imagines himself to be the sole custodian of Nur's poetry and feels that he should salvage it for posterity. It is this desire to assume the responsibility of preserving and perpetuating the Urdu couplets of Nur, now an inconceivably decadent poet, that worsens Deven's lot and makes him suffer undeservedly. As Jasbir Jain comments with regard to Anita Desai's novels "Roles become facades, they cloud the reality, they confine and blind and order the behaviour of the characters."[7]

The dramatic motivation (or demotivation?) provided by natural conditions is central to every aspect of *In Custody*. It defines the style of the novelist: page after page displays a wrought density of texture that emerges not from any specific verbal quality but from the actual motivational impact of the natural surroundings that often turn squalid to match the human low that plagues Deven when he is conscious of the shards of his shattered literary aspirations all around him. Symbolic depth in the novel is communicated by the physical surface of things with unhampered transparency as in the following lines:

> ...There was nothing to be heard but the water rushing past the banks.... He could slip in if he was not careful.[8]

On the other hand, the homeliest conviction of fact is convincingly preserved: "Dust lay heaped in smell piles around her."[9] All these together become aspects of Nature that assume almost dramatic causational necessity guiding the protagonist's course of action.

The natural environment in *In Custody* sets the tone of the novel to be dark and sombre, communicated to us as a symbol of Deven's inexorable circumstances that impede the realization of his literary ideals. So, Nature in this work is not a passive backdrop but an existence that intensifies and enhances the native proclivities of an individual struggling to survive with a modicum of dignity. The dilemma of Deven as to whether he should pursue his artistic yearnings or renounce them to provide the minimal comforts due to his wife and child is the dilemma of a morally individualizing consciousness in its earthy blend, a condition restraining man from soaring high in an imaginative and enterprising flight of fancy.

Dr. R.A. Singh, in his exhaustive study of the existential characters of Arun Joshi and Anita Desai, refers to five inter-related operational conditions which determine the plight of the modern man in a hostile world, namely, "powerlessness, normlessness, isolation, self-estrangement and meaninglessness."[10]

All of these are fully operative in the life of Deven in *In Custody* and Nature seems to be in connivance with all these factors in threatening to corrode every sphere of life, in reducing him to dust, the word 'dust' in the text assuming multiple connotations.

McIntosh, in his elucidation of Shakespeare's use of "grammatical clues" to characters, has endorsed "the widespread implication of every slight linguistic nuance", which is "capable of yielding its import to us."[11] Anita Desai, too, is fully conscious of the possibilities of the medium she has chosen to write in. Indepth studies and critical interpretations of her novels have strengthened the belief that

> ...an analysis of linguistic correlates of her characters' psychographs is most likely to reveal interesting correspondences between characters and the language used by them and *about them.* (italics mine)[12]

The language of *In Custody* is equally revelatory of the psyche of her protagonist, Deven, and of the problems that he encounters in the pursuit of his literary objectives. The imagery in the novel is in terms of dull, drab and subdued colours like black and grey. This is corroborated by expressions like "a grove of blackened acacian trees"[13] and "the grey clay."[14] These expressions suggest a stifling atmosphere everywhere.

In *In Custody*, too, as in Anita Desai's world of women in her other novels, we witness

> a world where the central harmony is aspired to but not arrived at, and the desire to love and live clashes—at times violently—with the desire to achieve harmony.[15]

Deven often finds himself on the verge of neurosis in trying to happily bring together his domestic world and the world of artistic aspirations. His efforts to create in his life "cosmos out of chaos",[16] as N. Ramachandran Nair puts it, do bear fruit when he fortifies himself at the end to fight his battle alone:

> He had imagined he was taking Nur's poetry into safe custody, and not realized that if he was to be custodian of Nur's genius, then Nur would become his custodian and place him in custody too. This alliance could be considered

> an unendurable burden—or else a shining honour. Both demanded an equal strength.[17]

At the end, however, Deven proves equal to the situation and displays a rare kind of confidence and resolution born of physical and psychological agony. He decides unreservedly to be the guardian and trustee of Nur's poetry, come what may:

> He turned back. He walked up the path. Soon the Sun would be up and blazing. The day would begin with its calamities. They would flash out of the sky and cut him down like swords. He would run to meet them. He ran, stopping only to pull a branch of thorns from under his foot.[18]

Despite the fact that the male consciousness torn apart by acute psychological agony is not Desai's forte, she has communicated to us the agonies of the wounded self through powerful perceptions and engrossing nature descriptions doled out in a vibrant style. The primary mode of narration is largely dependent on the use of Nature as metaphor, nature as a symbol for the disastrous conditions of life. Deven, in his final run, after pulling out the thorns from under his foot, affirms the eventual assemblage of his shattered self into one who could confront life with equanimity and poise. He realizes the existence of the symbiotic relationship that prevails between Nur and himself. The canal water turning "concentrically in a whirlpool"[19] is a symbol for this convergence of his co-extensive attitudes towards Nur—his admiration for his poetry and his consciousness of the decadence that had set in—to arouse his stable self, which is now instilled with a new clarity and vision.

The novelists' depiction of Mirpore, like E.M. Forster's delineation of Chandrapore in *A Passage to India* is "a deliberate focused evocation—only more detailed and more heavily laced with irony."[20] The two lines which describe Mirpore in a nutshell are not without an inherent sense of irony: "...Although it lacked history, the town had probably existed for centuries in its most basic, most elemental form."[21]

What made this place "enduring" and never essentially inclined to change was the fact that

> ...the dust beneath was always present, always perceptible. In fact, it managed to escape from under the asphalt and to rise and spread through the town, summer and winter, a constant presence, thick enough to be seen and felt. During the monsoon, always brief and disappointing on this northern plain, more than a thousand miles from the coast, it turned to mud. But the Sun came out again very soon and dried it to its usual grey and granular form. The citizens of Mirpore, petty tradesmen rather than agriculturists, could not be blamed for failing to understand those patriotic songs and slogans about the soil, the earth. To them it was so palpably dust.[22]

Dust, thus, becomes the predominant imagery in the novel. No resident of the place can ever escape "the ubiquitous dust of Mirpore."[23] This overwhelming consciousness of the presence of dust in everything associated with Mirpore emanates from what R.K. Gupta identifies as "the clear unambiguous images of this novel which are precise in their visual quality."[24]

The novel, thus, proceeds with the help of images, metaphors and symbols, most of which draw from the world of Nature. There is an abundance of colour imagery but the colours are almost always toned down or given a negative connotation by the use of epithets that detract from the normal vibrant colour. We have, in the novel, expressions like "acid-green" "pale-yellow", "withered and grey", "yellowed foliage", "pale-flash", "yellow-grey sky", "flattened grey world", "spittle-flecked red lips"—all suggestive of a kind of blight that seems to have struck them. This, perhaps, is in conformity with the protagonist's state of mind.

Bird and animal images in the text of the novel relate, almost invariably, to the central character's despair and suffering and foreground the "greyness" in his life. The sight of the dead stray dog, when on his way to Delhi, unnerves Deven as he sees prefigured in it his own prospective predicament. The reference to crows alighting on the dead dog connotes prey-predator images suggestive of Deven's situation in life where he is always cast in the role of the hunted. There are multiple references to

Deven imagining himself to be "like a caged animal in a zoo" or "a trapped animal."[25]

The image of the pet pigeons of Nur turns from being "a symbol of flight and song"[26] into an impending threat to the very spring of poetry in him:

> My pigeons are dying...when the last of my pigeons is gone, I will cease to write poetry forever. I will go with them.[27]

In another bird image in the novel, the parrot symbolizes a rare moment of joy and pleasure in an unexciting and drab stretch of life—"one brilliant feather of spring green fluttered down through the air and fell at their feet in the grey clay."[28]

Nature in *In Custody* is again symbolized by the 'neem' tree growing outside the wall of the courtyard of Deven's house. Because of its "yellowed-foliage" it does not provide much shade; rather, it is a liability that obstructs the passage of fresh air: "No message came whispering on a nocturnal breeze; every leaf on the neem tree hung stiff, lifeless."[29]

The most characteristic feature of the countenance of Mirpore is its dryness and aridity, suggestive of infertility. Mirpore, we are told at the very outset "spared no effort to give an impression of total aridity."[30] The town lacked a river and there stood in the shabby municipal park "an empty fountain painted blue."[31] In brief, we are given an inescapable impression of "Mirpore's addiction to total dehydration".[32] All this is clearly suggestive of the desolation in the monotonous life that Deven was almost compelled to live in Mirpore. His flights to give form to his immense literary yearnings are always impeded by the grim realities of the demands made on him as husband, father and lecturer.

Malashri Lal, in her essay on "Multilocality: International Themes in Women's Short Stories in English", categorically states that "Anita Desai's world is imbued...with psychological density."[33] This is said of her short stories but is equally true of her novels. The density of the mind referred to is as stated earlier, communicated to us in *In Custody* through a profuse use of Nature which reinforces her depiction of the life and character of her protagonist, Deven. Imperceptibly the novelist blends external nature and human life together in the couplet she quotes as a composition of Nur coming to Deven's mind: "Night ends, dawn breaks, and sorrow reappears, addressing us in morning light, with a cock's shrill crow."[34] Rarely did a morning scene appear to be positively idyllic, and when it did, the idyll was soon demolished.

Anita Desai's novels, then, are clear expositions of her belief in the correspondence between the inner landscape of a character and his external environment. As in Tennyson's poetry, in her novels, too, Nature is subordinated to the varying moods of man and presented from the human standpoint. Desai has the rare power of giving atmosphere to a novel, of suggesting correspondence and interaction between the mind and its surroundings, between the situation and the subjective stance, at the time of a crisis in life. Nature, to her, though it appears to be dominant, is essentially a mirror that reflects human sentiments. Sorrow and disillusionment, in varying degrees of poignancy and cognition provide her the inspiration for some of the most absorbing scenes in *In Custody*.

K.R.S. Iyenger, in his assessment of Anita Desai's novels, states that—

> ...the inner climate, the climate of sensibility that lours or clears or rumbles like thunder or suddenly blazes like lightning, is more compelling than the outer weather, the physical geography or the visible action.[35]

Yet "the outer weather" certainly does reinforce the experiences of exhilaration or desperation as experienced by the protagonist. Nature seems to observe and reverberate the vacillations of human emotions that are recorded on the sensibility graph.

NOTES

1. Anita Desai. "Flight of Forms", *India International Centre Quarterly*, Vol. 10, Number 4, 1983.
2. Ketaki Sheth's interview with Anita Desai, *Imprint*, June, 1984.
3. Anita Desai. *In Custody* (New Delhi: Penguin Books, 1984, rpt. 1999), p. 39.

4. *Ibid.*, p. 38.
5. *Ibid.*, p. 204.
6. *Ibid.*
7. Jasbir Jain. *Stairs to the Attic: The Novels of Anita Desai*, (Jaipur: Printwell, 1987), p. 134.
8. Anita Desai. *In Custody*, p. 202.
9. *Ibid.*, p. 193.
10. R.A. Singh. *Existential Characters of Arun Joshi and Anita Desai* (Bareilly: Prakash Book Depot, 1991), p. 81.
11. Angus McIntosh. *As You Like It*: A Grammatical Clue to Character", *A Review of English Literature*, 4/2 (1963).
12. R.S. Pathak. "Anita Desai's Fiction: Character, Semantic Space and Linguistic Correlates", *Modern Indian Novel in English*, (New Delhi: Creative Books, 1999), p. 95.
13. Anita Desai. *In Custody*, p. 64.
14. *Ibid.*, p. 73.
15. Jasbir Jain. "Anita Desai", *Indian English Novelists: An Anthology of Critical Essays*, ed. Madhusudan Prasad (New Delhi: Sterling, 1982), p. 23.
16. N. Ramachandran Nair. *In Custody*: The Road Not Taken", *Indian Women Novelists*, Vol. 4, ed. R.K. Dhawan (New Delhi: Prestige Books, 1991), p. 94.
17. Anita Desai. *In Custody*, p. 203.
18. *Ibid.*, p. 204.
19. *Ibid.*
20. E.M. Forster. *A Passage to India* (Harmondsworth: Penguin Books, 1924, rpt. 1975).
21. Anita Desai. *In Custody*, p. 19.
22. *Ibid.*
23. *Ibid.*, p. 20.
24. R.K. Gupta. *The Novels of Anita Desai: A Feminist Perspective* (New Delhi: Atlantic Publishers and Distributors, 2002), p. 134.
25. Anita Desai. *In Custody*, p. 131.
26. *Ibid.*, p. 48.
27. *Ibid.*, p. 200.
28. *Ibid.*, p. 73.
29. *Ibid.*, p. 131.

30. *Ibid.*, p. 21.
31. *Ibid.*, p. 22.
32. *Ibid.*
33. Malashri Lal. "Multilocality: International Themes in Women's Short Stories in English" *Signifying the Self* ed. Malashri Lal, Shormishtha Panja and Sumanyu Satpattry (New Delhi: Macmillan India Ltd., 2004), p. 157.
34. Anita Desai. *In Custody*, p. 65.
35. K.R. Srinivasa Iyengar. "A Note on Anita Desai's Novels", *The Banasthali Patrika* ed. Rameshwar Gupta, January, 1969, No. 12, p. 64.

Multiculturalism in the Recent Australian Short Fiction: An Indian Point-of-View

17

Pradeep Trikha

The contemporary Australian short story has been an influential literary form in the continent. The paper aims to discuss the stories written between 1960s and 1990s by the writers like Colin Johnson, Murray Bail, Frank Moorhouse, Michael Wilding and Joan London for they have given new direction to the Australian short story. The period between the 1960s and 1990s is the one during which Australian society experienced transmutations. The writers concentrated on Australian identity even though Asian locales provide suitable medium for their stories. No wonder Bennett aptly pointed out, "...it has been a suitable vehicle for the perceptions, feelings and attitudes of many that have not had the time, energy or inclination to write novels. But a good short story is as difficult to write as a good novel and it calls for special power of insight and organization" (Bennett: 1977). During the sixties short fiction experienced the breaking down of the repressive censorship legislation, eclecticism and rich literary culture. These 'new wave' writers "...were stimulated by resurgent radicalism of anti-Vietnam protests, counterculture and the influence of contemporary American writings" (Turner: 1964). They display a common desire to find access to the 'new horizons'[1] of self-definition/realization, warding-off Lawson-Furphy tradition. They influenced and directed public opinion and have a large following. They express their deep-seated skepticism about Australians as well as the society of the Indian sub-continent.

Bennett, congruously points out that a short story "...places both the writer and reader in the role of spectator rather than participant: a degree of aesthetic distance is necessary if the story is to have validity..." (Bennett: 1985) beyond a certain period of time. In other words, a story does not become just a sensational news item, it sustains the test of time. Australian writers have fictionalized encounters with Indian subcontinent settings. C.D. Narasimhaiah, an Indian academician, reiterates: "It is because these Australian writers have striven to preserve and promote the criterion of what "human wholeness" is that they have a claim to our attention" (Narasimhaiah: 1975)[2]. The aesthetic dimension in the stories by Johnson, Bail, Moorhouse, Wilding and London lies in their treatment of the moment of crisis[2].

Patrick White was perhaps the first Australian writer to include Gandhian thought as an epigraph to *Happy Valley* (1939). "It is impossible to do away with the law of suffering, which is one indispensable condition of our being. Progress is to be measured by the amount of suffering undergone the purer the suffering the greater is the progress" (White: 1939). There is little dignity without suffering, and Gandhi's life is a manifestation of sufferings. The novel portrays inner life of wide range of characters that suffer and attain spiritual sublimation[3]. There are a number of ways in which Colin Johnson, Murray Bail, Frank Moorhouse, Michael Wilding and Joan London have found Indian themes relevant to the people of Australia. They are indebted to Asian vicinity and not to the other British (post) colonial ones. Colin Johnson visited India in 1964, and then in 1968-75, worked for a Buddhist Journal in Calcutta. His story "A Missionary Would I Have Been" relates a rite of initiation of a trainee, as he is unable to overcome his desire of fantasizing sex with local girl in a teashop. The description of mountains, clouds and rain is ecstatic; reflect the swell of his unfulfilled desires. He travels to Darjeeling indulges in sex with a prostitute, decides to give up missionary pursuits, there is a huge flood and en-masse' destruction and suffering. Yet he thinks:

> Perhaps one day he would be classed as: Jesus Christ, Indian god of Euro-Semitic origins. Only the sword could cleanse this land and me!

After his first indulgence in sex, the narrator moves from spa to spa:

> Tibetan gods leered down: sought to possess, to hold to conquer, Heathen demons: ugly, corrupt—beyond corruption. Dancing on corpses—on death.... I was lost! Hideous scene—beautiful scene of my damnation. NO of my purging! Arak more Arak what matter—desire! The demons entered my heart and danced in my body.
>
> ("A Missionary Would I Have Been")

Johnson makes a significant comment on Australian counter-culture that often had inclination towards neo-Buddhists groups in India and suggests sexual repression can never lead to liberation or emancipation from the chains of desires be it in India or in Australia.

Murray Bail is a short story writer of substance, his collection *Contemporary Portraits and Other Stories* (1975) has stories like 'AB-Z' and 'The Dover's Wife'. Most of his stories are drawn from 'Suburban Australia'. 'AB-Z' deals with fictionalizing process and also divulges frailties of man-woman relationship. It has striking postmodern opening lines:

> I select from the letters [alphabets] pressing my fingers down. The letter appears....
>
> It signifies little or nothing; I have to add more.... The words match either my memory...or a picture of the object the word denotes. I am writing a story.
>
> (*Contemporary Classics*, 56)

A unique beginning compels the reader to read on and on. The characters Kathy Prindham and Syed Masood belong to two different cultures and nationalities but are in search of compatibility due to their common interests. Prindham, an Australian, is working as a librarian at the British Council Library, Karachi. She feels attracted towards a local artist Syed Masood. Unable to apprehend his 'natural self,' falls-out with him after living together for few months, and months later receives a self-portrait of the artist, which is also his masterpiece. The story suggests that for an artist his work of art is a social mode of communication. He tries to decipher the mystery of life;

self-portrait is an expression of self-realization by him. In order to comprehend this process Prindham will have to undergo transformation from a materialistic being to spiritual and intuitive being. Bail divulges that the work of art in the East is the source to interpret, rediscover, and explain the intuitive being and natural instincts of an individual.

Frank Moorhouse and Michael Wilding have played a significant role in shaping current attitudes to short fiction in Australia. They experimented with the form and content of the short story. They have found Indian themes relevant to the people of Australia in a comic and skeptical vein. Like C.J. Koch, Moorhouse sees the essential Australian experience is one:

> ....Where European consciousness, with European ancestral memories is confronted by the mask of a strange land and by a society no certain of its style.... (Koch: 1980)

It is also characterized by a "pathos of absence". Moorhouse longs for the other landscape and the other society and the other meaning. He finds that India offers a better understanding of life and behaviour of mankind in contrast to his own opinion against America's involvement in Vietnam and also exposes American hypocrisy, which drives an individual to the verge of nothingness.

"The Commune Does Not Want You" "The Mystery of a Time Piece" and "The Oracular Story", are narratives in which Moorhouse expresses his concern for Americanizing and Asian-izing of Australian youth. He contrasts two schools of Beats: the one which experiments with mysticism to attain spiritual heights and the other that advocate; sensuality to experience life. The narrator in these stories realizes that wherever one look; there is mystery and has potential for growth and exploration. In "The Oracular Story" he attempts to decipher the mystery to Hestia (a common friend of the narrator and his: associate Milton) that the birth and death are things which exist as parts of the universal scheme of which man knows just a fragment: He is also aware that there is no final answer. He suggests four functions of mind—intuition, thought, feeling and sensation.

"The Oracular Story", is an account of leisure time pursuits of Hestia and the narrator. Their imagination conjures incredible variety of fun. They form their own group separate and away from Milton's, adopt hippie cult which takes into account continuities and discontinuities of their lives, that includes

> ...The shoulder chains and the leather of the greasy bike heads; the starch of the blue psychiatric nurses, the bunch of domino players; the semi-conformist middle class some daring to wear beads; radicals in battle dress...
>
> ("The Oracular Story", 108)

The narrator becomes a Beat artist and Hestia his Beat audience. For him the society is a "closed room in which there are no values but rejected rat race..." he helps Hestia to overcome inhibitions, moralistic judgments and realize the potential of her individuality. Milton believes in self-restraint and man's collective existence, while narrator consider restrictions as life denying in spirit. He is in favor of individual's emancipation while Milton thinks individuality is an illusion. Moorhouse's narrator further helps Hestia overcome existential vulnerability by answering her questions:

> My problem....is that I don't know what to do with myself...
>
> Make an arbitrary decision. Respond then to the challenges set in motion by arbitrary decision.... Everything is contained within us...in degrees as every proposition contains the whole universe.... We contain our opposites and alternatives—the man in every woman...sometimes they are exclusive but not always.
>
> Hestia asks him:
>
> "What would you tell your children?"
>
> "I will tell them about great polarity of symbolic depiction of this..."
>
> "For what purpose"
>
> "Once realized it gives the state of resignation and diminishes urgency"
>
> "What are these symbolic representations"
>
> "Sleep/Walking, victory—defeat, silence—sound, passive—active."
>
> ("The Oracular Story", 112-11)

He explains to her that death is 'the changing of form—we become part of living soils and continue in cycles'. The setting of the story is equally important i.e. in a 'Golden Lake'. An interesting parallel can be drawn between Moorhouse' narrative and an episode of 'The Enchanted Pool' in the Mahabharata in Aranyaka Parva, in which Yudhistra is asked series of questions regarding day to day life of man and his relation to the universe. In Moorhouse's story Hestia makes similar queries to the narrator. The striking differences in the two tales are Yaksha and Yudhistra are males and unlike Hestia and the narrator he does not swim in the pool. Yudhistra answers Yaksha's questions to redeem his four brothers from Yaksha's spell and the narrator answers to redeem Hestia from Milton's spell.

Michael Wilding's story "The Silence of the Seer" is about the Eastern philosophical notion that, "purity can be achieved through silence and withdrawal from the world". The story is a dispassionate record of the man's retreat into silence, followed by his curious suicide. Wilding concludes on the note of undercurrent irony and skepticism:

> And so on 5 January 1970, he died by his own hand and his own necktie. His followers as his greatest sign took this, the final utterance he had been preparing for through forty years. In death he spoke more clearly than ever. They disseminated his message to all mankind and each year millions made their pilgrimage to his grave, from which that took away inspiration, a fore taste of infinity, and a glimpse of truth.
>
> (*The West Midland Underground*)

Joan London's "Burning off "too has synchronous theme i.e. 'the Inner Light Grows in Silence and Concentration'. The story is about city v/s country dichotomy. The characters go to live in the country far from the madding crowd in search of peace and solace. London, presents young Australians lacking strong convictions, and who out of lust, for power and certain curiosity, have entered active politics while being at university, unable to sustain the process of transition from Whitlam to Frazer. The narrator is a sensitive Australian youth:

> I lay on the mattress on the floor and tried to think... 'The Inner Light Grows in Silence and Concentration'
>
> In the city, in the big house where I had met Wes, the walls carried sign like a political meeting place. Indian gods behind the kitchen door. Over the stove, a newspaper cutting of Whitlam and Barnard waving after they had announced the conscription amnesty. A big mandala above the fireplace. What had come to be called the meditation room?
>
> (*Contemporary Classics*, 379)

London's protagonist suffers in order to arrive at self-knowledge. He appears to have succeeded in his search for solace in the Eastern philosophical system i.e. Inner Light Grows in Silence and Concentration[5]. The image of mandala is symbolic of totality its protective circle is a pattern of order super imposed on psychic chaos. The story concludes with a sudden change in political scene of Australia, i.e. Fraser assuming charge from Whitlam. Perhaps in order to heighten the moment of crisis we come to know about great forest fire[6]:

> The fire in the country took over. The house was darkened. I ran from room to room shutting the windows. A room seemed to run under the roof. I heard the wind chimes futile alarm. I stood by the kitchen window watched the flames pass the house in vast erratic tacks across the grass.
>
> (*Contemporary Classics* 390)

London suggests that Australian youth do have penetrating insights and are involved in social and political changes, self-conscious as they are in order to overcome their spiritual crises they turn to the Eastern philosophy. The fire signifies superiority and control, an expression of spiritual energy. It also symbolizes transformation and regeneration. It is capable of stimulating growth and the well-being of man. It is symbolic of spiritual strength as suggested in Indian Puranas.

The writers like Patrick White, Colin Johnson, Murray Bail and Joan London looked into Indian philosophical systems, as positive solutions to overcome counter-culture influence on Australian youth, while Frank Moorhouse and Michael Wilding are skeptical, ironic and quizzical. They question the meaning and value of the Eastern mystique. These writers have added notably to the tradition of Australian short story by enlarging the scope of the form so as to capture areas of Australian experience that the novelists had ignored. Moorhouse observes, "It can be an intense form which releases complex vibrations, not readily reducible to a single political and moral analysis." (Moorhouse: 1973). Though the observation was made in 1973 but it is still relevant because each new author is "very conscious of the main current"[7]—almost all of them are aware of the tradition to which they belong. They have transcended the geographical boundaries and reached to the people all over the world but the conjectural question is how many of them will pass the test of time.

NOTES

1. *New Horizons*: It was during 1996 Australia launched its New Horizons project with a single refrain "we have a shared love of cricket". But, since 1992 then AIC has been working like a missionary to promote cultural and business ties—nay the New Horizons between the two countries and has several new promises to keep.
2. Before analyzing the Recent Australian short fiction it is worthwhile to review the Australian point of view in Bruce Grant's, book *The Australian Dimension* (1983):

   "The dilemma of Australian civilization is that Australia is white, capitalist and thus inhibiting the growth of an Australian nation. Christian is a part of the world subject to ancient and powerful Asian influences. Cherishing western values, Australians have become intellectually and materially dependent on the power centers of the western world to protect them from Asia. Grant however does not ignore the fact that the immediate neighborhood is culturally rich and offers tremendous potential for the writers to undergo the process of cultural self-discovery".
3. Patrick White's early story "The Twitching Colonel" seeks to present India as a "state to the man's dualist dilemma and hence the answer to the question about the native reality". Later, White in *The Tree of Man* (1953) and *Voss* (1977) further expand Indian philosophical dimensions, which are relevant to the study of man. Unlike western society that depends on all reality and rationality norm, Indian society has a room for the intuitive and mythical.
4. Though Australians have made their presence felt on various occasions both on national and international fronts. Though Writers and

academics opposed censorship of laws left over an era before Whitlam Government against the freedom of expression. They reacted sharply against Americans aggression against Vietnam. More recently Australia resented against India's nuclear tests at Pokhran.

5. Mahatma Gandhi, throughout his life observed a weekly 'fast' unto silence during which he would introspect and self analyze. His effort grows inwardly.
6. Judith Wright's poem "Fire Sermon" has her pleasant memories of her encounter with Indian landscape.
7. To use T.S. Eliot's phrase drawn from his essay 'Tradition and Individual Talent', *The Sacred Wood*, London: Faber & Faber, 1979.

WORKS CITED

Anderson, Don. *Contemporary Classics*, 1965- 1995 Sydney: Vintage 1997.

Bennett, Bruce. "The Short Story", *Australian Literary Studies.* 8 No. 2 (1977) 164-182.

Laurie Hergehan (ed). "Perception of Australia, 1965-1988" *New Literary History of Australia* Sydney: Penguin 1985 (443-453).

"Asian Encounters in the Contemporary Australian Short Story." *World Literature Written In English*, Vol. 26 No. (1986), 49-61.

Brockman, Hennerita Drake "The International Symposium on the Short Story", *Kenyan Review*, Vol. 30, No. 4 (1968): 443-490.

Eliot, T.S. "Tradition and Individual Talent", *The Sacred Wood*, London: Faber & Faber 1919, p. 69.

Grant, Bruce *The Australian Dimension*, Sydney: Penguin, 1983.

Heseltine, H.P. "Thirty Years of Australian Short Story" Rajasthan University *Studies in English* XV (182-83).

Johnson, Colin. "A Missionary Would I have been" *Westerly* No. 1 (1975).

Koch C.J. "Literature and Cultural Identity" *The Tasmanian Review* No. 4 (1980); 85-89.

Moorhouse, Frank. *The Americans Baby* Sydney: North Ryde: Angus & Robertson, 1972 *Tales of Mystery and Romance* Sydney: North Ryde: Angus & Robertson, 1977.

Narasimhaiah, C.D. "An Introduction", *The Flowering of Australian Literature*, Mysore: Dhavanyaloka 1978, p. 6.

Pauline, Tom. "Specks of Unhistorical Time" *Times Literary Supplement*, 24 April 1961 (442-447).

Radhakrishnan, S. "Introduction", *Mahatma Gandhi*. Bombay, Jaico Pub House (1977).

Ross, Bruce Clunies. "Some Developments in Short Fiction 1969-1980", *Australian Literary Studies*. 10, 2 Oct 1981, p. 177.

Tiffin, Helen. "Indian Motifs in the Novel of Christopher Koch", Rajasthan Univ. *Studies in English*. Vol. XV 1982-83, 57-63.

Turner, lan. "Introduction", *The Literary History of Australia*. Geoffrey Dutton (ed) Ringwood: Penguin 1964.

Wilding, Michael. "The Silence of the Seer", *West Midland Underground*. Brisbane: University of Queensland Press, 1975.

White, Patrick. *Happy Valley* London: Harrap, 1939, p. 6.

Patrick White, 'The Twitching Colonel' *A Critical Symposium*. Ron Shepherd & Kirpal Singh (ed) Adelaide: CRNLE, 1978, p. 29.

Teaching Achebe and Conrad at the University of Burundi in Bujumbura

18

Athanasius Ayuk-Ako

The third-year students of the Department of English in the University of Burundi, like nearly all the students in that institution, have been tremendously affected by a conservative educational system where pedagogues conflate academics and culture; hardened and rendered gloomy by years of civil strife and seething poverty, these students' responses to Chinua Achebe and Joseph Conrad are in part influenced by their experiences.

The students in this university where not permitted to ask their professors any questions because this is seen as a sign of disrespect of and challenge to their authority and a travesty of their culture. Their contact with us[1] was to be the first time they would be at the center of any lecture, where their own opinions would be heard, and sometimes considered. It is within this classroom situation that I introduced my course on Chinua Achebe's *Things Fall Apart,* a novel that is at the center of African writings that evoke the encounter between the West and Africa.

A better understanding of the subversion of the African culture as Achebe portrays, can only be had against the background of European fiction that denigrates and distorts the image of Africa. Such fiction includes Joseph Conrad's *Heart of Darkness*, which Achebe argues, questions "the very humanity of black people" ("Image" 330). In putting this novella side by side *Things Fall Apart*, the instructor can help the students to understand Achebe's main purpose—capturing the dignity of a downgraded race—rather than continue to see it as a mere presentation of anthropological facts.

The danger exists that if not carefully handled, the discussions may degenerate into the partisan and polarized reception that both Achebe and Conrad have suffered and still do unfairly suffer both in the classroom[2] and in professional criticism. This explains why I usually start the class by cautioning the students on the importance of reading and responding to what they read as objectively as possible. The reason, to quote Ray Stevens, is that the responsibility of the instructor "is to assist in opening minds to various possibilities for critical interpretation, not to close them by trying to superimpose a critical or philosophical schema" ("Approaches" 22). To students who for the first time have been given the opportunity to fully participate in class discussions, the euphoria that this engendered, ultimately leads the students to levels of responses and analysis that make the class the more interesting.

The aim of my class lies in laying bare Achebe's attempts at debunking European tropes that misrepresent Africa and gauging students' responses to this unending question of difference and subversion. I introduce the class with the students and I briefly review such European texts, as Rider Haggard's "She", and King Solomon's "Mine", Joyce Cary's "Mister Johnson" that paint a refracted image of Africa. My intention is to suggest to students that what Conrad did was not new, being part of a continued process of denigration of a continent and a culture Europeans possibly did not fully grasped.

Equally, as a prelude to the class, I usually assign Patrick Brantlinger's essay "Victorians and Africans: The genealogy of the Myth of the Dark Continent" and Achebe's "An Image of Africa." Both articles help students in understanding the context in which both Conrad and Achebe wrote. I agree with John A. McClure and Padmini Mongia that no reading of *Heart of Darkness* should ignore Achebe's essay[3]. I will not hesitate to add that no such reading should equally ignore Patrick Brantlinger's. Both essays stimulating as they are, help us on the one hand to understand not only the forces which pushed Conrad to give in to what Rhino Zhuwarara describes as "the predilections of a readership whose imagination and sensibility have been for a long time indisposed towards anything black and anyone non-white" (230); and on the other hand to come to terms with Achebe's claim, "that the story we had to tell could not be told for us by anyone else no matter how well-gifted or well-intentioned" (qtd in Ojinmah 1).

Brantlinger argues that the Myth of the Dark Continent was a Victorian invention:

> ...as part of a larger discourse about empire, it was shaped by political and economic pressures and also by a psychology of blaming the victim through which Europeans projected many of their own dark impulses onto Africans. (80)

This conclusion helps the students to appreciate Achebe's novel in terms of its being a response to a colonial discourse that for its own political and social reasons unapologetically mis-represented the image of Africa. Conrad's *Heart of Darkness* was just part of this dominant discourse that according to Zhuwarara amounted to "a very cheap way of entertaining a jaded Europe afflicted by self-doubts" (239). It is, therefore, necessary for the students to know to what extent Conrad's narrative destabilizes the normal order of things in Africa. *Things Fall Apart* can better be understood within this framework as both novels reflect opposing images of Africa. Although Achebe's desire to become a writer was instilled by his reading of Cary's Mister Johnson, yet it is with *Heart of Darkness* that he expresses his anger, not for the purported exploitation of the Africans, but for the sheer ignorance of its writer, who refused to acknowledge the humanity of Africans.

Achebe's greatest accusation of Conrad is that he is "a bloody racist" ("Image", 328), whose story is one in which "the very humanity of black people is called to question" ("Image" 330). This charge of racism so grave, partly because of Conrad's own ambiguous rendering of the narrative, has since, sparked off a wave of counter rhetoric that either tends to defend or oppose either Conrad or Achebe. This has unavoidably led to a polarized and bipartisan attitude towards both authors. It is the first time that my students are reading this text, which they will read again in detail in a different context at the fourth level in a Modern British Author's course. The excitement in class is obvious and understandably so because the Congo, which shares the same colonial experience with Burundi, is just next-door.

In spite of numerous attempts at rescuing Conrad from Achebe's charge of racism, the facts still stare at one, each time the text is read. The students and I read portions of the text, which are littered with some of the most annoying misconceived descriptions of Africans. This is because students need to understand these descriptions if they have to understand Achebe's anger, and the world he creates in *Things Fall Apart.* Such derogatory descriptions of blacks as "creatures" (32), "nigger" (38), "a whirl of black limbs" (50), "prehistoric man" (50), "savage", "improve specimen", "a dog in a parody of breeches and a feather hat, walking on his hind legs" (51), with faces as "black death-mask" (62), speak for themselves.

Descriptions like these, irritate the students to the point where they ask to know why a book that dehumanizes the African still continues to be in the university curriculum and a canon for that matter. To these students whose colonial heritage is simmered in blood and anger, it is a tremendous challenge to justify the continuous existence of an apparently racist text in their school curricula. Some students even argue that my justification for the continued teaching of the text can be understood against my own country's historical and intellectual background. It becomes a very serious issue trying to convince them that teaching a text does not necessarily mean that the views in it are consonant with one's views. I indicate to the students the centrality of *Heart of Darkness*, on the grounds that for Africans to objectively represent their image, they must first of all understand the context, and the history of their own false representation. This will of course help them to better appreciate counter-discourses that attempt a re-orientation of the warped image of Africa and Africans.

The narrative refuses to give Africans any human authenticity. Passage upon passage, students read evidence of how Marlow refuses to give the Africans a language and a voice simply because he considers that they have none. He reduces their language to "a very loud cry, as of indefinite desolation..." or "a complaining clamor" that "modulated in savage discords" (54) as "they shouted periodically together strings of amazing words that resemble no sounds of human language; and the deep murmurs of the crowd, interrupted suddenly were like the responses of some satanic litany" (83). The doubt about Africans' humanity (51) echoes strongly in the narrative. I suggest to students that Marlow possibly meets people whose language sounds strange to him because it does not resemble any that he is conversant with in Europe. Students easily dismiss this arguing that being educated as he is, he should have known that there are other languages elsewhere other than those he knows especially as they believe, he knew that there is no race of people living on the surface of the earth that is dumb. To them, difference does not or should rather not mean inferiority or non-existence.

The interest of the evidence against him lies in its relevance to understanding Achebe's counter-discourse. The aim of reading Conrad thus is not just to concord with the fact of his racism, but also to demonstrate how his narrative unavoidably does what he might have wished to avoid. I equally call the students attention to the author's condemnation of the colonial exploitation of the colonized. Generally, by the time we are done with *Heart of Darkness*, the students are equipped with the knowledge and the context that gave birth to novels such as *Things Fall Apart*.

In writing *Things Fall Apart*, Achebe writhed under the possibility and necessity for change. Today, my students face that same dilemma. My students are offended by Stereotypic images of Africa but also by some moribund aspects of their culture. The teaching of *Things Fall Apart* therefore helps them to express their bitterness at what they detest in their own culture.

More than just an anthropological treatise as Charles Larson has indicated, and the tragedy of a clan and its hero Okonkwo, or a portrayal of the clash of civilizations and its consequences, *Things Fall Apart* is monumental in objectively debunking the myth of Africa as perpetrated by nineteenth century Europeans. The novel is equally important in its being the first real attempt at giving a precise picture, or of even attempting to shore up another discourse, one contrary to that of the colonizer.

The starting point for me is a quotation from Achebe's third novel *Arrow of God*. In the chiaroscuro of events that characterize the abovementioned novel, Ezeulu, the chief priest makes one cardinal statement that remains to me the most important in understanding Achebe's colonial and postcolonial novels. Wearied by the unavoidable presence of the white administration, the chief priest contends, "The world is like a mask dancing. If you want to see it well, you do not stand in one place. My spirit tells me that those who do not befriend the white man today will be saying had we known tomorrow" (46). How well is this wisdom and how well this reflects Achebe's own sentiment with regards to the clash of civilization is important in the discussions in the classroom. The statement reflects the very anxiety that characterize my students as they struggle to come to grips, with European stereotypes about them, and at the same time reject some moribund traditional values that impinge on their own very existence as human beings.

Things Fall Apart gives an image of a tranquil society with its own laws, rules and systems of worship, in fact, its own cosmogony. The very first part of the novel upholds the heterogeneous society of Umuofia that early critics apparently refused to recognize. They continued to see that first part only in terms of its anthropological relevance. No surprise therefore that Charles Larson in discussing the novel underscores the fact that "African writers have largely ignored Western literary modes of writing" (19), seeing the first part of the novel as being "heavily anthropological" (30). This kind of reading of course seriously undermines the text's importance as a counter-discourse with its own aesthetic merits.

No doubt, one can make that claim and correctly too, as to the anthropological significance of the text. But to think that it is the novelist's only purpose will be to forget Achebe's real intentions. His novel portrays a society, which is heterogeneous, with people coming to a life of their own. I suggest to the students that we should read this first part of the novel against the background of the negative images of Africa that Conrad portrays. While this first part reveals a lot of the positive sociological characteristics of African life, it equally reveals some of its horrific and detestable aspects.

Usually, at this level, the students find themselves hedged between the passing away of this festive traditional African society immersed in the revelry of feud and feast, and a Europeanized one with its attendant problems. They are quick to condemn the barbarity that had actually characterized Africa and in some parts still does. Since I suggest to my students that Achebe's Africa is very close to the truth, I challenge them to pick out aspects of the society, which they consider are moribund, harmful and therefore, not necessary in a more and more changing society. Responses here are usually varied and sometimes very strange. Understandably, some, if not most of the responses are conditioned by the students' own heavily patriarchal culture and their attitudes towards it. The female students are quick to condemn Okonkwo's heavy handedness; and his involvement in the cruel killing of Ikemefuna receives almost unanimous condemnation, all of this being a way of condemning their own heavily patriarchal society. Responses to the Ibo tradition of presenting heads of people as a sign of bravery in war or the use of human heads as cups are varied. Here I can understand that these varying responses depend on the various backgrounds of the students. Most of the male students in my class see this as an expression of genuine might, while a majority of the female students albeit their own participation in their civil strife, regard it as a barbarous and outmoded practice.

A major issue in the teaching of this novel, and which generates serious debates among the students is the whole question of the conflict between Western and traditional systems of beliefs. For a good number of my students, African traditional gods were too severe, and exacting. They argue that this severity though it served as an instrument of moral control, yet, made life very difficult for the inhabitants of the Umuofia people. In a country where more than 90 per cent of the people are Christians, one can understand the students' concern about traditional religious practices. Sometimes, it is surprising to hear some students argue that Christianity is also at the roots of Africa's problems. It is difficult at times to come to terms with this group of students who having fresh memories of the Rwandan[4] experience see this religious practice as yet another instrument of Western control of the Africans. To these students, Africans should develop their age long religious practices, and make them conform to the changing times. Achebe himself in evoking the inevitability of change underscores not the complete eradication of African traditional methods of worship, but their adaptation to the changing phases of their lives. His interview to National Educational Television, testifies to this:

> The weakness of this particular society is its lack of adaptation, not being able to bend.... I think in this time the strong men were those who did not bend and I think this was a fault in the culture itself. (Qtd in Larson 61)

In sampling the various opinions of students with regards to the various religious confessions, the challenge rests in coping with students who on the one hand are skeptical about the potency of their own religious traditions and on the other are uncertain about the real purpose of Western religious practices, in a world continuously taken hostage by Western idiosyncrasies. I suggest to the students that to cope with this dilemma, perhaps the best thing to do is to coalesce positive aspects of traditional religious practices with Western religious forms.

Some of the students relate the experience of Christianity in *Things Fall Apart* to that of present day Evangelism that they fear has a hidden agenda. We read the conversation between the old man Akunna and Mr. Brown, as an example of the white man's refusal to acknowledge that Africans had a defined system of worship. To some, this attempt of Christianity to subvert the traditional modes of worship in Umuofia was good in that it possibly helped in discarding certain acts of barbarism and atrocity, which were common currency in Umuofia. However, even these students who are generally Christians, and who do not see anything wrong in the Christian colonization of Umuofia, are not comfortable with the fact of the Christian colonizers not always considering that Africa had its own religious culture.

Students are shocked by such cultural attitudes as the throwing away of twins and albinos because they were believed to herald ill luck. Responses of disapproval to these types of issues are predictable. But this disapproval is informed not sometimes by the students' sense of decency, but by their sense of parenthood. The female students are particularly revolted by this attitude, because maternity is much respected here. The students regard the throwing away of twins and albinos as abominable.

The ostracization of the "osu" or slaves is regarded with the same contempt. In a country where the dichotomy between the ruling class (the Tutsis) and the ruled (the Hutus) is so evident, where the memory of years of atrocious wars are still fresh, separation on the basis of any form of inferiority can be detestable. This, to the students, resembles some form of Apartheid in traditional Umuofia. Naturally, many of them acknowledge the ignorance that has characterized some African societies. It is time they argue, that they do away with this, and erase the line between the marginalized and the powerful.

In *Chinua Achebe: New Perspectives*, Umelo Ojinmah argues that:

> Achebe portrays Umuofia of *Things Fall Apart* as a pluralistic society, which admires energetic, aggressive, and ambitious members, one that is patient, tolerant and forbearing, entrenched in the wisdom of its ancients, yet flexible and adaptable when necessary. (13)

At first value, the students have the impression that Okonkwo represents such values, and in some respects they are right, because he fits Ojinmah's description of the strongman. He is brave, daring, and energetic. But he lacks flexibility upon which the very survival of his tribe depends, and it is precisely this that will lead to his demise. A remarkable feature of Okonkwo's personality is that in spite of his rashness he at least attempts to check the white man's encroachment into Umuofia and in this way affirms the dignity of his people. Some students sanction his show of force, which they argue is a deterrent to the unmitigated Europeanisation of Umuofia. To some, he is a man betrayed by his people, and therefore worthy of our sympathy. Opinions on him are divergent, depending on the perspective and some times the social and even political backgrounds of these students.

In an interview given at the Afro-American Research Institute at the University of Texas at Austin, Achebe himself disapproved of Okonkwo when asked what he thought of Ezeulu, the hero of Arrow of God. He argues that unlike Ezeulu who was an intellectual and understood the need to adapt to change, Okoknkwo did not have the same vision. He

> ... was not an intellectual and did not see what was going on. Okonkwo just saw his duty to protect his own and stand against the assault. So he failed. Ezeulu said, "Right, I have seen this thing; these people are powerful but that doesn't mean they are superior to me. I will make use of them" But he failed too, that's a pity. (8)

Here Achebe presents a dilemma, which is also not only akin to my students. Like Ezeulu, these students are caught between a derogatory representation of their values, and a culture that can no longer uphold its own. Gruesome memories of the students' own military experience informs their perception of Okonkwo as a victim of historical forces about which he has no control. He equally represents to them the symbol of Africa caught in the whirlwind of change and struggling to come to terms with it. I suggest to students that Okonkwo fails because his fight is gratuitous. He has no fixed alternative to the encroachment of Christianity; he undertakes a rather personal struggle for his own glory and to avenge his personal disgrace at the hands of the white man's administration. In spite of his failure, Okonkwo is history's own statement on the inevitable passage of time.

Okonkwo's world I suggest to the students is full of contradictions, and it is precisely these contradictions that destroy him. Obierika, his friend captures his predicament when he says: "why should a man suffer so grievously for an offence he had committed inadvertently" (25). I suggest to my students that in many respects Okonkwo's fate is ours. If we do not come to terms with some of the changes occasioned by globalization then that can be our own end. Okonkwo's demise is the result of his failure to acculturate. Many students wonder whether in killing Okonkwo, Achebe has not accepted defeat for the people of Umuofia. I equally call their attention to the fact that in any case what happens to Umuofia was inevitable, and in accepting death, Okonkwo has just made his own personal decision to it.

In his very succinct essay "Realism, criticism and the disguises of Both: A Reading of Chinua Achebe's *Things Fall Apart* with an evaluation of the criticism relating to it," Ato Quayson argues with convincing evidence that femininity pervades Achebe's narrative as "The clan's cultural values institute the feminine in a very powerful position within the governing symbolic system, taking care to suggest a subtle interfusion of the two principles of male and female" (27).

However, overall, Umuofia is a society pervaded by male chauvinism. Female students are quick to denounce this. In a society where women are only beginning to express themselves freely, this is an opportunity for them to speak out against the heavy chains of patriarchy that continue to affect a great majority of them. A good number of the male students continue to sanction and celebrate this male chauvinism. Some even justify this by explaining that Europeanization of women fails to take cognizance of African reality. In fact, this is one issue in my teaching of this text where opinions between the male and female students are sharply divided.

The whole idea of the invasion of Umuofia constitutes a very political issue to the students who see in this infiltration, the source of Africa's continuous conflicts. Usually, I call the students attention to the inevitability of the encroachment as part of the cyclical nature of history. A good majority of the students are usually skeptical about the importance of the relation between African and European countries. Students generally acknowledge that the Europeanization of Umuofia helped in discarding the unwanted aspects of the culture that hamper the smooth evolution of the society, but at the same time, it brings with it such ills as would equally denigrate the society.

In all, teaching *Things Fall Apart*, in this university comes with many challenges. These challenges reflect both the problematic nature of the text and the patterns of students' responses when given a free hand to do so. On the one hand, the students are revolted by the warped picture of Africa given through an imperial discourse determined to occlude the objective truth about Africa, and on the other they are equally angered at some of their traditions which continue to exist, and which impinge on the true political, social and economic development of Africa. Objective responses to Achebe's novel are sometimes determined and at the same time undermined by the culture of the students. In many ways, the students see the texts as the medium through which they can express their own anguish. But may be the more difficult task is trying to show the extent of the relevance of Achebe's novel in a society in which the clash of cultures is already a fait accompli. However, through it, students may come to a better understanding of their own history and equally what I consider to be Achebe's main purpose: re-orienting Western images and metaphors of difference and falsehood.

NOTES

1. We were a group of four Cameroonian lecturers sent to the University of Burundi in October 2003 as part of an exchange program between our two universities.
2. See Agbaw, S Ekema's "The dog in Breeches: Conrad and an African Pedagogy". *Research in African Literatures*. 29.1 2000, 185-196.
3. See Approaches to Teaching Conrad's *Heart of Darkness* and *The Secret Sharer*. Eds. Hunt Hawkins and Brian Shaffer (New York: The Modern Language Association, 2004) 40-47,104-110.
4. Here we are talking of the involvement of the Catholic Church in the genocide in Rwanda.

19

White Man at the End of History: A Comparative Study of Nadine Gordimer's *The Conservationist* and J. M. Coetzee's *Disgrace*

Arpa Ghosh

The sixties in South African history was a difficult time for the blacks with the new Prime Minister Dr Hendrik Verwoerd laying out details for the launch of 'grand apartheid'. It was the decade of the aftermath of Sharpeville Massacre (1959) in which ANC and PAC activists were mowed down by police for their mass protest against the notorious pass laws. In the wake of the Massacre, marches, mournings and boycotts were organized on a daily basis. Pretoria, in sharp retaliation, declared emergency, banned ANC and PAC and arrested prominent African leaders.

Outlawed in its land, the ANC held its first conference in Botswana in which it openly advocated armed struggle. PAC, a militant group from the first, established itself in Basutoland. Pretoria reacted by increasing its stranglehold on black population within South Africa and tightening border vigilance. The iconic first generation leaders of black struggle, Mandela, Sisulu, Mabeki and others were behind bars; the new-generation leaders had not yet come into prominence. The freedom movement within South Africa had suffered a severe setback. Across the borders, however, there was a slow but steady gathering of forces. Black fugitive ambassadors used the American and English media to influence world opinion even while failing to garner the Security Councils' support for the armed struggle.

The Conservationist,[1] written in 1974 marks a deepening of Gordimer's vision and commitment vis-à-vis the anti-apartheid movement. Deeply sensitive to the changing face of South African politics Gordimer uses the novel as a vehicle of prophecy to warn the reigning pro-apartheid capitalist government of South Africa against alienating itself from the majority indigenous black population. Moving away from her usual practice of portraying well-intentioned white liberals, Gordimer attempts to understand the secret fears and desires of the reigning white Nationalist in South Africa through her portrayal of Mehring a white pro-apartheid capitalist.

Mehring is a wealthy, influential, jet setting Afrikaner colonizer who lives off the fat of the land benefiting richly from the Nationalist Party's apartheid policies. The title is profoundly ironic indicating Mehring's desire to conserve the infertile, unproductive landscape of the farm at the cost of the Zulus who depend on it for sustenance, and in the larger context, apartheid, at a time when black history is swiftly altering its course.

The novel operates on three narrative planes. The stream-of-consciousness technique is used by Gordimer with a specific political purpose to unravel Mehring's totally self-absorbed, predatory, aggressive and abusive consciousness that neglects to take stock of the changing historical scenario. Lukacs criticizes the ahistorical nature of the stream of consciousness technique that gives precedence to individual consciousness at the expense of the individual's historical role and identity in history. Gordimer positions Mehring's narrative within a larger matrix of the omniscient narrative to bring out in sharp relief the latter's ignorance of his diminishing historical role.

The second narrative plane makes use of symbols that are intricately tied up with Gordimer's dialectical approach to history—black history in contestation with white history with the latter eventually collapsing under the press of the former. A black dead body, perfunctorily buried by white police, keeps resurfacing in the northern part of Mehring's farm. South African readers of Gordimer's novel will immediately recognize this as a symbolic reference to Namibia and Angola's independence from Portuguese rule around this period. The white man's grip over Africa is loosening and thus in Mehring's nightmare the corpse is an invasive presence together with terrifying images of drought and flood. The symbols used are archetypal and organically connected with Zulu kinship conventions.

The third plane is a sensitive amalgamation of realist narration and mythic prophecy. The black world is the focal point of this plane. The poverty, hunger and meagerness of the life of the Zulu labourers of Mehring's farm are as real as their strong and vital connection with the soil as a source of sustenance. The Zulu community is close-knit where survival is a collective enterprise. The psychic link of the Zulus with their ancestors as a source of knowledge (a subtext of Zulu mythology with its stress on family, kinship, and continuation of bloodline) runs contrapuntal to Mehring's egotist, sterile ruminations.

The three narrative planes are interconnected by the common thread of Gordimer's vision of African history as exclusively belonging to the blacks. In later novel's Gordimer sees whites playing significant roles in the history of the South African postcolonial nation, but in this novel the future belongs exclusively to the blacks. Mehring, with his grasping attitude to the land which he seeks to conserve in its sterility to flaunt as a showpiece to his friends and mistress, is a man virtually as the dead end of history. This impression is fortified by his status as a divorced man. He has a son who comes to visit him in the farm, but the son shows no interest in the workings of the farm and will definitely not stay back to foster it. Moreover, the son betrays signs of homosexuality. Therefore possibly, Mehring will die heirless. His liberal mistress Antonia, after mouthing a few harsh truths about Mehring's growing insignificance in the political arena of South Africa, and flirting with fashionable politics, leaves South Africa using her influential lover's connections to bail herself out on an exit visa. Gordimer's disillusion with the impotent, opportunist liberal stance and its secret entente with apartheid-enforcers find expression in the portrayal of Antonia, Mehring's liberal girlfriend: "Always promising what you can't give, your kind" (136). Mehring's labourers, indifferent to his presence or absence, solve their own problems and eke a pared livelihood from the farm without relying upon his assistance or patronage: "He and his son with woman's hair came and went away, leaving nothing, taking nothing; the farmhouse was empty" (172). Mehring's lust for the terrain of Africa, with its infinite material possibilities, parallels his lust for young, nubile women, preferably keyed in to his male pleasure. He admits that there is "a special pleasure in having a woman you've paid.... It's very clear-cut. For that one night, or that one afternoon or day, whatever it is. You've bought and paid for everything" (77-78).

Two black adversaries are pitted against the male, rapacious, egotistical and sterile persona of Mehring—the supine yet menacing solid mass of the black corpse with its face in the mud, a violated, tortured, mutilated Africa returning to reclaim its lost ancestral place, and a Zulu seeress, Phineas' wife who, troubled by hallucinations sleeps peacefully only after the corpse is buried.

Gordimer uses the corpse-metaphor to underline the resurging of erased, mutilated black history. The corpse is described thus:

> One of them. The face is in the tacky mud; the tiny brown pinstripe ears, the fine, felted hair, a fold or roll where it meets the back of the neck, because whoever he was, he wasn't thin. [...] the face, which struck a small break or pocket between clumps, his body isn't actually on the earth or pocket between clumps, but held slightly above it on a nest of reeds it has flattened, made for itself. (15)

Face buried in the mud the body represents an oppressed race, its individuality stifled by torture and oppression. Its corporeality threatens Mehring the white supremacist who is at a loss as to how to dispose of the body. Its location draws the South African reader's attention to the recent independence of South Africa's northern neighbours Namibia and Angola. The secondhand clothes handed down possibly by a white master indicate the exclusionist strategies of the whites who hoard the best for themselves as also the threat in the back of every white man's mind of the black man ultimately usurping his place. However, the most powerful symbol is the bed of reeds on which the body rests, the reed being a Zulu totem for the ancestor.

The other image is that of a black female diviner referred to as Phineas' wife, a name that underlines her social role, who unlike Cassandra (interestingly a western mythical female diviner who is scorned and ignored by patriarchs till too late), is a respected figure in black community. The diviners' psychic disturbance that lasts as long as the corpse lies unclaimed, points to her strong affinities to community and cult, affinities that Mehring knows nothing of.

The body is finally given a burial in keeping with Zulu and Christian rites by the labourers of Mehring's farm, even as Mehring's self-centred, material and sexually predatory grip over reality slackens and he succumbs to a series of gruesome delusions. The description of the funeral of the black corpse is simple and evocative, removed from the convoluted and egotistical stream-of-consciousness narrative of Mehring (266). The evocative language celebrates the restoration of the corpse to its rightful place in time and history preceded by ancestors and followed by children. Interestingly, the slogan of ANC was "Mayibuye Afrika!"—"Africa will come back!" The corpse is a potent symbol of resurgent black African history acting as a link between the past and the present. The concept of the family for the Zulus is a larger, kinship concept spanning generations, clans and the spirit world. The solemn acceptance and burial of the corpse as one of their own points to the deeply emotional relationship the Zulus share with the land and its black inhabitants.

In contrast to the organic relationship between the Zulus and the soil, Mehring's relationship with the land is governed by concerns of conquest, profit and male prowess:

> The dunes of the desert lie alongside the road between Swakopmund and Walvis Bay. Golden reclining nudes. Torso upon torso, hips sweeping from waist, smooth beyond smoothness, suggesting to the tactile imagining only the comparison, in relation to the hand, of the tongue when some substance evanesces on it. (103-4)

Characteristically, Mehring associates sterile desert landscape with the sensuality of the female body. Both for him are objects of acquisition. Towards the end of the novel, Mehring's hold on reality, never strong at its best disintegrates irredeemably. The concluding sections of the novel take on the shape of phantasmagoria in which Mehring confuses reality with secret psychological fear, actual occurrence with dreadful hallucinations.

Four years later, against the backdrop of Soweto Revolt, Coetzee would create a female protagonist Magda[2] whose spurious, tenuous grasp over reality would also crumble under the pressure of change. The common point of resemblance between Magda and Mehring is that both, of a sudden, find themselves in the leeward side of history, severed irrevocably from the larger community life. Extreme isolation breeds neurosis in both.

The Conservationist is Gordimer's firm rebuttal of the fascist methods of governance adapted by the white Nationalist government post-Sharpeville. It is an unequivocal affirmation of black history as coming of its own and ousting the techno-savvy, capitalist white history at a time in the early seventies when no such actual possibility was at sight, either within South African borders or in the international forum of the UN. The novel marks the victory of Gordimer as visionary artist over Gordimer the chronicler of socio-political events and their repercussions on private life.

Gordimer reveals her Marxist leanings by foregrounding the economic question of whites depriving blacks for economic gain at a time when the question of profit was glossed over by white liberals, who emphasized interracial personal relations and friendships. Stephen Clingman describes *The Conservationist* as a rejoinder to Olive Schreiner's "The Story of an African Farm". Clingman writes:

> For if Schreiner's work, drawing in an unspoken past, represents the uneasy settlement of a colonial order, then it is the dissolution of this order that Gordimer's work, telling a history of the future, prophesies. Critically, the question of possession comes to the fore; here the African farm that Schreiner settled at once so assuredly and uncertainly returns to those from whom it was dispossessed in the first place; the material and mental hold of the European on Africa is loosened, as the land comes back to its people and they to it.[3]

But unlike Mehring who is blinded by his acquisitiveness, Antonia his liberal mistress acts as the novelist's mouthpiece by prophesying that, "That four hundred acres isn't going to be handed down to your [Mehring's] kids, and your children's children.... That bit of paper you bought yourself from the deeds office isn't going to be valid for as long as another generation. It'll be worth about as much as those our grandfathers gave the blacks when they took the land from them. The blacks will tear up your bit of paper. No one'll remember where you are buried" (177). Antonia is clearly speaking in Gordimer's voice linking in her discursive warning the issues of race, family and economic disparity. The fragility and provisionality of the white man's ownership of African land over the strength and legitimacy of the black man's claim over the same is emphasized in no uncertain terms. It is evident that Antonia, while retaining her sexual relation with Mehring, has a low opinion of his politics. Man-woman relationships in the context of apartheid are thus shown to be emotionally sterile and tainted with opportunism and mutual recrimination.

Compared to the Mehring-Antonia sections, the sections devoted to the description of black life in the farm are oddly inadequate and stripped of detail. In these sections Gordimer uses the pared narrative framing the blacks in a timeless setting. The phallocentric, hypermasculine persona of Mehring is countered by subversive, eruptive energy stemming from two sources. One is the supine, apparently lifeless corpse that paradoxically turns out to be the most potent entity in the novel reinscribing erased, mutilated black history. The other is Phineas' wife whose powers are intuitive, mystical, oral and deeply embedded in the folk culture of the Zulus. Both these entities are at counterpoint to Mehring's increasingly hollow, ineffectual authority that springs from economic oppression and rides piggy back on the divisive and unjust economic policies of the apartheid state.

Through the figures of the corpse and Phineas' wife, we see how the concepts of kinship, ancestry, and the intuitive, emotive power of women, are brought in to counter the intimidating money power of Mehring. Gordimer is keen to drive home Mehring's destructive masculinity by narrating an encounter between the city-smart, high-powered executive Mehring with his penchant for young, nubile women as sexual toys, and his more rustic, agrarian but equally domineering counterpart the Afrikaner neighbour farmer De Beers who comes to visit him with his brood of subdued, baby-producing women. By drawing attention to De Beers' sexual equipment: "The retaining wall of belly and bunch of balls part the thighs majestically. Oh to wear your manhood, fatherhood like that, eh, stud and authority" (51). Gordimer emphasizes the underlying resemblance between the two characters. Both are men, who by subjugating, alienating (Mehring is a divorcee) and commodifying women have jeopardized their links to the African soil. The white woman in the novel is either submissive (the women of the De Beers family) or absconding (Mehring's wife and mistress). The black woman, Phineas' wife, is a far more grounded, focused presence in the novel.

Two important occasions are described even in the pared narrative: feasting and funeral, timeless group activities that reinforce the bond of brotherhood and interestingly evoke the Dickensian narrative of Scrooge's Christmas vision of the penurious clerk making merry in his virtuous, Christmas home, while he is excluded from its warmth by virtue of his mammon worship.

> All the farm was dark except for where they gathered the life of the place together for themselves.... Stamping slowly, swaying from one foot to the another, dancing conferred a balance of its own that drunkenness could not fell, and those who felt blows gathering in their fists mostly could not find their target. The night stood back from them; their voices, their treading feet and thumping drums spouted from it in plenty. (172)

Against the self-centred stance of Mehring, augmented all the more by the stream of consciousness narrative that issues from him, the land stirs into life with the unearthing of the black corpse that refuses to stay buried. The novel's narrative energy stems from the fact that the black corpse is a locus of profound symbolism. On one hand it stands as the symbol of exploitation and torture of the black in the hands of the white minority through centuries. This is brought out powerfully when towards the end Mehring is scared by the imagined grip of a ghost hand on his foot:

> He [Mehring] must get his leg out of the mud.... It...holds him in a cold, thick hand round the ankle. A soft, cold, black hand. Ugh. It's simply a matter of getting enough leverage, with the other leg and the rest of his body, to pull him free. As he heaves, the mud holds him, holds on, has him by the leg and won't let him go, down there.... It's absurd; he's begun to giggle with queer panicky exasperation. (228)

For a moment it seems as if the body is pulling him down to the degradation of shallow burial, to the injustice of being denied basic human rights. In the context of the gathering force of the changing tide of history, the body is an object of veneration and adoration by the Zulu farm hands. It is also an emblem of the deep tie that black Africans experience for their progenitors. Finally, the nameless corpse is gathered within the community and given a decent burial by the resident blacks. An organic, fertile connection is thus established between past and present:

> The eyes of the children moved with the spade. Phineas's wife's face was at peace, there was no burden of spirits on her shoulders as she watched Witbooi, Izak, Solomon and Jacobus sink the decent wooden box, and her husband shovel the heavy spatter of soil, soft and thick. Without consulting Jacobus, Witbooi had privately provided a pile of medium-sized stones to surround the mound as he would mark out a flowerbed in a white man's garden.
>
> The one whom the farm received had no name. He had no family but their women wept a little for him. There was no child of his present but their children were there to live after him. They had put him away to rest, at last; he had come back. He took possession of this earth, theirs; one of them. (267)

Lost land and lost history is restored to the blacks, in this case emblematically the plot of land that is initially denied to the corpse. Continuity is sought to be established between past suffering and present peace. Also, the corpse, Mehring's Manichean opposite, is drawn into the center of black community.

He is no longer a nameless tramp, but the ancestor of the black children in Mehring's farm. In contrast, Mehring's sexual aggression is fruitless as it begets no heir. Rather, in the airplane episode, his predator-like conduct towards the under-age Portuguese girl (126-132) in retrospect seems a barren, absurd act that demeans him as a human being without really touching his victim in any way.

On a return trip from one of his business meets Mehring molests a passive underage girl. The incident takes place in an unspecified hour between night and dawn, on vague terrain neither Europe nor Africa, the plane suspended in midair. "The plane is privately veiled, hidden in sand, buried in space. Nothing is disclosed" (126). The girl is passive, unresponsive. She allows herself to be molested and in the morning silently leaves Mehring's side to rejoin her mother unaffected by his overture. Mehring realizes that it was an "insane risk" (132) that left no lasting impression on the girl. "Her fluid on his hand as one says a man has blood on his hands. She screamed, or got up and told her mother.... A prosecution for 'interfering' with a young girl;...the girl has no name" (131). The episode illustrates Mehring's insignificance in African history. The predator-colonizer thinks he has power over a "female" Africa, but his sense of power is a delusion having no base in reality. Self-absorbed and blinded by self-interest he fails to see that the tide of history has swerved in a direction that will finally render him economically, politically and sexually redundant.

The plane episode is central to the narrative design of the novel. The active-male/passive-female binary that recalls the classic binary of the colonizer/colonized is played out literally in vacuum. "The finger was in no hurry to broach the question; the thighs must be anticipating that it was coming...whatever time this was—an hour between the hour of Europe and the hour of Africa...and whatever place this was" (129). Mehring's sexual overture towards the Portuguese girl in the plane hanging in midair leaves no lasting imprint, begets no offspring and exists outside the realm of history. The encounter is a symbolic comment on the Afrikaner short-lived impact on African history. Also as the underage girl is young enough to be his daughter, Mehring desecrates the parental-filial bond by molesting her. Familial bonds that are honoured by the blacks are desecrated by the white Afrikaner.

Mehring's frequent hallucinations about a close, brotherly interaction with his black foreman Jacobus is tainted by the luxury of self-indulgence. Even though he owns the farm, he does nothing to upgrade the lives of the black dependents. In the final analysis Mehring is the conservationist of delusory power and false, static history that has no lasting worth or meaning, cut off as it is from the soil of Africa, from the organic history of the land.

Unlike her younger compatriot J.M. Coetzee, Gordimer does not regard fiction as a substitute of history. Her links with political activism and her identification with the black cause are too strong for her to take this standpoint. In *The Conservationist* she penetrates surface reality to seek the more profound links between history, myth and prophecy that will help to impart a greater momentum to the black movement that had suffered a severe setback after the Sharpeville Massacre. Drawing from the resources of Zulu myth and folklore and connecting these to a present that points to the bankruptcy and growing insanity of white capitalist culture, a firm affirmation in the eventual success of the black struggle is registered. Such an affirmation comes long before any such actual change was to be noted in South African surface reality. In an address to PEN Congress delivered in 1986, Gordimer voices her belief in the power of imagination to construct the future:

> ....in instances where time and history appear to have met, this has been, so to speak, before the event: the writer's imagination has visualized an ordering of human lives that seems to be attainable by the projection of a state not yet created.... But once the State is established, the duality between Writer and State opens up again. Why? I do not think the whole explanation is to be found in the stark fact that the ideals of a revolution are at best difficult to realize and at worst are betrayed, when the revolution itself succeeds. The Writer himself knows that the only revolution is the

permanent one—not in the Trotskyite sense, but in the sense of the imagination, in which no understanding is ever completed, but must keep breaking up and re-forming in different combinations if it is to spread and meet the terrible questions of human existence.[4]

Mehring's story is less important than his position in the perspective of the changing political scene, particularly the growing demand of the South African blacks for freedom and the independence won by South Africa's neighbour Mozambique from age-old white domination. In this novel, Gordimer undoubtedly attempts to surmount the difficulties posed by the realist mode, which has a history of being an effective ideological tool in the hands of exploitative and colonizing class in the nineteenth century (Theodore Adorno's argument). The refractory nature of the modernist interior monologue serves a double purpose. Firstly, it helps the narrator to render problematic the white's position in the South African scenario of the seventies without falling into the pitfalls of realism. Secondly, one of the charges Marxists bring against modernism is its refusal to take into account the political and historical movements in society. The modernist, according to Marxist critics, highlights the individual psyche at the expense of historical reality. Mehring's self-engrossed narration is, therefore, evidence that he has neglected to take stock of a reality that has outstripped and jettisoned him. Caught in a time warp, Mehring is in the blind alley of history.

The Conservationist is Gordimer's first novel in which the white protagonist is a colour conscious Afrikaner. In Mehring's disintegration is contained the seeds of the disintegration of oppressive white apartheid-ridden power. This is the first novel that symbolically points to a future overthrow of white powers in South Africa. As Clingman points out, Mozambique is to the north of South Africa and this symbolism could well point to its recent freedom from colonial exploitation. The time warp in which Mehring get caught at the end of the novel where his actions get constantly repeated, is a definitive shift from realism to emphasize his ahistorical position. The collapse of Mehring's familial configurations is off-set by the reassembling of the larger community of Zulus at the funeral-feast.

Disgrace (1999)[5] is the first post-apartheid novel by J.M. Coetzee that also has as its central consciousness David Lurie, an authoritative, sexually predatory Afrikaner professor of literature who, expelled from his university post for sexually abusing a female student, goes to live with his daughter Lucy, a lesbian woman who has set up a farm in the countryside far away from the din and bustle of Cape Town in a bid to live a simple, self-effacing existence. *Disgrace* is a writing back to the Afrikaner popular fictional mode of the plaasroman that stresses the idyllic beauty and possibilities of the countryside farm. During David's stay, Lucy is gang-raped by three black youths. Lucy finds herself with child and refuses to abort the unborn child. Nor is she ready to leave her farm "in the back of beyond" (David's words), even though as she herself recognizes it, her life is in danger. As the only remedy to a bad situation, Lucy meekly accepts the marriage proposal of her black farm assistant Petrus as under the circumstances this is the only way in which she can safely stay back in the farm. Lucy's humiliation is compounded by David's suspicion that possibly her ravishers are henchmen of Petrus who set them upon her to put her in her place and possibly to scare her away from the farm.

David Lurie, finds his position shifting from that of a sexually aggressive, predatory male with a penchant for nubile, passive females, to that of a helpless powerless father who lacks the ideological means to defend his daughter from her humiliation. Now that the blacks have equal right to the land, Lucy sees her fate as a form of penance for the collective crime perpetrated against the black majority population by the white Afrikaner. Not only is she disinclined to bring her tormenters to justice, she goes a step further by consenting to marry Petrus, her black foreman, hand over the land to him in exchange of male protection and live as one of his numerous wives, thereby relinquishing her "Western", independent womanly status for a more humble "African" one. Lucy's one desire is to blend in with the post apartheid South African milieu.

Lucy eludes and frustrates classification, evaluation and assessment by remaining a closed text throughout; a text that David, the aggressive male colonizer newly stripped of his powers, tries and fails to read.

David Lurie, in the beginning of the novel is a self-conscious Eurocentric intellectual. However, life with his daughter teaches him that in order to survive in Africa one needs to lose one's Eurocentric distinctiveness and start from the bottom rung. Lucy is the only white character in the oeuvre of Coetzee's fiction who makes a determined effort to cross over to the black world. It is characteristic of Coetzee's skeptic, hesitant world view that he should make no attempt to portray Lucy from the inside.

David Lurie's distress at Lucy's resignation to and acceptance of an ignominious fate marks a shift in his position. From the grasping male who is habituated to exploit the services of women under his control—Soraya, the non-Afrikaner prostitute whose services he pays for and later whom he harasses by stalking her when she is with her two children, and then his student Melissa, whose vulnerability as student he sexually abuses as teacher—Lurie finds himself increasingly feeble and helpless, an impotent witness of the calamitous events that overtake his daughter's life.

> He [David] speaks Italian, he speaks French, but Italian and French will not save him here in darkest Africa. He is helpless, an Aunt Sally, a figure from a cartoon, a missionary in cassock and topi waiting with clasped hands and upcast eyes while the savages jaw away in their own lingo preparatory to plunging him into their boiling cauldron. (95)

Effete, feminized terms like "Aunt Sally" and "a missionary in cassock and topi" reinforce David's helplessness in a reversed situation beyond his control in which he is the victim and the helpless on-looker stripped of all powers of intervention. As a father, he is completely unsuccessful is saving her daughter from physical and social rape. The power equations of the patriarchal family go awry.

The family structure is scrutinized in the perspective of the changed socio-political scenario of post-apartheid South Africa. The lesbian mother-to-be, Lucy, by accepting her bleak fate as the mother of an unborn coloured child, and the consort of her social and intellectual inferior, moves out of the order of her father into a completely new sociological set up: "I cannot be a child for ever. [Lucy says] You cannot be a father for ever. I know you mean well, but you are not the guide I need, not at this time" (161). A new kind of family structure is posited where the male authority, now black instead of white, (Petrus instead of David) is as self-centred and rapacious as the former, but where the mother is capable of crossing the colour bar and making courageous gesture towards reconciliation.

Disgrace is a novel where old assumptions are systematically denied and ciphered. The first among this is the concept of the farm. The Afrikaner plaasroman has idealized the farm and its life. Ownership, preferably white male ownership, is an idea integrated to this concept. Man's relation to his animals is regulated by the same ownership laws. Animals are for blind servility and consumption. The ordered, hierarchical existence of the farm has as its nodal point the white baas. In sharp contrast, Lucy refuses to call her habitat by the name; "Stop calling it the farm, David. This is not a farm, it's just a piece of land where I grow things—we both know that" (200). Elsewhere she says, "[T]hat is what I must learn to accept. To start at ground level. With nothing..... No cards, no weapons, no property, no rights, no dignity...Yes, like a dog" (205).

A couple of decades ago Gordimer had written *The Conservationist* questioning the white assumptions of the plaasroman. There, Mehring's farm was depicted as being a travesty of the Adamic concept of the farm as ordered, meaningful, idealized, above all innocent existence. The absurdity and meaninglessness of Mehring's hollow, egotistical existence was stressed.

In *Disgrace,* the narrative movement is towards anagnorisis at a tragic, elemental level. Lucy and Bev Shaw, two women, who have chosen to eke an existence for themselves outside the wrap of white male authority, strive to find new meaning in their lives while denying the old, time worn conventions of male-dominated society. Theirs is an empirical existence. Lucy says: "They [Bev Shaw and her husband Bill Shaw] are not going to lead me to a higher life, and the reason is, there is no higher life. This is the only life there is. Which we share with animals. That's the example that people like Bev try to set. That's the example I try to follow. To share some of our human privilege with the beasts. I don't want to come back in another existence as a dog or a pig and have to live as dogs or pigs live under us" (74). Lucy, unlike Magda, is keen to arrive at some meaning surrounding her existence in post-apartheid South Africa. Of greater importance is the fact that along with her, David Lurie too finds some kind of significance in the life he is going to lead in the countryside henceforth as Lucy's aging father.

David's relationship with Lucy gradually moves from the realm of the public to the private, to a point where David's only residual identity is that he is Lucy's father. The novel ends with the lines "Yes, I am giving him up" (218). David says this when he finally gives up the lame dog for euthanasia, a lame stray dog for which he had started feeling affection and would have liked to keep alive. At the start of the novel David as specialist in Romantic literature loses his preeminence as no one likes to be taught the Romantic poets anymore. From the stripping away of sexual pleasure that he derived first from Soraya, then Melissa, to the gradual stripping away of his social position as professor of literature, his livelihood, his dignity when he becomes the butt of joke of the campus and his ex-wife, and finally to the travestying of his pride as an educated, superior "Westerner" when his daughter sends him as emissary to Petrus to convey her acceptance of Petrus' marriage proposal—David's trajectory is one relentless, denudation of rights and privileges. Even the pitiful cur that followed him about has to be relinquished. However, the one right that David refuses to give up, in fact the right that he rediscovers along the route of surrender is that of fatherhood, not as an authoritative, patriarchal right as the Afrikaner convention sees it, but as the basic, human right of the father to share his daughter's troubles.

> So: once [Lucy] was only a little tadpole in her mother's body, and now here she is, solid in her existence, more solid than he has ever been. With luck she will last a long time, long beyond him. When he is dead she will, with luck, still be here doing her ordinary tasks among the flowerbeds. And from within her will have issued another existence, that with luck will be just as solid, just as long lasting. So it will go on, a line of existences in which his share, his gift, will grow inexorably less and less, till it may as will be forgotten. (217)

Occurring towards the end of the novel when David returns for a second time to spend the rest of his days with his daughter and stand by her through her pregnancy, these lines convey a strong sense of affirmation. Lucy, by her patience, acceptance and sacrifice clings to her piece of land, roots herself in post-apartheid South Africa in a manner that appalls and impresses David. So when he is giving up the dog, his act can surely be interpreted as his volitional surrender of his ideological beliefs.

> He and Bev do not speak. He has learned by now, from her, to concentrate all his attention on the animal they are killing, giving it what he no longer has difficulty calling by its proper name: love....
>
> "It gets harder all the time", Bev Shaw once said. Harder, yet easier too. One gets used to things getting harder one ceases to be surprised that what used to be hard as hard can grow harder yet. He can save the young dog, if he wishes, for another week. But a time must come, it cannot be evaded.... (219)

David Lurie's own life, replete with promiscuity, cynicism and an adherence to Western conceptual modes of living and thinking has led to a sterile mode of life. It has yielded little meaning or satisfaction. In contrast, his daughter's way of life free from the burden of western ideology is more attuned to the rhythms of Africa. In a moment of searing anger and cynicism David sees Lucy's rape in the light of history:

> The gang of three. Three fathers in one.... Lucy called them rapists.... Well, Lucy was wrong. They were not raping, they were mating. It was not the pleasure principle that ran

> the show but the testicles, sacs bulging with seed aching to perfect itself. And now, lo and behold, the child! Already he is calling it the child when it is no more than a worm in his daughter's womb. (199)

Words spoken in hatred are yet veracious words. By taking the difficult and complex decision to give the child life and love, Lucy turns an act of "personal hatred" into an act of affirmation. When David asks her: 'Do you love him yet?' Lucy replies: 'The child? No. How could I? But I will. Love will grow—one can trust Mother Nature for that. I am determined to be a good mother, David. A good mother and a good person. You should try to be a good person too.' (216)

To this simple, touching resolution and entreaty, David's reply is equally honest: 'I suspect it is too late for me. I'm just an old lag serving out my sentence. But you go ahead. You are well on the way.' To himself he says, 'A good person. Not a bad resolution to make, in dark times.' (216)

From the ordeal and negative hype of public mortification, shame and disgrace David Lurie moves to an intensely private space of personal shame and disgrace as an aftermath of the rape of his daughter. However, his passage does not end at this point. Even at a cross road where he feels he cannot go on any further, he discovers to his surprise that the end point is in fine a starting point and that possibly he has to revise all his known beliefs and practices, unlearning all he has learnt so far:

> Narrating an intensely private story of a father's agony at his daughter's capitulation to her suspected tormentors, Coetzee examines the white dilemma in post apartheid Africa in his own preferred private domain. Like Michael K.[6], Mrs. Curren[7] and the Magistrate[8], David Lurie too has to work out his own destiny outside the purview of politics and mass movements.

Gordimer's *The Conservationist* prophecies a bleak future for South African whites. Africa in this novel is viewed as a land entirely belonging to the blacks. But in later novels, Gordimer rectifies this stance by discussing the contribution and sacrifice, of whites committed to the case of eradication of apartheid and their stake in its future. In contrast to her standpoint, the deep pessimism that informs all of Coetzee's novels originates from the radical disjunction of known, recognizable structures of human relationships. These shattered structures are not replaced however by more radical, experimental structures as found in Gordimer's later novels. The legitimacy of established human structures is questioned and displaced by Coetzee in minute, intricate ways. The white colonizer's gradual diminution and powerlessness as social entity, and informed passivity in the theatre of a politically turbulent South Africa is the subject of analysis and observation in Coetzee's novels. Coetzee's novels follow the classic tragic pattern of impediment, peripety, suffering and anagnorisis. Notably, tragedy is a pre-capitalist genre concentrating on the inner, psychological workings of the human mind, its desire for immortality and its losing battle against inchoate, yet omnipotent cosmic forces. A reason why Coetzee prefers the desert archetype as his setting could be that such a backdrop is relatively free from the taint of capitalist life style. He also views the desert as symbolizing the failure of human relationships. Speaking about the desert archetype in an interview Coetzee says:

> The desert archetype is about a lack of society and the lack of a shared culture, a feeling of anomie, a feeling of solitariness, a feeling of not having human ties with the people around one.... We find ourselves living in a country of fragmented oar obsolete cultures: African culture is fragmented, Afrikaner rural culture is equally fragmented, and the cities are just agglomerations, with no distinctive urban culture. So for the people whose roots have been cut, who have no sense of identity to the extent of not even knowing what their roots were, the image of the desert in which one is solitary has a lot of meaning, and yes, I would say that socially it has a lot of relevance.[9]

His characters too, are prototypes rather than strongly etched individuals with individual eccentricities. If there is one common trait his characters share, (and this is probably gross simplification) it is a fierce desire to cling to their personal world, forge their own private language and idiom referring to their heartfelt emotions and experiences and working out their private destiny in a socio-political set-up that is clinically hostile to such cravings and aspirations.

NOTES

1. All textual quotations are taken from Nadine Gordimer, *The Conservationist*. London: Penguin, 1978.
2. Magda is the heroine of Coetzee's novel *In the Heart of the Country*. GB: Martin Secker & Warburg, 1977.
3. Stephen Clingman. *The Novels of Nadine Gordimer: History from the Inside*. (London: Allen and Unwin Ltd., 1986) 136.
4. Nadine Gordimer. *Living in Hope and History*. (Great Britain: Bloomsbury, 1999, Paperback Edition 2000) 193.
5. All textual quotations are borrowed from J.M. Coetzee, *Disgrace*, London: Vintage, 2000.
6. The protagonist of J.M. Coetzee's *Life and Times of Michael. K*, GB: Martin Secker & Warburg, 1983.
7. The protagonist of J.M. Coetzee's *The Age of Iron*, GB: Martin Secker & Warburg, 1990.
8. The protagonist of J.M. Coetzee's *Waiting for the Barbarians*, GB: Martin Secker & Warburg, 1980.
9. J.M. Coetzee in interview with Stephen Watson, *Speak* 1, (Number 3, 1978) 22, in Dick Penner, *Countries of the Mind: The Fiction of J.M. Coetzee*, (NY, London: Greenwood Press: 1989) 58.

Indigenous vs. Non-Indigenous: Cultural Interface in Multicultural Australia

20

Jaslene Dhaliwal

Australia—a land of flora and fauna has one of the most culturally diverse societies in the world. The new statement of Australian government's multicultural policy is "Unity in Diversity," which aims at promoting communal harmony, and repudiating prejudice and bigotry. Wrapped up in a new vision it is not just rhetoric of the "colonial elites," but is essentially designed to ensure respect, justice and welfare for all. The overall image is one of a plural and varied society with a majority of population aligning to culturally diverse elements. However, in reality the relations between indigenous and non-indigenous Australians are indeed very disharmonious. There is a clear cut cleavage between the two races based on the misplaced cultural assumptions and perceptions of Blacks being inferior, "useless savages" and "ignoble heathens," while the Whites are conceived as possessing counter virtues. Over the years this divide has acquired a sharper edge and there seems to be a bleak chance of it ever being smoothened in the near future. Labeled as "living fossils," the subsumed indigenous communities are living on the fringes of the mainstream society accommodating to the marginalized status accorded to them by the Whites.

The colonial encounter between the Aborigines and the Europeans commenced in 1788, when Capt Arthur Philip and the First Fleet landed at Botany Bay with the overspill of British criminals to be deported to the dungeons of the earth. Their arrival is now considered as "invasion of Australia" rather than settlement. Prior to them the Aborigines were the sole occupants of the Continent. It is estimated by the Western archaeologists that the Aborigines have been living in Australia for more than 40,000 years or perhaps as long as 60,000 years. The gold rush of the 1850's lured many fortune seekers from all over the world who later settled in this country. Since World War II, immigrants from over 150 countries have made Australia their homeland. To a great extent diasporics have settled considerably well in the new country enjoying a respectable status, but unfortunately the Aborigines are placed at the bottom rung of the social ladder.

Before the arrival of the European settlers, the Aboriginal and Torres Strait Islander people inhabited most areas of the Continent. Each language group had distinctive lifestyle, religious and cultural traditions in diverse regions. Anthropologists may have vacillitating answers to the origins of the Aborigines, but the Aboriginal people believe that their origins lie in the Dreamtime, a metaphysical concept. It refers to a remote period in the distant past when reposing superhuman beings resembling one or another creature in appearance stemmed out of the featureless plain, and began to wander randomly over the countryside. During this period, these emerging mythical beings treaded the land, metamorphosed the landscape, and returned to the land where their spiritual presence persists for all times. They possessed life-creating powers, hence wherever they carried out any action, some natural creature—a mountain, an isolated hill, a waterhole, a riverbed or even trees originated to signify that place. The Aborigines looked upon these mythical creators as their forebears, referring to them as "Ancestral Beings." It was a strong belief among them that the creator ancestral beings inhabited the land they possessed. To understand the law and culture of the Aborigines and their relationship to the physical and the spiritual world, one must begin with their special affinity to land. Everything about Aboriginal society was inextricably woven with and connected to land. The connection between the Aborigines and the land was expressed in terms of "being related to" rather than "owning." The land nurtured them and they, in turn, had sacred responsibilities to protect it. As mother is to a child, land was to the Aborigines a symbol of maternal love and belonging. It was hard for them to cut off the umbilical cord and stay away from it indefinitely.

During the pre-contact times Aborigines were basically semi-nomadic gatherers and hunters who moved from one place to another in search of fresh hunting grounds. The family was a part of a band called "Tribes," and they could be distinguished from one another by differences in customs, laws and myths. In their society the relationship between man and woman was based on partnership, that is, they were partners in sharing all economic, cultural and social responsibilities. They were both equally integral to the sacred life of their community, though in certain matters men had more powers and authority than women.

Art and music were significant components of Aboriginal culture branching out a spiritual dimension. There was a spectacular array of art forms including body painting and personal ornamentation, ground sculpture, bark painting, wood carving, rock painting and engraving. Paintings were done on bodies or sand, whereas music was a part of their ceremonial dancing and chanting. Their songs were like the song cycle of "Moon-Bone", which were not in script form. They were memorized and passed on orally from generation to generation.

It was in 1788, that Australian history recorded the most traumatic cultural interface between the Aborigines and the Europeans. The paradigmatic cultural benchmarks became major determinants of racial superiority and inferiority. For the Whites, culture is dipped in Christian values and materialistic considerations, while for the Aborigines, culture has a spiritual quality: it is a source of life with a religious core. This ideological disparity sets a cultural dichotomy in contemporary Australia. At the outset itself the incompatible cultures or temporalities of European "modernity" and Aboriginal "antiquity" marked the substantial rift between the two races. This direct conflict was underpinned by a belief in the superiority of the Europeans and inferiority of the Aborigines. The Whites saw Aboriginal culture and practices as being undesirable aspects of a pagan culture and set about to replace them with European culture. Consequently, there was a tendency to react and resist than to re-adjust. The inferiority of the Aborigines was seen as cultural which could be overcome by civilizing the primitive natives and converting them to Christianity. For this purpose, policy of assimilation was put into practice. The use of laws to justify and support the deliberate destruction of Aboriginal society and the ruthless slaughter of Aboriginal men, women and children had serious implications on Black-White relations.

In the wake of colonization ensued multiple setbacks to the Aborigines and their culture. Their dispossession by European colonizers was legally justified by invoking the doctrine of "terra-nullius"—that Australia was the land belonging to no one and could be taken by anyone, who would put it to productive use. This became the substratum of the claims of the mining companies and apostles of commercial enterprise against the original custodians of the land. The pastoralists moved into the Aboriginal lands, pushing the natives to the periphery of their tribal territory. Clashes marked situations as the Aborigines and the Europeans pursued conflicting interests. The divide was noticeable, and there was a little chance of it being bridged. In the chain of events, the seizure of their land had the most disastrous impact on the Aborigines because they not only lost their source of food but spiritual sites as well. The invaders perhaps never realized the centrality of land to the cultural survival of the Aborigines as a race. The towering edifices European civilization built were nothing but jungles of concrete, iron, cement and bricks. The Blacks looked upon them as glorified graves of their own culture and civilization on which they had been raised. The intemperate White geographical annexation of territories in a few decades precipitated the disintegration of the Aboriginal society as it had existed for thousands of years. With their land gone, and their traditional life pattern shattered, Aboriginal people lost the will to live. They had to struggle to adapt to new situations under extremely adverse circumstances. The Aborigines now became reliant on European goodwill and received allowances of the invading culture in terms of blankets, clothing, provisions and alcohol. The Europeans mixed poison with wheat flour and distributed it among the unsuspecting Aborigines killing them in thousands. The import of foreign deadly diseases, such as influenza, tuberculosis, venereal infection took their toll on the susceptible Aborigines, who had no immunity to these afflictions. Thus, in the garb of kindness, the guileful Europeans unleashed hostility.

The Christian Missionaries took upon themselves the responsibility of imposing their religion on the Aborigines. This was both a physical invasion and an "invasion of the mind." Started in 1910, the policy consisted in surreptitiously taking away of the Aboriginal children and placing them in religious institutions. This severed their familial ties and cultural affiliations. Here, these children were used as free labour and evangelized; the juvenile girls were tutored to become "good wives" for White men. This irredeemable policy of segregation marked the extinction of Aboriginal culture and left ineffaceable scars for its victims. In the words of Mudrooroo Narogin:

> A terrible future was forced on us without a qualm, for the Masters knew what was good for us. Many of our children were placed in those orphanages he had constructed for his own bastards, and even had special places constructed for them where they might be far from us. They were to be disciplined and educated in what was called "Civilization." (*US Mob-History, Culture Struggle—An Introduction to Indigenous Australia, p. 21.*)

The displaced Aborigines who were taken away from their families as children suffered from acute identity crisis, depression and alcoholism. Humiliated and disconcerted by feelings of shame and ignominy, many of the melancholics committed suicide, while others resorted to violence. To reclaim their identity and gain acceptance in Aboriginal society they had to imbibe new values and overcome complexes of their own unrefined Aboriginal heritage.

The White colonizers perpetuated the downfall of the Aborigines and their culture, simply because of the racist connection of supposed cultural inferiority with natural inferiority. They had an interest in negating the very existence of the Aborigines as humans, describing them as a missing link between human and animal, destined by divine logic to give way before European settlement. According to them, the Aborigines had no recognizable form of governance and culture, and were considered as "lesser breeds without law." The belief that the Aboriginal problem would be solved by the dying away of all the Aboriginal people was the comfort of Australian racists of the century. So the notorious policy of assimilation was constructed as "soothing the dying pillow." This was also a deliberate policy of cultural genocide—Aboriginal culture would eventually disappear as full-blooded Aboriginals were expected to die out in competition with the superior "Nordic" White race, and the probability that the "half-castes" might gradually assimilate in the White community could not be overlooked. Delving on this thought Mudrooroo writes:

> Our culture was not enough for the humans to live in, our languages were not enough for humans to speak by, our methods of oral transmission were not enough for continuance. Our very being had to be inscribed and imprisoned on the pages of books. It was as if our souls had been imprisoned in another language, in another way of recording and other ways of formation. Not only had our bodies to become settled but so had our spirits. (*ibid*, p. 2)

After the Europeans set their foot on the Continent, the Aboriginal women lost their privileged position in society. Many female roles that existed in the nomadic lifestyle were completely taken over by men especially in the economic sphere. The west actually minimized the age-old cultural roles of Aboriginal women. On the pretext of making them civilized, native women were employed as domestic servants and sexually exploited by their White masters. It resulted in miscegenation and a terrible future awaited the "half-caste" children who were brought up in the foster homes.

The mind boggling disclosures by the Royal Commission into Aboriginal deaths in custody bear testimony to the fact that Australia is one of the "last outposts of institutionalized racism." The Aborigines are at the receiving end of racist attitude not merely at individual but at the structural and cultural levels also. Their domination, subordination and exploitation is justified and rationalized by the emergence of racial ideologies which become institutionalized throughout the structures of society.

The cultural and racial biases form the basis for repressive legislation and administration which seek to separate and exclude the Aborigines from White society. They have to live on day-to-day basis with "degree of pin-pricking domination, abuse of personal power, utter paternalism, open contempt and total indifference." The ideology of imperialism, which assumes the right of White people to rule the world, sets them against the Blacks. The Europeans continue to define themselves in imperial terms, as champions of world conquest. Filled with ethnocentric arrogance they rate themselves as the paragon of unequalled moral and intellectual caliber simply because they are "Whites." The Black activists believe that modern structures totally contaminated with racism cannot be toppled completely, nevertheless they urge resistance. This is true of people of all Black races, who have waged war against imperialism in their countries.

It is ironical that a country that adopted the policy of multiculturalism to assert that it believed in the peaceful co-existence of different ethnic groups, should exhibit profound discordance with human beings who are not "Whites." Given the context of racial discrimination, it is hardly surprising that there has been so little progress in breaking out of welfare dependency for the Aborigines. The hegemonic control exercised by the Government agencies ignores the interests of the Aborigines which have neither been accommodated nor protected. The State and Territory Governments also have operated to sabotage the Aboriginal efforts to control their resources and establish an independent economic base. Despite a myriad interventions and programmes aimed at addressing Indigenous socio-economic disadvantages, the Aboriginal population remains to a large extent culturally differentiated and discriminated. They have shown a sluggish pace of progress in economic, social and political spheres.

In the present day multicultural Australian society Aborigines are still coming to terms with the historical legacy, which has been left to them. They are still cast as "primitive" because they do not uphold Western values. The White Australians refuse to acknowledge the fact that the Aborigines are the "First People" and therefore their unique status as the first Australians needs to be recognized—"being first" is very crucial to their identity. In the new social set up, the Aborigines do not include themselves in the mix of ethnicity because the others do not possess the spiritual ancestry, which they have, and is alien to the people of other diverse cultures. The irony is that even United Nations Organization recognizes their status but the White population of their own country still maintains and supports its own claims. The extent of discrimination meted out to the Aborigines in all the government agencies, be it Parliament or education sector, proves that racism still looms large casting its demonic shadow on the lives of the marginalized. As Ruby Langford Ginibi has written "We have never been one nation—ever because Aboriginal people have always been excluded in white social enclave in this country. Even the people who migrate here are on a higher social level than we are. We are classified as the lowest of the land, and we are the first people of this land" (cited in Meridian Vol. 17, No. I, May 1998, p. 26).

Such passages demonstrate contradictions of multiculturalism and the tensions generated by the revitalized hierarchies of Australian society. The country may have escalated in terms of its economic progress, but the social status of the Aborigines is languishing on the hierarchical graph. The most distressing fact is that the Aborigines have withstood the tumultuous jolt of the White usurpation, acknowledged the reality of non-Indigenous, yet their numbers are dwindling. They constitute about 2.4 per cent of Australia's total population. Life expectancy of Aboriginal men continues to be fifty seven years, while that of women is sixty five years which is 15-20 years lower than non-Indigenous people. Most of them die of diseases, while others are trapped in the enclaves of alcohol and drugs. There are no initiatives taken to rehabilitate them through de-addiction measures or provide them with adequate health facilities. They suffer from high rate of infant mortality, have higher unemployment rates and are over-represented in custody and arrest figures. Education seems to be a distant dream for a majority of them. Without effective English literacy, the Aborigines have clogged opportunities in seeking employment. Schools in Aboriginal communities turn out students who are functionally illiterate in English, that is, readability factor is strong but understanding of the concepts is very weak. As a result, one does not find many Aborigines employed in hotel and tourism industry, shops and public transport sector. Social justice is about rectifying the injustices heaped upon the Aborigines, improving health services for them and ensuring their democratic inclusion into the mainstream society. There is an impending need to grant special rights to the Aborigines so as to reinstate their distinctive cultural identity vis-à-vis the other Australians.

Despite the emergence of new theories, the psyche of the Europeans cannot be overhauled as they adhere to the racist notion that their culture is more highly valued socially than the Indigenous culture. The desponding Aborigines have no illusions about the enormous challenge they face at the crossroads of such a cultural interface. Thrust into powerless position the Aborigines are still clinging tenaciously to their limping cultural identity "seeking changes that sustain and not weaken Aboriginal culture". The vision of an Arcadian Aboriginal life lived in harmony with the land is being shattered. The question arises, whether in the coming times the Aborigines would be able to retrieve their pristine primordial culture, especially when tradition comes face to face with modernity. The answer remains elusive and the dust raised by the winds of change further blurs the vision. It is one world on the throes of extinction. And the other, it seems, is unlikely to be born. It can be summed up in the words of Kath Walker "I would like to state that a multicultural society could only successfully occur in this country when seventh generation Australians recognize the Aboriginal culture" (cited in Mudrooroo, *The Indigenous Literature of Australia*, p. 67.) It is through "integration" and "inclusion" that the indigenous and non-indigenous can homogenize their cultural polarities and make multiculturalism a reality in Australia.

NOTES

Blacks/Aborigines—Original inhabitants or indigenous population

Whites/Europeans—Non-indigenous population

REFERENCES

Attwood, Bain. *Telling The Truth About Aboriginal History*. NSW: Allen & Unwin, Australia, 2005.

Broome, Richard. *Aboriginal Australians*. Sydney: Southwood Press Pty Ltd, 2001.

Docker, John & Fisher, Gerhard, (eds) *Race, Colour & Identity*. Australia: University of New South Wales Press Ltd., 2000

Bourke, Colin, Bourke, Eleanor and Edwards Bill. *Aboriginal Australia*. Australia: University of Queensland Press, 2003.

Narogin, Mudrooroo. *US Mob-History, Culture, Struggle: An Introduction to Indigenous Australia*. Australia: Angus & Robertson, 1995.

Parbury, Nigel. *Survival: A History of Aboriginal Life in New South Wales*. Australia, Ministry of Aboriginal Affairs (New South Wales), Sydney: 2000.

ARTICLES

- "Multicultural Australia: The Way Forward-States, Territories & Wider Community", downloaded from http://www.immi.gov.au/media/publications/multicultural/issues97/macpape3.htm
- "Racism. No Way: Fact Sheets", *Multicultural Australia: Unity in Diversity*. Downloaded from http://www.racismnoway.com.au/cgi-bin/printversion/classroom/facts

The Dialectics of Enchained Sensibility in *The Foreigner*

21

Basavaraj Naikar

Arun Joshi's novels explore the tragic predicament of their protagonists struggling to realize 'a fix on reality' that could arrest their descent into 'the dark incoherence of the mind.' The novel, *The Foreigner*, opens with the death of Babu Khemka and the response of its narrator-protagonist, Sindi Oberoi to it, "They uncovered his face and I turned away in spite of myself" (p. 3). What follows is the unfolding of his experiences leading up to it as events flash back and forth in his consciousness. Sindi Oberoi like Camus's Mersault in *The Stranger* retreats from contact with his environs feeling as Roquentin in Sartre's *Nausea* has felt, "We were a heap of existents unconvinced, embarrassed by overselves, we hadn't the slightest reason for being there, any of us, each existent embarrassed, vaguely all at ease, felt superfluous in relation to the others."[1] Sindi wonders, "...in what way, if any, did I belong to the world that roared beneath my apartment window" (p. 65). Since he felt the same wherever he was—in Kenya, London or India to which he eventually returns, "Perhaps I felt that because I was a foreigner in America. But then what difference would it have made if I had lived in Kenya or India or any other place for that matter? It seemed to me that I would still be a foreigner. My foreignness lay within me and I couldn't leave myself behind wherever I went" (p. 61). He thinks that his very birth was a joke, "Somebody had begotten me without a purpose" (p. 61) as the sheer insanity of his existence depresses him, which makes him appear strange to others, as observed by June on meeting him for the first time:

> There is something strange about you, you know. Something distant. I'd guess that when people are with you, they don't feel like they're with a human being. May be it's an Indian characteristic, but, I have a feeling you'd be a foreigner anywhere. (p. 30)

Sick of life, Sindi even contemplates suicide but is dissuaded by his uncle and the realization that "suicide is the end of a battered old road, not the beginning of a new one" (p. 75). Feeling that 'his life in Nairobi had virtually ended" (p. 167), he tells himself: "I might as well try my luck elsewhere" (p. 167). Going to London to study Engineering, he finds it equally unavailing, "I wanted to know the meaning of my life. And all my classrooms didn't tell me a thing about it" (p.167). He, therefore, gives up his studies and becomes a dishwasher at a nigh-club in Soho and as fate would have it, it is during his stint as a barman that he has a tortuous love affair, which brings him "...face to face with pain, which seemed to permeate everything, like the smell of earth in the epidemic. All that 1 had thought was pleasurable had ended in pain, and after all this I was as far from finding the purpose of my life as I had been to start with" (p. 170). Bewildered, he seeks an answer, which he seems to find after three months of introspection while being in Scotland:

> All love—whether of things, or persons, or oneself was illusion and all pain sprang from this illusion. Love begot greed and attachment, and it led to possession. (p. 170)

He realizes that

> There is another way of loving. You can love without attachment, without desire. You can love without attachment to the objects of your love.... Love is real only when you know that what you love must one day die. (p. 171)

Imbued with a philosophy of life based on detachment, he goes to America only to realize that America is a place for well-fed automatons rushing about in automatic cars. He finds himself to be an alien even after five years' stay:

> My fifth Christmas on these alien shores. And yet all shores are alien when you don't belong anywhere...twenty five years wasted in the search of wrong things in wrong places

> ...and what did I have to show for achievement: a ten stone body that had to be fed five times a day.... This was the sum of a life-time of striving. (p.91)

His thoughts are echoed by his friend, Arun, who articulates them while they and their friends, June and Karl, are relaxing on the beach:

> All freedom is illusion. You had no choice in your birth nor do you even choose your death. And in between is vast expanses of lawless sands that pile up where the wind blows.... Random events happen around you forcing you to make decisions propelling you on through life. It is only our vanity that makes us imagine that we are leading our destiny. (pp. 75-76)

Losing faith in himself as a 'free agency,' he becomes increasingly neurotic and isolated, and determines to avoid involvement, especially after his involvement with Anna and Kathy, which left a 'bleeding wound' in his heart. Reflecting on his affair with Kathy, he observes:

> I had loved with the piercing, all-caressing love of an adolescent and it had shattered the very roots of my existence. (p. 121)

Sindi's resolution gets broken when he meets June Blythe at a dance and although he struggles to avoid getting involved with her, he finds that the "commitment had already been made the moment I had seen June at the dance" (p. 60). He uncannily visualizes the outcome of their affair:

> Our hands would soon give place to our bodies and then the worst will come, our souls get involved.... I could already see the death struggle of our souls as each of us tried to claim his own destiny.... I could smell the decay of love, the sudden realization that the end has begun. And worse, the tear that there might be another beginning.... I wasn't afraid of getting hurt, but to hurt June would have been unbearable.... If only I had the strength to act as what I knew was right. (p. 69)

Unfortunately, he does not have the strength to act in time as he opts "for the excruciating moments of ecstasy in a woman's body" (p. 117) in preference to the preservation of the tranquillity of his soul. Trying to rationalize his involvement with her, he feels that he is drawn to her because she symbolizes all that he was not "and couldn't hope to be. May be that is why I later fell in love even as I wildly struggled to remain uninvolved" (p. 62). As for June, she is fascinated by his quaintness and eccentricity and falls in love with him despite the witty warning, "Take care Honey, you might as well fall in love with a shadow. You can't love a stranger now, can you?" (p. 8l). Leading a life of loneliness and barrenness, June hopes that his love may impart meaning to her life and feels so insecure that she repeatedly wants to be assured that Sindi loves her.

Sindi receives a jolt when June proposes marriage, since he is afraid of possessing anybody and of being possessed which marriage means. When exasperated June asks him, "what is wrong' with possessing or being possessed?" he answers:

> There was nothing wrong with it. It was just too painful for some people and the point was whether one was built to take the pain or not. I didn't think I could, and that more or less settled the matter for me.... (p. l06)

He tries to convince her that their loneliness cannot be resolved through marriage. He gently tries to convince her of it:

> Marriage wouldn't help, June. We are alone, both you and I. That is the problem. Our aloneness must be resolved from within. You can't send two persons through a ceremony and expect their aloneness will disappear. (p. 124)

Sindi's intransigence stems from his fear of committing himself as also that of being crushed by the value system of American civilization based on materialism and individualism of which June herself has been a victim.

Shocked by Sindi's indifference and infected with 'materialistic entropy' which renders her incapable of overcoming her aloneness, June in desperation turns to Babu Khemka, son of a rich industrialist from India, who appears to be a contrast to the cold and reserved Sindi. Babu comes to America with his head filled with fantasies of women and sex, "What is the good of coming to America if one is not to play with girls?" (p. 19-20). Such young Indians do not realize, as Sindi observes, "They forget that one couldn't play around without playing with oneself and that would be fatal" (p. 20). Sindi was right in his assessment, since Babu's naiveté, which initially attracted June eventually leads to the break up, "This naiveté in a large measure made and subsequently broke up the bond of affection which grew between them" (p. 90). Being brought up in an orthodox family, Babu could not contemplate marriage to an American girl as his father would be 'very angry if I married here" (p. 89). His heady affair with June soon ends in bitter disappointment and frustration, aggravated by his failing in examination after examination which demoralizes him as also by his not finding "Americans congenial towards foreigners" (p. 9 I). When he turns to Sindi for sympathy he is repulsed by his cynicism, "Sindi is always willing to listen to me, but he is so terribly cynical I am afraid he will make fun of me if I took my small problems to him" (p. 52). A victim of an orthodox and hypocritical society which puts a premium on a foreign degree, Babu is haunted by the fear of social ostracism and ridicule if he goes home a failure, "Everywhere I turn I am faced with deficiencies. When I consider how much you all expect of me, my heart sinks within me" (p. 52). But lacking the will to improve, he continues to feel miserable indulging in self-pity, "They would all be ashamed of me" (p. 110). Faced with the threat of dismissal from the college, he seeks Sindi's help. Seeing him crying, Sindi is disturbed despite his being cold and detached, "His crying had shaken me up. I tried to brush it aside as none of my business but I couldn't help imagining how lonely and miserable he must have felt. Angrily I wished, he was not so damned afraid of his father and that he had not got me involved" (p. 112). Sindi is humane enough to promise Babu that he would see the Dean and request him to give Babu another chance.

Babu's plight moves June, who feels that in helping Babu overcome his unhappiness she will be able to fulfil her ideal of being useful to someone. But her unstinted love and tender care prove inadequate as Babu's depression get deeper with his continuing to fail academically and receiving letters from his father, who threatens to disinherit him if he marries June. Sindi's advice "not to rush into a wrong thing for a temporary need" (p. 116) goes unheeded. His neurosis taxes June's endurance and saps her emotionally as she is not able to gauge his needs, "I wish to God I knew. I just don't know.... I have given him all that I have, but it does not suffice.... But there is just one long drawn-out agony. Each minute is loaded with the throbbing of a climax, which never comes" (p. 160). Unable to withstand the strain she steadily goes to pieces.

The final blow comes when Babu is expelled from the university for having failed again, which shatters him, despite Sindi's warning, "You are not in a fairy land, where you can get what you want just by wishing it. It is high time you ceased to be an innocent little rich father's boy and got down to doing something." (p. 154). Increasingly becoming peevish and temperamental, Babu has a showdown with June, who tells him of her relationship with Sindi with whom she has been sleeping, which shocks him so much as to drive him to suicide. It is American materialism, which destroys Babu as it does June later on. Babu's death fills Sindi with a sense of guilt, "All along I had acted out of lust and greed and selfishness and they had applauded my wisdom. When I had sought only detachment I had driven a man to death" (p. 4). It also drains out his conscience in himself and the world, "Babu had kicked out all my beliefs and disapproved all my theories" (p. J 75).

Sindi and Babu are but two sides of a coin, since both are self-centred blatantly exploiting June's generosity for meeting their own ends. While Sindi regards love as an emotion to fill the void of existence, Babu draws on June's love to escape from the consequences of his failure brought about by his shortcomings and deficiencies. Brought up under a system of values different from those he encounters in America, Babu gets confused and wage a desperate struggle to retain a foothold on life in the face of mounting disappointment, failure and frustration As Sindi tells his angry father in India after Babu's death:

> Babu was frantically trying to fight his Gods the short while I knew him in America...you might have taught Babu to be afraid of the demon within him instead of saddling him with a set of make-believe values that made sense in

> your circle. Babu got baffled when he found that they didn't work. (p. 140)

Sindi survives because of his being able to safeguard sanity and self by projecting an image of "Americanized male ruthlessness" through his indifference to everyone and every thing in life.

In taking away his life in spite of his knowing of June's pregnancy, Babu shows his cowardice, which is set off by the courage displayed by June, who writes to Sindi:

> I have written this letter twice before, but each time, at the last minute I lost courage. And what I am going to do calls for a measure of courage that I do not possess.... This is a kind of courage that comes with despair and I suppose that is happening to me. Sindi, I am carrying Babu's child and I don't know what to do. It is nearly four months now. He knew it when he went off that night but I can't blame him; it was all my fault.... I didn't tell you before because I didn't want you to get involved.... I'm sure I'll find a way out. (p. 182)

Sindi finds himself shattered when June dies during her abortion and raves about Babu's ghost:

> Babu, You miserable, miserable fool.... See what wretchedness your innocence has perpetrated.... Behind Babu lay the stupidity and innocence of his father and his sister and his entire civilization. I hated every thing that was Indian, as if the whole nation had conspired to debauch June. (p. 183)

June seems to have paid the price for Sindi's achievement of enlightenment, since he observes:

> Detachment at time meant inaction. Now I had begun to see the fallacy of it. Detachment consisted of right action and not escape from it. The Gods had set a heavy price to teach me just that. (p. 192)

Sindi tells the caretaker at June's cemetery, "The dead teach you how to overcome their death though" (p. 194). In hoping to begin life anew in India, Sindi soon realizes the absurdity of his assumptions as it is not possible to escape from a part of himself that seemed most decayed, "by hoping from one land mass to another" (p. 177). Working as a director in Mr. Khemka's company, he soon finds himself implicated by Mr. Khemka's unscrupulous ways and unlawful activities but refuses to pay for his sins when he is trapped in the dragnet of the Income Tax officials. He tells Mr. Khemka:

> You have prostituted my ability for a whole year for your diabolical aims. And now you want me to go to prison for you. Is this what you treat me to be grateful for? ...I am not afraid of going to prison but this time it is your turn. (p. 215)

He learns from Sheila Khemka that he could not be detached from the world and remain attached to himself. With this belated realization he sets out to work for the welfare of the men of Khemka's organization, which gives him a measure of sense of fulfilment. His statement at the end that he had a feeling "we were beginning to understand each other" (p. 229) refers not only to his relationship with Sheila but also to that with life.

It may, thus, be seen that while in Babu Khemka June encounters 'a terror of aloneness' generated by his inability to live up to the demands of 'the false prestige value system,' enjoined upon him by his family, in America, she finds in Sindi Oberoi the terror of indifference and that her tragedy is due to her being unable to understand the nature of aloneness from which they all suffer as also her hoping to overcome her aloneness by giving herself to Babu or Sindi. Sindi's self-discovery that his detachment implying objectivity "was just another form of vanity" (p. 118), proves shattering in that he asks himself:

> Wouldn't Babu still be living if I had not surrendered my body to June that night we went out for a ride? I thought I was acting out of detachment but was it not merely a desire to prove that I still had the key to June's happiness? (p. 196)

He realizes that whereas Kathy and Anna had taught him to be detached, "June's death finally broke my attachment to myself" (p. 195), which proves liberating in that it helps him break out of his shell of indifference and insularity. His condition symbolizes that of contemporary man, who looking inwards sees much that is rotting in his consciousness and whose hope lies in his being able to rid himself of it.

NOTES

Arun Joshi, *The Foreigner*, Bombay: Asia Publishing House, 1968. (All the page references are to this edition.)

1. Jean Paul Sartre. *Nausea*, Tr. R. Baldick, Penguin Books, 1965, p. 184.

List of Contributors

Nandini Sahu, Reader in English (Editing), IGNOU, New Delhi.

Emmanuel N. Ngwang, Associate Professor, Mississippi Valley State University, Itta Bena, Mississippi.

Ernest L. Veyu, English Department University of Yaounde 1, Cameroon.

Devika, Asst. Prof., Languages Group, BITS Pilani, Rajasthan.

Purnendu Chatterjee, Research Scholar, Rabindra Bharati University, Kolkata.

Alessandro Monti, The Department of Oriental Studies, University of Turin, Italy.

Natalie Wall, University of Calgary, Canada.

Anita Myles, Reader in English, D.D.U. Gorakhpur University, Gorakhpur.

Elisa Armellino, University of Turin, Italy.

Sushila Rathore, Lecturer, Languages Group BITS, Pilani,

Meenakshi Raman, Associate Professor and Group Leader, Languages Group, BITS, Pilani.

Rosalyn M. Mutia, Department of English, University of Yaounde 1, Cameroon.

Srutimala Duara, Senior Lecturer, Department of English, Handique Girls' College, Guwahati, Assam.

Ranu Uniyal, Reader, Department of English, Lucknow University.

Anita Singh, Reader, Department of English, Banaras Hindu University, Varanasi (UP).

Shubha Tiwari, Head, Dept. of English, A.P.S. University, Rewa, (M.P).

Reena Mitra, Senior Reader, Department of English, Christ Church P.G. College, Kanpur, Uttar Pradesh.

Pradeep Trikha, Department of English. Dayanand (PG) College, Ajmer.

Athanasius Ayuk-Ako, Senior Lecturer, Department of English, University of Yaounde 1, Cameroon.

Arpa Ghosh, Senior Lecturer in English, Vivekananda College for Women, Barisha, Kolkata.

Jaslene Dhaliwal, Senior Lecturer, Department of English, Guru Gobind Singh College for Women, Sector 26, Chandigarh.

Basavaraj Naikar, Professor and Chairman, Department of English, Karnataka University, Dharwad. 580 003.